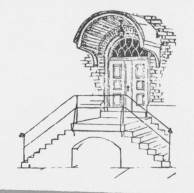

THE LAST RADIO BABY

A memoir by
Raymond Andrews

Illustrated by
Benny Andrews

PEACHTREE PUBLISHERS, LTD.
ATLANTA

PEACHTREE PUBLISHERS, LTD.
494 Armour Circle, NE
Atlanta, Georgia 30324

Cover illustration by Benny Andrews
Interior design by Candace J. Magee

Manufactured in the United States of America

10 9 8 7 6 5 4 3 2 1

Library of Congress Cataloging in Publication Data

Andrews, Raymond.
      The last radio baby : a memoir / by Raymond Andrews ;
illustrated
   by Benny Andrews.
          p.   cm.
      ISBN 1-56145-004-9 (hardcover)
      1. Andrews, Raymond—Biography—Youth.   2. Novelists,
   American—20th century—Biography—Youth. 3. Afro-Americans-
   -Georgia—Social life and customs.   4. Country life—Georgia.
   I. Title.
   PS3551.N452Z464   1990
   813'.54—dc20
      [B]
90-41751
                                                                  CIP

"Is it true that when you grew up there was no television?"
"Not where I lived."
"No TV? My God! What did you do?"
"Watched radio and scratched on the walls of the cave."

From a conversation the author had with a young medical student in New York City in 1984.

"You and I were too naive to know we couldn't make it."

My brother Benny recently revealed to me.

My only memory of our living on Missis Mamie Hampton's place: 1934-1935

Less-than-a-year-old me lying on the bed raptly watching my older brother playing with a broom in the brightly burning fireplace.

"What are you doing in there, Benny?!" Mama is calling from the other room.

"Nothing!"

Benny is dragging the broom out of the fireplace and leaning it against the wall in the corner before running into the next room to show Mama he was doing nothing. This leaves me in the room alone to enjoy the fire on the broom beautifully lighting up the wallpaper. Suddenly, Mama is running in to watch the fire with me, only to run back out and return with a bucket of water to splash out the pretty light.

Mister Jim's Place:
1935-1943

BENNY ANDREWS
DEC 27, 1989

I. Flashes

In 1935 a house was built about a hundred yards or so from Grand-mama Jessie's house for Daddy, Mama and us—then—four children. Grandmama Jessie was Daddy's mama.

I remember when I was about three running into the kitchen of this house. Reaching up and digging my hand into an open can that sat on the edge of the table, I pull out a fistful of its contents to slap into my awaiting mouth. Mama stops making her strongly smelling lye soap and grabs me roughly by the scruff of the neck along with a jar of vinegar, which she pours down my throat to catch and kill the potash on its way down.

Mamas!

ᶜᵌ

I don't remember that day in 1936 when the first baby, Shirley, was born in our new house, but I do remember two years later:

"Both of y'all gonna have a lil' 'Joe Louis' baby brother," Grand-mama told my first cousin June and me in the kitchen of her house. A Joe Louis, the World Heavyweight Boxing Champion, all my own! I couldn't wait!

Excitement kicked its heels atop the tin roof of our house. Daily we children scanned the sky looking for the long-legged stork that Daddy said would be bringing us our own Joe Louis. (Those were the days when storks made house calls, before the mother had to make a trip into town to the hospital to pick out the child of her choice and bring it home herself.)

One day while we children were playing outdoors there erupted a loud baby cry from our house. Shortly, Grandmama appeared in the back door calling us to come inside. Standing around Mama—who lay in bed looking asleep in the middle of the day—we five children all stared wide-eyed at what Grandmama held in her arms. A wrinkled, twisted-up thing that looked like a big o' blind red worm. "This is Joe Louis," said a beaming Grandmama.

"That ain't Joe Louis. It ain't even got on boxing gloves!" hollered a disappointed me before turning and running from the room.

That evening Sister ran up the road to meet Daddy, who was returning home from work on the WPA. "Daddy, today I saw the stork who brought us Joe Louis, who was wearing no boxing gloves!"

A few days later, June's "Joe Louis" was born. I didn't see him—only saw the shoebox June's daddy, my uncle Bubba, carried, along with a shovel, down into the wood behind Grandmama's house to the babies' graveyard. June's Joe Louis had been a girl.

Our Joe Louis lived and cried...and cried... More proof he wasn't the real Joe Louis.

Joe Louis's given name was Harold (even Mama and Daddy weren't fooled) and he was the sixth child born to the family. The first five of us, in order, were Harvey Christopher, Benny, Valeria Belle, me, and Shirley, all born two years apart. Besides Harold's nickname of Joe Louis, Valeria Belle was called "Sister" and I was called "Brother." Grown-ups called my Daddy (George Cleveland) "G." My first cousin, June (short for Junior), born less than two months after me, was named Fred after his daddy.

His daddy's nickname was "Bubba" but many of the grownups called him "Tampa Red" (or just "Red" because of his light skin), for he picked the guitar and sang the blues just as good—or so everyone said—as the real Tampa Red. Aunt Bea, the sister of my Daddy and uncle Bubba, had the real name Beatrice. Everybody was called some-body else.

ॐ

Several of us children were down at Grandmama's one special Saturday night for her sixty-ninth birthday. We were all allowed to stay up for an ice cream party, since to eat any of the ice cream that took hours to make with the hand-turned freezer, we had to stay up late. We sat around the crackling fireplace that cold March night eating cold ice cream while Grandmama talked to us about back when she was a girl. I was stunned! I sat there wondering, well, if Grandmama had been a girl like she said, then who back then had been our Grandmama? I thought Grandmamas had always been Grandmamas. Never girls!

That night Grandmama told us children that her earliest memory was of her mother tying her long hair in one big, ropelike plait that hung way down her back. She told us about one winter day when a fire had burned in the fireplace and Grandmama's half-sister, whose hair was short and nappy, had asked their mother, "Mama, why don't you plait my hair long like you plait Jessie's?" She did not remember what her mother had replied but her half-sister's daddy had been in the room at the time and when he heard her he shot out the back door and returned with mule shears. Without a word, he yanked young Jessie around by her long plait and cut off the thick rope of her hair right at the nape of her neck and then threw the braid into the fire. Since that time, whenever Grandmama smelled hair burning, she said her mind raced back to that day.

II. Mother Jessie and Mister Jim

What Grandmama Jessie didn't tell us that birthday Saturday night:

Jessie was born in Maxey, Georgia, on March 7, 1872, to Minerva Jones, who never married yet solved the secret to birthing by having seven children by more than one man. On record, Jessie's father, whose family name she took, was Charlie Brightwell. Off record, Jessie's—and her younger brother Will's—father was half-white, half-Indian (probably Cherokee). He tacked "Wildcat Tennessee" onto the name of his daughter Jessie Rose Lee, who supposedly looked like him with her long, straight black hair, high cheekbones, and beige skin. Minerva's other three daughters, Ella, Matt, and Cora, and her son, Cleveland, were Brightwells—at least in name. Minerva's baby boy, Selma, was a Campbell. Except for Jessie and Will, all of Minerva's children were dark-skinned black like her. In the South, as in the rest of America (the world?), the shade of one's skin color has always made a difference.

At the age of eleven, Jessie's mother brought her approximately thirty miles from Maxey in Oglethorpe County to settle in the small black farming community of Barrows Grove. For more than three quarters of a century following the end of slavery, Madison, the county seat of Morgan, located in north-central Georgia, served numerous small farming communities surrounding the town. Jessie grew up between Barrows Grove and Plainview, another mostly black community located a few miles up the road closer to Madison. Jessie was a free spirit and grew up precocious in both body and mind, but she was remembered most for her long-haired beauty:

"Mama, I just saw the prettiest girl in the whole wide world sitting on a log down at the creek." This was the reaction of young Mamie Hampton, one of Jessie's peers, upon seeing Jessie for the first time.

"Was she with a white man?" Mamie's mother wanted to know.

"Yes, Ma'am."

"Oh, that was nobody but Jessie."

Legend had her to be the most beautiful woman ever to roam the region or strut the streets of Madison. Jessie, like many small-town rural black women of her day, was heavily recruited as a mistress, or concubine, by white men. This meant white men of means—the landed gentry—since owning a black mistress was too rich for the blood and, especially, the pocketbooks of po' white trash (grandpappies of the redneck). Southern custom of the day called for rich, ruling white men to have themselves a black mistress as proof of their manhood.

During the early half of this century when one of these men of means in the town of Madison didn't own himself a black concubine, it made news. Not newspaper news (these men owned the newspapers) but "talk"—talk among the white men and the black—then "colored"— community, for such conversations were definitely not for the ears of white "ladies" and their children. Talk was that Madison owned such a rare individual during the first half of this century —Mister Vason—who for this reason alone was greatly respected throughout the colored community.

By sleeping with these white males and having their babies (along with those of their husbands), many black women (like Mata Haris) got to know these ruling men more intimately than did their white wives. The white Southern male of the day felt it was his God-given duty to protect his wife and children, especially daughters, from the world of reality—the black world in particular.

Meanwhile, blacks couldn't escape the real world... Much of it many of their women carried around in their bellies. The colored community of yore was indeed colorful, consisting of tar, brown, yellow, pink, red, and even white-skinned folks with nappy, curly, and straight hair. They all black. According to the law of the South a baby is born whatever race its mother is (except that if the mother is white and the daddy is black, automatically assumed the result of a rape, then the baby reverts to whatever race the father is). Another part of this real world was the reality that many of the white men's private whims, wants, needs, fantasies, fetishes, and kinks were passed along by their black gals and swept through the colored community by word of mouth—shocking enough to make blush a much later-day supermarket magazine rack.

Jessie's only marriage was to a fellow Barrows Grover—Eddie Andrews. Other than his marriage to the most beautiful and sought-after woman in the area, nothing is known about Eddie Andrews at this time except that he had a sister who died giving birth...and that he worked two miles up the road at the "Orr Place" (later Oaks Plantation) for one James Jackson Orr, or "Mister Jim."

☙

I was playing with the other children in Grandmama's front yard when the man called me up onto the front porch where he sat reading the newspaper in between watching us play.

"You know you got a hole in the seat of your britches?" He said to me as I reached back to my seat and felt meat. "Come here and let me see what size you wear."

He then proceeded to order for me two pairs of brand new blue overalls from the Sears & Roebuck catalog.

He had just come down from Virginia and was staying in Grandmama's house until Daddy, Uncle Bubba, and some other men finished building his house down the hill and across the branch into the woods back of Grandmama's. The branch was to separate him from the rest of us. All of us, including Grandmama, whose room he was then staying in, called him "Mister Jim."

❦

Mister Jim of the Orr Place —its front road had been a route of the Yankee Soldiers—was born on December 17, 1879, to William Jackson Orr and Sara Angeline (Babe) Few Orr. Mister Jim had an older brother, William, a sister, Susie Elizabeth, born in 1882 (who died with the married name of Beale in 1919), and a younger brother, John Kenneth, born in 1891 and later married to a Carrie Morgan. Even as a young boy, Mister Jim had been considered a maverick. Completing Madison's public school (which opened in 1895), he'd gone on to several colleges throughout the South and as far away as Virginia. While his father and older brother ran one of the area's largest cotton plantations, located three miles from Madison, the young Mister Jim roamed the country aboard his favorite mode of transportation—the then fairly new and very popular bicycle. Once he led a group of his peers on a cycling trip to Texas and across the border into Mexico. Shortly after the turn of the century, Mister Jim, while in his twenties, had a daughter by a black woman named Queen. The child, Kate, for whom Mister Jim is said to have shown great affection, went North as a young girl. She returned once many years later, then left for good. Talk was she was "passing."

One day, shortly after Kate's birth, Mister Jim was out in the yard of the Orr place talking to his hired hand Eddie when up the road came walking Eddie's wife, Jessie Rose Lee Wildcat Tennessee. She was seven years Mister Jim's senior but that didn't stop him from falling heels over head in love with the long-haired, beautiful black gal. A possessive, quick-tempered individual, Mister Jim from that day onward made it known to all concerned—including Eddie—that Jessie was his.

Lord knows, after having several ruling white men of the region eating out of her hand and literally fighting over her, not to mention her being married, this declaration of Mister Jim's put a serious crimp in the free-spirited Jessie's style. As Missis Mamie Hampton, who lived to be a hundred and two years old, said, "Jessie was so beautiful that every time you saw her you were sure to see a white man, or more, following her, even in public."

Since Mister Jim was a white man of means and, according to lore, willing to duel anyone over her, Jessie knew, if she wanted to stay in the area, that she would have to be his "gal."

From this point onward no one remembered Eddie...other than to say he loved Jessie very much, and, like most colored men of the day, kept a low profile, never knowingly interfering with his wife's lifestyle. In 1917, Eddie Andrews, age unknown, died. Jessie had no living children by Andrews, but it is believed she had two by him early in their marriage. On occasion she was heard to talk about a Sidney, whom she said died at age two, and a Robert, who also, according to her, died as a baby. Both are believed to have been Eddie's children.

Jessie and Mister Jim were now in the spotlight, under which they were destined...or doomed...to dance and duel for the next fifty years. Amen.

Mister Jim's and Jessie's first child was a girl, Christine, born in 1907. Petite, beautiful, and blond, like her father, Christine was the apple of Mister Jim's eye. He spent much time with her and planned to eventually send her away to a private girls' school. But at the age of seven Christine came down with diphtheria. The story goes that on doctor's orders the child was not to have any sweets. Supposedly her mother gave her some sweets when she was ill and shortly thereafter the youngster died, causing some to say, "Jessie killed her child." Others have felt that this story was untrue, believing that Jessie, the eternal giver, simply found it impossible to deny her child anything she had that the daughter wanted. Whatever the cause, it is rumored that Mister Jim never forgave Jessie for Christine's death. There was only one picture made of Christine, which Mister Jim kept until his death...after which Grandmama had it, but it was lost a few years later when a fire burned down her house.

The couple had six other children, of whom three, Mamie, Quiller, and Gary, all died before the age of eight (child death was common at the time). Of the three children who lived to adulthood Fred, the oldest, born in 1909, was Jessie's pet. At an early age he fell in love with the gas buggie and in his teens became the proud owner of a Tin-Lizzie, Model T Ford.

George Cleveland, the second oldest, loved the land, the farm, and its animals. A horse-and-buggy man. The youngest, Beatrice, was born in 1917 and grew up spoiled by her mother... She also became the community's most sought- after female since the days of one Jessie Rose Lee Wildcat Tennessee. (Except for an occasional mentioning around her family, Jessie never talked about, nor used, the Wildcat Tennessee, "Indian" part of her name. I assume this end of her name was superfluous to the non-hoarder, light traveler, Jessie.)

In 1916 the new, second, Plainview Baptist, or "Upper" Church was completed (having broken away from the older "Lower" Church, just on down the road a piece). The Upper Church was built on two acres of land donated to the colored community for the purpose of a house of worship by Jessie's white man, Mister Jim. This act catapulted her to the position of leading female, or "Mother" of Plainview's Upper Church. Thereafter, it was "Mother Jessie and Mister Jim."

After having a house built for Mother Jessie, Mister Jim hired a colored couple, Rance and Ida Henderson, to work on her farm, land that was given to her by Mister Jim. Mother Jessie didn't have to do so much as milk a cow. Nor did her children. All the other youngsters of the community worked in the fields, but Fred, George, and Beatrice had only to go to school. Most local blacks didn't begrudge Jessie and her children their special status. She was constantly giving to the neighborhood needy much of what was given to her. The common view of the time was that colored folks got whatever they could from white folks, most of whom only handed out a bad time to blacks. Survival was foremost.

Mister Jim wanted Fred, George, and Beatrice to finish high school, preferably at the newly opened Booker T. Washington High School in Atlanta. He promised Mother Jessie he would take care of all expenses if she would just agree to send them. Booker T. Washington, or BTW— thanks mainly to the famed black educator and principal, C. L. Harper from Sparta, Georgia—had become Atlanta's first public high school for blacks.

Before BTW, public schools for blacks in the city only went as far as the sixth grade. (There were a few private high schools—Morehouse

College offered one, for example.) With the nearby Atlanta University System supplying BTW with some of the nation's top black teachers, the high school stressed college preparation courses rather than vocational courses. Students entered BTW from all over Georgia and many other sections of the South, and the country. BTW became and remained for many years the nation's largest and best-known black high school.

Unfortunately, Mother Jessie, besides not wanting her children out of her sight, felt that such an education would be too pretentious for her children. She didn't want them acting superior, or "putting on airs," around the community's less educated. Thus, Fred and George, both bright students, dropped out of elementary school after learning the three Rs, to the disappointment of Mister Jim, without any interference from their mother. Beatrice did go on to high school but she did not attend Booker T. in Atlanta. Instead she attended Burney Street, the county colored high school in Madison, but she never graduated.

Mister Jim eventually left his home on the Orr Place for a smaller, unpainted, shingle house built for him on Orr land about a half a mile from his mother...and even less distance from Mother Jessie. This was a move for appearance only, since everyone knew Mister Jim spent most of his time in Mother Jessie's house, where, among other things, she cooked for him. Why did Mister Jim pretend he wasn't living with Mother Jessie in a society where a white man of his standing could do anything he wanted with his black gal? Well, not quite anything.

It was the Code of the Old South for the ruling white men to have their colored gals. In fact, it was common practice for these white fathers to entrust their virgin sons to the "care" of their black women, or another black female, to ready them for a marriage to a "chaste" white lady.

But Mister Jim went completely against the Code. That is, he never married a white lady to raise a "legitimate" family while keeping his black gal on the side for sport. Instead, for his black gal, Mister Jim had a large new house built, painted white, and outfitted with fine furniture and "a rug on every floor." He also gave her farm land with animals and hired hands to work it, a riding horse, and a buggy. He supported her in a posh manner unique to most whites, much less blacks, of the area, and offered to have their children educated.

Lord, this was too much for the Southern White Man's Burden, or Old Code, to bear. The Code meant for no real man to treat his black gal like his wife, like a real woman, a white woman! The Old-Coders fumed and accused Mister Jim of being a "traitor to his class." By defying the Code and choosing not to marry a real woman who could produce him real children and by choosing not to use his nigger gal purely for pleasure, Mister Jim so angered his peers that, by a gentleman's agreement they—the region rulers—excommunicated him from their ranks. Amen.

Lord, once word of this gentlemanly agreement to disown one of their own leaked out (intentionally?), the doings of Mister Jim became fair game for any of his white critics to attack. (Incidentally, colored folks dug him.)

Inevitably came that late night when Mother Jessie was awakened. She heard her name being hollered outside and upon opening her front door she saw, in the flickering light of the lamp she carried, Mister Jim's worst critics...the Ku Klux Klan. Astride horses in her front yard, their identities hidden behind their pillowcase masks, they warned Mother Jessie to keep her "mixed-bred bastard children" from parading around town with the darker- skinned niggers where all the decent white folks and their children could see them. If she didn't heed their warning, they—the Ku Klux Klan—would hang her and all her bastard children from the same rope. Then, in their white bedsheet uniforms, the guardians of "white makes right" rode off into the night.

The KKK continued to make house calls on Mother Jessie in an apparent attempt to catch Mister Jim in her bed. But he was never caught, thanks to his ever-watchful black neighbors and Mother Jessie and their children and, most of all, thanks to the hideout. The front room of Mother Jessie's house had a large, deep closet. Shortly after the Klan began visiting Mother Jessie, Mister Jim had its wall moved forward, leaving a small space behind...large enough for him to stand up in. On a nail on the back wall of this closet hung year 'round a thick winter coat which shielded from sight the narrow door to his hiding space. Mister Jim hid there whenever he was at Mother Jessie's and the KKK came calling. Ever ready to run, Mister Jim wore his cap at Mother Jessie's at all times.

The Klan visited Mother Jessie's house where there lived only a woman and children. They never went to Mister Jim's house, which was just down the road, to catch him alone. They knew he carried a gun.

Meanwhile, Mother Jessie was having other problems with the Klan, having to constantly hide her children from them. She hid them with the neighbors, in the woods, fields, and barn, under the house and the beds, and in the closet hideaway. The KKK wanted to take them away from her. They told her that her children "looked too white for niggers." The bedsheeted brigade felt that this was especially true of Beatrice—a little girl they claimed was seen too often in the company of "big buck nigger boys"—and of George, about whom the delivering doctor had said to his mother at his birth, "Jessie, I doubt if this baby got a drop of Negro blood in him."

Mister Jim's and Mother Jessie's relationship was doomed to bring hardship on the Orr family socially and, eventually, economically.

After Mister Jim's father died in 1910, at the age of seventy, and following the arrival of the boll weevil to the region on the tail of World War One (along with other financially complex matters), most of the Orr's land was sold. (Included in these complex matters was much talk about Mister Jim's drinking and gambling—playing the stock market—and owning a big house outside of Atlanta in Stone Mountain, where, under the pretense of being his cook, Grandmama had often visited him.) Even though his maverick actions were the chief cause of the societal and financial ruin, not to mention "public embarrassment," that beset the Morgan County Orrs, Mister Jim wasn't ostracized by his family.

In fact, Mister Jim's mother, called "Babe" by her friends (and called "Miz Babe" by the blacks), took an immediate liking to Jessie and, later, to her children, the white lady's "colored" grandchildren. When the Orrs sold the plantation house in 1918, along with 171 acres of its land, the then-widowed Miz Babe moved to the town of Madison, and thereafter Mother Jessie commuted three days a week to attend her. The white woman was continually giving Mother Jessie clothing and, especially, household articles and furnishings for her and her children. Most of these gifts were in turn given by Mother Jessie to other less fortunate members of the community of Plainview.

Living with Miz Babe at the time was her granddaughter, Mana Manelle, or "Nell," born in 1913, the child of Miz Babe's oldest, deceased son, Will. Young Nell, like most of the children of Plainview, loved Mother Jessie and spent much time visiting with her and her children. Nell grew up very close to Fred, George, and Beatrice—her "colored cousins." She also played with many of her cousin's friends, who became her friends...while she was young. It got so that Nell wanted to spend all her time out in the country with Mother Jessie, her children, and their friends. Occasionally Mother Jessie would feel forced to send for someone to come and get the little girl and take her home. (Local social custom called for white girls—"little ladies"—not to spend the night with their colored cousins.) If no one was available, Mother Jessie herself would take little Nell the four miles into town, usually arriving past sundown at Miz Babe's.

Many years later, I was to hear my mother say of Nell, "She was a very, very sweet young girl...but very confused." (As a young married woman, Nell—then Smith—committed suicide.)

Despite the posh—for the time and place—lifestyle he provided for Mother Jessie and their children, Mister Jim was by no means a saint.

He undoubtedly loved Mother Jessie, but apparently he was much too possessive, too particular, and too much the perfectionist for her ever-wanting-to-be-free-as-the-wind soul. Jessie Rose Lee Wildcat Tennessee lived for the moment. A "grasshopper." Also, Mister Jim drank... He even went away to take the cure once. Often, when he hit the bottle he hit Mother Jessie. The last time he did this, Fred, still in his teens and owner of the same temper as his father, told Mister Jim that if he ever hit Mother Jessie again he would kill him. This threat by his colored son was strong enough to provoke Mister Jim to change his will, which was originally worded to leave the house and farm to Fred and move Mother Jessie out of the big white house into the smaller, unpainted, shingled house he had been living in. Meanwhile, Mister Jim moved into Mother Jessie's big white house with his mother, whom he had brought from town to live with him. Now Mother Jessie had a shorter commute, only a few minutes walk from her smaller, unpainted house to attend Miz Babe...and...Mister Jim in the big white house. Mother Jessie and her children soon started spending most of their time at their "old" home attending to the new residents.

Many years later, in a rare unburdening for her, Mother Jessie opened up momentarily to my mother, saying what a "hard time" it was being the woman of a white man and how she would never wish such an affliction on her daughter, Beatrice.

Eventually, Miz Babe moved back to town, whereupon Mister Jim sold Mother Jessie's former big white house and land to his first cousin, Mattie Allen—a mulatto—and her black husband, Wesley, or "Wes." Mattie Allen was the daughter of Mister Jim's father's brother. Mister Jim was then left with just over fifty acres of the original Orr land, which had once stretched within the county from Plainview to the community of Buckhead, land so vast it was discussed in terms of miles rather than acres. Shortly thereafter, Mister Jim left for Virginia to work for a railroad company. From Virginia, he sent money back monthly to Mother Jessie and the children, whom he continued to support. Mother Jessie went back to commuting to town to care for Miz Babe and the teenager Nell.

When the Depression, or "Hard Times" hit, Mother Jessie became the local—and later the county—official black midwife. Every black baby born at home, which included practically everyone, in Plainview (and many outside) was delivered by Mother Jessie, who kept a log recording the time and date of all births and took care to see that this information reached the Madison courthouse. These children became "her" children, many of whom she named, thus confirming to both the young and the old that Jessie Rose Lee Wildcat Tennessee was the true "Mother" of Plainview. Amen.

III. Miz Babe

June and I sat in Uncle Bubba's car outside Miz Babe's house in town watching our daddies bring her things out and put them in the car.

Now that Mister Jim had returned from Virginia and his house down the hill and across the branch into the woods in back of Grandmama's was finished, Miz Babe was moving in with him. Minutes earlier I had gone into Miz Babe's house and it had looked different from our house. Her house was much bigger and prettier than ours.

🍃

One day I went across the branch with Grandmama to Mister Jim's house. He and Miz Babe were sitting and talking out in the sun of the front yard. Miz Babe smiled and talked to me. She was real nice but when she got up to walk she moved so slow. She was very old. I didn't think she was too well.

The oldest daughter of Mister Jim's brother, William, was named Valeria (for whom Sister was named) and was married to Mister Albert Whitaker, who ran the hotel in town. They would bring their two young boys with them out to visit Mister Jim and Miz Babe. Once they brought a dentist to pull Mister Jim's teeth, with plyers. Valeria and her family seemed to like Grandmama and the rest of us. They always brought us children something. When the war started they moved to Florida and I never heard any more about them.

🍃

Every Sunday when we went to Grandmama's there would be a lot of men coming to see Aunt Bea. I didn't know why. Every time I, or one of the other children, tried to talk or play with one of these grown-ups, Aunt Bea would tell us, "Go outdoors and play!"— even if it was raining. Aunt Bea had a gramophone that stood on the floor with a tall stack of records beside it. She and some of the men and another woman or two (often the neighbor Missis Mary Allen) would dance—even on Sundays—to the blues, mostly sung by Tampa Red whom most of her records were by. Sometimes Aunt Bea and her friends took drinks from a bottle, and then they would talk and laugh even louder and dance much faster, and this would make Aunt Bea shoo us children out of the room more often.

Aunt Bea's main boyfriend was J.B. Hampton, Missis Mamie's youngest son. Sometimes J.B. even came to see Aunt Bea during the week. Daddy subscribed to the *Atlanta Constitution* newspaper. But before he, or we children, saw the daily paper, it was taken to Mister Jim, who after he read it sent the paper back to Grandmama's house. We children would pick up the Constitution and bring it home to Daddy, who read it first, then Mama would read us the funnies until we each learned to read them ourselves. One day Benny and I ran down to Grandmama's only to find her house locked! Panic! We knocked hard on all the doors and looked in all the windows but couldn't see anyone! It was dark inside. Yet we heard somebody in there. Benny said it was Aunt Bea and J.B. We hollered in to them that we wanted the paper. No response. But after much, much more of our loud hollering, the front door abruptly sprang open and out flew the newspaper, its pages scattering over the porch and the wind blowing it clear across the yard. Man, we were happy! But I was puzzled over how Aunt Bea and J.B. could read the funny papers in the dark?

Aunt Bea, who went to the picture show all the time, took me to see my first one. She took Sister and me to see Tarzan (Uncle Bubba drove us to town). In this show Tarzan and Jane, who was so pretty, took in a little boy they had found in the jungle whom they named Boy. I wanted to be Boy. After the picture show we stopped at W.H. Adams's garage, where Mister Les Edwards worked. Aunt Bea had to see him about something. Mister Les gave Sister and me a nickel each. I liked going with Aunt Bea because she knew a lot of men who liked to give us children nickels.

But my very first nickel had come from Daddy. One day he came home after getting paid by the WPA and gave all of us children a nickel apiece. So happy was I over this sudden, unexpected fortune that I hollered to the top of my voice and ran down to show the nickel off at Grandmama's, where I lost it.

❦

Until my first day of school I had no idea the world was stocked with so many children. Every bit fifty! When Benny took me there that first morning these children were all over the yard and in the schoolhouse! Lord! Enough to make you want to run back home and hide under the bed! When the teacher later let us all out of class to eat lunch, I followed Benny around the schoolyard until he told me, "Go play with the little boys"— and then he disappeared with the big boys. That's when I went running and crying for more than a mile all the way back home. Mama was against me too, sending me right back to school. But I walked back. That night Mama and Daddy talked seriously about what had "happened" that day. I felt much better knowing by the way my Mama and Daddy looked and sounded that they were going to do something about that schoolhouse with that schoolteacher and all those strange children. I was hoping they were deciding I wouldn't have to go back. Then, Lord, I discovered they weren't talking about me and my predicament but instead were talking about somebody called "Hitler" who had picked my very first day of school to start fighting a war somewhere a long way off. I was very disappointed in both my Mama and Daddy for not taking my schooling seriously.

❦

Grandmama had a cow, Peg, who didn't like little children. She was always chasing us away from the barn, especially when she had a little calf. Grandmama didn't milk Peg. Mama did. Peg didn't chase Mama. Peg's milk and butter were divided among three houses, Grandmama's, Mister Jim's, and ours. Uncle Bubba and his wife, Aunt Marie, and their one child, June, lived in Grandmama's three-room, shingled house. Aunt Bea lived with Grandmama too. Before Grandmama lived in this house, Mister Jim, everyone said, lived there.

Our tin-top house only had two rooms. In the bedroom where the fireplace was located, Mama and Daddy slept in one bed and Sister, Shirley, and Joe slept in another. This was where I had slept before Joe stopped sleeping with Mama and Daddy. Harvey, Benny, and I slept in a bed in the other room—the kitchen.

Grandmama gave Mama one of Peg's calves, which was mean, like her mother. Red and built more like a bull than a cow, she chased us children even as a calf, and she butted us with her hornless head. Only Mama she didn't butt. Daddy built a stable for her while Peg continued to stay in the barn behind Grandmama's house.

Grandmama also had a pig but no pen to keep it in. Our pig had a pen that Daddy built. Grandmama had to keep her pig chained and tied to a tree or a stake. It was Benny's job to care for the pig. One hot summer day he tied the little pig to a stake in the shade. When he stopped drawing pictures long enough to remember his daily duty, he ran out to move the pig to another shady spot and give it water. But the sun had beaten him there and given the little pig sunstroke. The pig died and shortly thereafter Grandmama sold Peg. Thus she retired from the animal-raising business, finding it less troublesome to live from Mama's and Daddy's pig and cow...and chickens and garden.

ॐ

One early Sunday morning at breakfast, Daddy and Mama were talking about Aunt Bea getting married the day before—not to J.B., her regular boyfriend, but to Toodney Maxey, Missis Cora Maxey's son. Eating quickly, I ran down to Grandmama's to see what Aunt Bea looked like married. A smiling Grandmama let me into the room where on the sofa sat our new Uncle Toodney, smiling, and Aunt Bea, who wasn't smiling.

ॐ

Grandmama called June and me into her house to see another baby. This time it was Aunt Bea's. Aunt Bea was lying in bed in the middle of the day like all women with brand new babies seemed to do and Grandmama was smiling when she held out Betty Jean for June and I to see. To see that she, a girl, was bald-headed! Needless to say, I ran out of the room.

ॐ

It snowed that winter. We children sat in the kitchen doorway at the back of our house looking out at the pretty, cold, white snow. Mama walked through the snow every day to tend to Miz Babe, who was so sick.

One cold night when the snow on the ground made the night look almost as light as day, Uncle Toodney knocked on the outside of our bedroom window, awakening Daddy to tell him "Miz Babe just died," before walking the four miles into town to get the undertaker. This awakened me too and after hearing what Uncle Toodney told Daddy I whispered to Sister, who'd heard too, "Miz Babe gonna gitcha," sending her scooting way down under the covers.

When the undertaker came early the next morning, the ambulance could not be driven onto Mister Jim's land because of the deep snow.

We children stood looking out the back door of our house watching Uncle Toodney walk through the deep snow, toting over his shoulder a big black bag...holding Miz Babe's dead body. Out of the woods he emerged from Mister Jim's house, trudging across the branch and up the hill back of Grandmama's house on his way out to the main road, toting the big black bag through the white snow.

This is what Mama has to say about that time in her writings she's leaving for the family:

"After Jim Orr came home from Virginia Missis Jessie went to town to cook, clean, and wash for his mother, Missis Babe, and on those days, about twice a week, Mister Jim came to my house, where I cooked for him. A short time later, he moved his mother, once the mistress of the antebellum Orr Place, from town to his small two-room cabin in the woods down back of his colored mistress. Missis Jessie cooked the food in her house and took the food to them. Not too long after she moved in with her son, Missis Babe, who was eighty-six years old, took sick. Missis Jessie also took sick at that time. This is when I started to attend Missis Babe.

"That winter we had one of our biggest snows ever. The snow was very deep.

"Missis Babe knew she was dying and I knew it too. But Jim Orr did not know. He and I were the only ones with her when she died. I stayed alone with her while he went to get someone to go to town for the undertaker.

"The snow was so deep that the body had to be carried by Beatrice's husband, Toodney, for nearly a mile from Jim Orr's cabin in the woods out to the main road where the ambulance waited.

"Jim Orr had wanted me to stay there when the undertaker, Mister Hemperley, came so that the white undertaker could see that Missis Babe had had a colored attendant in her last days. When the undertaker left, I left Jim Orr in his cabin all alone.

"Later, Jim Orr gave me Missis Babe's nicest winter coat and many more of her clothes.

"Jim Orr did not go to his mother's funeral."

IV. Uncles

I often wondered why children had parents. Besides being dull, and despite their claims of having once been young, parents didn't understand children. Uncles and aunts did. Uncles and aunts should have had all the children, not undeserving parents. I wanted to grow up to be, not a father, but an uncle. Like Uncle Bubba.

The grown men called Uncle Bubba a "sport." But we children never once saw him box or play baseball, the two most sporting things one could do in our young boys' circle. Yet the menfolk insisted—and usually with a wink to one another—that Uncle Bubba "played the field." Well, he most certainly didn't play on our baseball field. But what he did do around us young boys of Plainview that we loved so well (and for some inexplicable reason so did most local girls and women) was to speed up and down the road in the sawmill truck hauling lumber from the woods to town; coming around on Saturday afternoon when everybody said he was "half-lit," do a buckdance and afterwards give us children each a stick of peppermint candy before hopping back in his top-rolled-back V-8 to go speeding down the road while pulling on his tail a big cloud of red dust; then later that night with his cap pulled down over one eye he, performing alongside "Kisser" Jones and Bo Gilbert, would pick his guitar while moaning as mean and low-down a dirty dog blues as could the real Tampa Red. Uncle Bubba knew how to be an uncle, Lord, Lord!

Uncle Bubba also loved cars. He always had one, and all of his jobs involved driving a car or a truck. Even the year he was on the chain gang working on roads, he drove the dump truck. He had been caught operating a liquor still. Sent to the chain gang with him had been Mister Marshall Morgan—a townsman who with Uncle Bubba had married two sisters—Minnie and Marie Sanford. Mister Marshall Morgan had had nothing to do with the whiskey making. One day he had come to visit Uncle Bubba, who was down in the woods in back of Grandmama's house busy at the still. Mister Marshall arrived just minutes before the law and both men were arrested at the site. My early childhood regret was that Uncle Bubba got off the chain gang the year I was born, thereby depriving me of seeing him wearing his convict stripes while driving the dump truck. They say he was something else.

One late Saturday night I woke up suddenly to see Mama holding a lighted lamp. All of us children were now awake. There were men bringing somebody who was moaning loudly into the house. It was

Daddy. He sounded like he was dying. The men had brought him home from Uncle Bubba's wrecked car, which had gone off the road full of, Mama said, "drunk" men. When Uncle Bubba took that curve too fast and his car ended up in the ditch, everybody got thrown out except Daddy. He was trapped beneath the wreck wailing that he couldn't move because his back was broken. Uncle Bubba stood in the road and hollered over into the ditch, "G, the car gonna blow up!"— which sent Daddy's head ripping a hole in the car's canvas top to get out of there.

Daddy did injure his back, but apparently had emerged from the wreck more scared, or—like Mama said—"more drunk" than hurt. Besides Daddy's shooting through the car's canvas roof, the most talked-about incident of the wreck was Mister Marshall (yes, the same one) and his link pork sausage. Getting nothing more than a big bump on the head himself from the wreck, Mister Marshall stood at the accident site crying upon discovering that his family's Sunday morning breakfast, which earlier that Saturday evening he had bought in town, was strewn up and down the dirt road. Mister Marshall had some bad luck around Uncle Bubba.

Talk was Uncle Bubba couldn't hold his liquor...or held too much of it. Like the Saturday afternoon when he drove home with the family's groceries and slung the storebought stuff all over Grandmama's front yard instead of taking them out of the car and into the house. Then he jumped back into the driver's seat and sped off to town. Looking at the yard decorated with colorful wrappings that Aunt Marie was busy picking up, I thought this was a normal way for one to bring home groceries.

The road located a hundred or so yards from the front of our house ran to the main road, called the "crossroads," which was about a quarter of a mile from our house and led to town. This is the road Uncle Bubba used while driving Daddy and himself back and forth to work on the WPA. On these return-from-work trips in the afternoon his car would appear around the corner of the trees along the road in front of our house. When it made the turnoff onto the road that ended beyond the side of our house down in Grandmama's front yard, June and I would run out and jump on the car's running board for the short ride down. Running board riding, especially "jumping" (while the car was moving) was—next to "cussing"—Mama's and Daddy's biggest DON'T YOU EVER LET ME CATCH, SEE, OR HEAR OF YOUs! We children always felt that running board riding and jumping was like a cowboy jumping off his horse onto a runaway stagecoach. Well, one day I jumped for the running board of Uncle Bubba's car and missed. The car tire rolled onto my big toe, which caused me to holler so loud that Uncle Bubba immediately slammed on the brakes...right atop my big toe.

Sister was also a running board jumper. Her most memorable jump involved the running board of Mister Wes Allen's grey 1936 Ford. Mister Wes lived down the road from us in a big house that folks said Grandmama and her children had once lived in. Mister Wes drove so slow that you could almost walk up and step on his car's running board while it was still moving. But when Odessa, Mister Wes's oldest daughter, came shooting up the road in this same car, you had to be on your mark. Dust, chickens, and children scattered when Odessa went through. She drove almost as fast as Uncle Bubba.

Mama and Daddy had told us that anytime Uncle Bubba, Odessa, or anyone else came along in a car while we were on the road we were to step back into the ditch and stand there until the car had passed. Well, one day Mister Wes crept up the road in his car and Sister stepped off the shoulder (no one stood in the ditch when Mister Wes drove by) for the running board. She missed. But instead of getting her big toe smashed, Sister fell to the ground and the car tire just ran, slowly, over her arm.

Sister's first words were to me: "DON'T TELL!" Then she hollered, quietly, in pain. Mister Wes didn't hear her holler so he continued creeping down the road. Meanwhile, I, of the yet-flat-as-a-pancake big toe, wasn't about to "tell"— the worst sin a sibling could commit upon another sibling.

The next day Sister's arm was swollen. Still, we didn't tell. Soon she couldn't use it and had to hide the swelling from view by wearing long sleeves during the hot summer. Still we wouldn't tell. Then the arm started turning blue. And still we didn't tell. Finally, the swelling started going down and the arm returned to its normal color and use, without our ever telling. But Sister never again jumped any more running boards. My personal feelings were that if you couldn't jump Mister Wes's slow-moving car's running board, then you should not have been in the running board jumping business in the first place.

Both old and young called him "Shorty." That is, all but we Andrews children, who had to call him "Uncle Selma," on strict orders from Daddy. Uncle Selma was Grandmama's youngest brother and

Daddy's uncle. Daddy called him "Shorty." (Behind our parents' back we boys called him "Shorty" too, while the girls called him "Uncle Shorty.") Due to Uncle Selma's short, though muscular, stature eleven-year-old Benny and seven-year-old I yearned to wrestle him, since we felt he was small and old enough for us to "throw."

Early one Sunday morning Uncle Selma was in a hurry. He had left the other men in the car up at the road to run down to our house to get Daddy, who was eating breakfast.

"Hurry up in there, G, we gotta go!" hollered Uncle Selma through the screen door of our front porch while Daddy hurriedly gulped down his food at the kitchen table. Mama invited Uncle Selma to come in and have breakfast with us but he politely no-thanked her while fidgeting and fussing out on the front porch awaiting Daddy. When it suddenly got quiet on the porch we inside figured Uncle Selma had gone back up to the road to sit in the car with the other men to await Daddy. Then, without warning, through the screen door came a loud snore. Uncle Selma had stretched out on the front-porch bench waiting for Daddy and had instantly fallen asleep. Daddy left Uncle Selma snoring on the bench, and he and the rest of the men in the car rode off that early Sunday morning for wherever they were bound without their Shorty. Later that morning when Mama and us children left for church, Uncle Selma was still snoring loudly on the bench. Mama told us children he'd been drinking.

When we returned home from church that afternoon, Uncle Selma was still snoring on the bench and Benny and I saw our chance. Convinced we now for sure could out-wrestle, or throw, a half-asleep and drunk old man, we woke Uncle Selma.

After quickly throwing both of us with one arm, Shorty laid back down on the bench and right away went back to snoring.

V. Aunts

I always thought of uncles and aunts as being independent souls, having to answer to no one but God...and sometimes a nephew or niece.

Daddy loved hot peppers. He, to the consternation of Mama, even cut them up over his grits. So hot would these peppers be that Daddy would sit eating his breakfast with tears rolling down his cheeks and into his grits. Whenever Mama asked why he punished himself so with peppers, he would whisper in a choked-up, hoarse voice "'Cause I love them."

The peppers would be picked from the garden and hung on the wall of the back porch or kitchen to dry and turn red, or redder, and hotter. One day on Grandmama's back porch I pulled one of these pretty red peppers from its string and with no one looking chomped down on it. And hollered. During my spitting, sputtering, and mouth-rubbing while running home, I somehow got a hot pepper seed, or more, into my eye. The eye burned, turned fiery red, swelled, and closed. Mama washed the eye the best she could, put a bandage over it, and sent me to bed. Word about my red-hot-pepper-seed-filled-eye spread and by nightfall several people, mostly grownups, came by to sit up with me, talk among themselves, and tell "eye" stories. One of the grownups there that night was Grandmama's sister, Aunt Cora, who was in her fifties. Aunt Cora had been married several times, but more importantly she had been to Savannah. As a young woman she had spent a week or two in the coastal city, but the older Aunt Cora got the longer she had stayed in Savannah. By now nobody around her could recollect anything from the past without hearing her say, "That reminds me of when I was living in Savannah..."

The only Aunt Cora Savannah story I recall from the night of the red pepper seed in the eye was the one she told when the subject of snakes came up...which reminded her of the time she was standing on a log in the middle of the Savannah River (with no mention of why she was out there in the water) only to look down and discover the log was a snake. That flat-out ended all snake talk that night. The next morning Mama said that if my eye still hurt I didn't have to go to school. The eye's swelling had gone down and even the pain was gone but I had so enjoyed all the special attention of the night before that I wanted to be a full-time invalid. But then Mama told me that if I stayed at home I would have to work around the house. I went to school.

Mama's oldest sister, Aunt Lula, would send us boxes of clothing from her home in Jersey City, New Jersey. Mostly these were clothes that her three children—Cozette, Frank Junior, and Marion (the youngest, born the same year as Harvey)—had outgrown. These clothes were usually too big for us but it never stopped us from wearing them. We often wore out the clothing before growing into it. Whenever we Andrews children showed up for school or church in clothes too big, everyone knew a box had just arrived from New Jersey.

Once our New Jersey cousin, Frank Junior, wrote and told us children that his family had a "tree" in their backyard. We Georgia children of the 1940s weren't at all impressed by anyone having a tree in the backyard. But if Frank Junior had mentioned having in his yard a car...

In the summer of 1945, Aunt Lula's daughter Cozette came with Aunt Polly's daughter Geraldine to visit us. We enjoyed Cozette in spite of her having told Benny and me the ending to the Humphrey Bogart movie Conflict, which we went to see the following week. Too, when Cozette left, Mama said her sister's child didn't understand us having an "outdoor" toilet. I couldn't figure out what there was to "understand" about our toilet.

Then, in 1949, Mama got a letter from Aunt Lula saying her youngest daughter, Marion, had died after a brief illness at the age of twenty-one. Aunt Lula, it was said, never got over the death of her baby.

Mama had a sister, Aunt Soncie, who lived in Madison. Aunt Soncie was married to Corris Mapp. Her family hadn't wanted her to marry him because they considered him to be too old for her (by thirteen years) and because he had been divorced. But we children loved Uncle Corris because he spent lots of time with us. Besides giving us rides in his car, Uncle Corris was one of history's great nickel-and-dime givers. He gave Benny and me our first dime, which we used to buy our first comic—or "funny"— book.

Aunt Soncie and Uncle Corris had no children and they, especially she, drove out to see us quite often. One year they drove all the way to Jersey City to see Aunt Lula's family, taking my sister Shirley with them, and while there they drove to New York City to see the World's Fair.

The rest of us older children never quite forgave the younger Shirley for being the first one of us to go to a big city, to go up North, to go to New York City, and to go to the World's Fair—all at once. The fact that she was too young (four years old) to remember much helped some...but still she had gone and we older ones had not. Of course, we didn't blame Aunt Soncie and Uncle Corris for Shirley's sin.

Uncle Corris, whose family owned the Mapp Funeral Home in Madison, lived with Aunt Soncie in a pretty house in town. Sometimes when Aunt Soncie drove out to our house she would take one or two of us children back to town to stay a few days with her and Uncle Corris in this pretty, yellow-with-green-top house. A social soul herself, Aunt Soncie always insisted we children who were visiting her house go outside to play with the children in the neighborhood. But we country children didn't right away take to strange, especially town, children. Besides, in the country we could play outdoors with other children whenever we wanted. Town was for indoors. So we would try to spend most of our stay indoors admiring Aunt Soncie's house. She had such pretty furniture, and a radio, a telephone, a daily newspaper that one could read without waiting until Mister Jim had read it, magazines, and a refrigerator that was loaded with good things to eat, including ice cream. To top everything off, you could go sit on her front porch and, looking straight across the yard and down the bank, see the train shooting past. (But to go to the toilet at Aunt Soncie's you still had to go outdoors. It was said there were many townfolks who had their outhouses in their houses. That must've felt funny, I thought, to go to the toilet inside the house.)

During one of my visits, Aunt Soncie was entertaining several of her women friends in the sitting room when one of them asked,

"Soncie, how old are you?"

"Twenty-eight."

"No, Aunt Soncie, you're thirty-two, Mama's twenty-eight," says me, correcting my forgetful aunt. There followed a deathly silence before Aunt Soncie spoke, in a tone of voice I'd never heard her use before.

"Brother! Go outside and play!" For the first time ever I went outdoors to play with the strange, town children.

Later, and in that same weird tone of voice I'd never heard her use before, Aunt Soncie said to me, "Brother, don't you ever, ever again mention my age to anyone, not even me! You hear?"

"Yes, Ma'am." Now I was doubly puzzled. Why didn't Aunt Soncie know her own age and why didn't she want to know it?

Mama's other sister, Aunt Polly, who was next to Aunt Lula in age, was "different." As a youngster she had cracked a black walnut between her teeth and had caught a fox which she killed with her own hands. (And when she would grow old she would carry a pistol in her purse.) Aunt Polly taught school and had more than one husband, but only one child. Her last husband was named Few. He fought in World War Two and came back shell-shocked.

But Aunt Polly was known most for her traveling, spending her years between Madison, Atlanta, Macon, Fitzgerald, Knoxville, Jersey City, and Chicago. While most of her relatives were working in the fields, Aunt Polly, the family's orginal "jet setter," would wave at them from the window of a streaking-on-down-the-road Greyhound bus. As the saying went,

> *She's living so high on the hog*
> *She can afford to ride the Greydog.*
> *Yes, Lord, she's catching the next 'hound*
> *'N gitting on to the next town.*

Besides always being prettily dressed, Aunt Polly herself was pretty. The grown men especially thought so. And talk was Aunt Polly had lots of boyfriends. More than Aunt Cora. And just as many as Aunt Bea. But most important, it was whispered, the men Aunt Polly liked best were preacher men. "Lord have mercy!" they all said. Such talk wasn't supposed to reach the ears of us children. But it did. Besides, we couldn't help but see that whenever our pretty Aunt Polly, dressed to kill, came to visit, a lot of menfolk happened to drop by to say hello.

Lawd, Lawd,
Greydog, Greydog!
Amen for aunts!

VI. IT

One beautiful spring morning in 1940 Uncle Bubba drove Aunt Bea into town to buy IT. They returned early in the afternoon with IT, and Aunt Bea carried IT in a box from the car into the house as gently as she would've a bomb. We children followed her every step and watched her every move as she carefully unpacked IT from the box.

IT was very small, built like a box, and black. Written on the front was the silvery word PHILCO. We crowded around to watch, and got in the way, as Uncle Bubba hooked IT up. Then Aunt Bea turned one of the two little round knobs on IT's front, and from out of the little black box came the sound of a man's voice. I had heard my first radio. So stuck did we children become to the little black talking-and-singing box that day that Mama had to call us home for supper and then again later that night for bed. Early that next Sunday morning we were back down at Grandmama's listening to Aunt Bea's radio.

I was convinced that there were little people inside the radio making it talk and sing like it did. I even sneaked a look at the back of the radio, which was sealed up except for a hole. By closing one eye I could look into it and did. I saw nobody. Then I thought that maybe these weren't the voices of "real" people. Maybe they were just make-believe voices that sounded like real people. I was never that curious about how movies operated because they were shown in the picture show in town where anything magical could happen. But here was a little radio talking and singing all by itself in Grandmama's house!

Daddy had owned the community's first radio. In the late 1920s he had bought a small RCA Victor radio that came with ear plugs that had to be inserted in order to hear it at all. Wearing these ear plugs, he'd walk down the road and suddenly break out into a wild buckdance, making people think he was "tetched" in the head. But only one person could listen to this radio at a time and when it eventually broke down Daddy never had it fixed. Yet he kept it wrapped in its original casing in a box under his and Mama's bed.

Shortly after Aunt Bea bought her radio, Daddy bought his second one, second-hand. This one was a larger box and everyone could hear it at once. But Daddy wouldn't let any of his children touch this brown, bigger-than-Aunt-Bea's-little-black box. Besides himself, only Mama was allowed to so much as touch this radio. Whenever he left home for work or elsewhere for any length of time he always disconnected the radio's aerial. But just as soon as he was out of sight we children, with the approval of Mama, who didn't believe us to be the bumblers Daddy thought we were, would reconnect the radio and listen to it until shortly before he was due home, when we would disconnect it.

It was Mama who told me there were no little people in the radio. She said the radio voices were those of "real" people coming from all over the world and when we turned the radio off the voices did not stop until we turned them back on to finish what they were saying or singing but instead kept right on talking and singing even though we couldn't hear them. I tried listening when the radio was turned off, but I heard nothing. I don't know how Mama knew all this but, I swear, this is what she told me.

Mister Wes also owned a radio, even before Aunt Bea, and his was the first one to which people in the neighborhood listened to hear the fights of Joe Louis (the real one). It was on Mister Wes's radio that the people of Plainview heard Joe Louis win the Heavyweight Championship and later beat the German, Max Schmelling. These were fights I was too young to go listen to. But since Daddy was a big boxing fan, the Joe Louis fight crowd started coming to our house to listen when Daddy got his radio. Mama was no boxing fan but she liked Joe Louis enough to stand, just on fight nights, the predominantly male crowd.

When Louis won the championship in 1937, I was only three years old and didn't remember the fight. But in the succeeding years I heard again and again about that June 22nd night when "Joe won it all." Unsure if I remembered or not, I constantly tried to remember so hard that I thought I remembered. What I do remember about the Joe Louis fight nights at our house were the crowds, my efforts to stay awake until the fight started, and static. Radio static.

Daddy, like a radioman attempting to contact sinking ships at sea, was always at the controls, down on one knee in front of the radio, continually trying frantically to bring in the sound of the fight through the never-ending noise of popping static coming through like rapid machine-gun fire mixed with exploding shells. Through all of this static shock, Daddy gritted his teeth and hung in there, to decipher—or guess at—the words of the fight announcer and relay them back over his shoulder to the anxiously-waiting-to-hear packed house. Daddy got better at announcing with each Joe fight. But what I'll never forget about those fight nights was the big WHOOP!!! that went up from the crowd at our house and could be heard nearly all over Plainview when the referee, or Daddy, announced, "The winner and still champion, Jooooe Looouisss!!!"

The next day I never failed to give my playmates a blow-by-blow, round-by-round, verbatim account of the fight...without the static. I was

almost as good as that other fight announcer, Daddy.

Joe Louis (the real one) made boxing the favorite participant sport of Plainview's young boys. That is, most of them. While Harvey and Benny put up their dukes against all comers practically daily during the noon recess hour at Plainview's one-room schoolhouse, the art of throwing punches bored me. Especially if the punches were being thrown at me. My trouble was that I couldn't take boxing lightly. To me it was no game. I never wanted to hurt anyone (nor get hurt) so at the beginning of any boxing match I suddenly found myself in I would automatically pull my punches. But if I got stung I would get mad, and if gotten the better of would start crying. And then, Lord, all hell would break loose (at least for me). I would stop boxing and start fighting, holding back nothing with my fists and letting everything but cusses loose from my mouth. Everyone always said that I took a little bloody nose, fat lip, black eye, or missing tooth much too personally.

But in a never-ending attempt to keep boredom at bay, while at the same time save face (along with the rest of my body), I worked myself into becoming the arranger, promoter, and referee of Plainview's Recess Hour Fistic Tournament of Elimination (after safely eliminating myself). As a result, this daily burden of having to look out for those who didn't know how to go about finding someone to fight at recess left me no time for any fighting of my own.

VII. The Neighborhood

Besides owning one of the few cars in Plainview, after Mister Jim sold the big white house to him and Mattie Allen, Mister Wes owned enough land to house several other families who helped work the land. Moving onto his land too were his parents, Mister Frank and Missis Marylou. Folks said Mister Wes took after his daddy, who could be ornery at times—so ornery that we boys never got up the nerve to ask Mister Frank to show us the hole in his lower leg where—it was said—yet lodged a bullet.

Mister Wes and his wife, Missis Mattie, who was Daddy's second cousin, didn't object to my spending so much time at their place. I liked it because their house had so many interesting things in and around it. Besides pretty furniture, a radio, a big kitchen where no one had to sleep and where Missis Mattie was always cooking something good, there was the car in the garage whose horn I was always trying to honk. Also there was a big barn and lot with mules, cows, and pigs, a two-horse wagon, a blacksmith shop, a shed full of all sorts of tools, a deep well, and plenty of apple, peach, pear, and plum trees. I wished Grandmama had kept this house.

Mister Wes was also known for his two pretty daughters, Odessa and Pauline. These were two "older girls" who went to school at Burney Street High, or "Town School." Odessa always appeared to be in a hurry and we boys loved seeing her driving her father's car fast. Also, Odessa had no time for children. Especially for Sister.

Once, on one of my daily jaunts to visit the Allens, Sister decided to join me. It was the day before Odessa's birthday. Sister had a way of finding out everyone's business, especially what others didn't want her to know. And, Lord knows, Odessa didn't want any children finding out about her having cake and ice cream on her birthday. But Sister found out. The cake and ice cream were scheduled to be eaten by the family Allen—alone—on Sunday, Odessa's birthday. But Sister, not wanting to chance missing anything, was awaiting Odessa when she stepped out of the car that early Saturday afternoon bringing, Sister swore, store-bought ice cream. Missis Mattie, Sister also swore, had already made the cake and put it in hiding. Enough to get my interest! Sister and I hung around the Allens' kitchen until past sundown just in case birthday-eve samples were given out but we saw no sign, nor heard any mention, of ice cream and cake.

That following day, immediately after Sunday school (an Andrews

must per Mama), Sister and I shot straight for cake-and-ice-cream land without stopping home. Odessa was waiting, determined that we two uninvited guests were not going to get any cake or ice cream. And Sister was just as determined that we were.

Came Sunday afternoon dinner Sister and I were still hanging tough...and hungry. The Allens invited us to dine with them but we were not interested in "regular" food. Sister and I came for the "real" food—cake and ice cream. We waited.

We sat in the kitchen amidst the aroma of food until the last plate was cleaned off, cleared from the table, washed, dried, and put away. Still no cake and ice cream. Sister began following Odessa about the house on the chance the goodies were stashed elsewhere. Meanwhile, on Sister's orders, I remained at my post in the kitchen. Still no ice cream and cake.

Finally, Sister said goodbye to all, took my hand, and we headed home. Or so my hungry stomach thought. Just around the bend, Sister suddenly stopped, quickly reversed directions, and, still holding my hand, scooted back to take a last peek in the window. No ice cream and cake. Desperate, Sister circled the house peeking in all the windows, still clutching my hand. No ice cream and cake! Sundown finally sent us home and while the two of us hungrily wolfed down cornbread and black-eyed peas, Sister, in between bites, told the rest of our envious family about the delicious cake and ice cream Odessa had served to us.

I still wonder how Odessa managed to hide that ice cream and cake from Sister.

❧

Mister Martin Dorsey's land was farther on down the road, and adjacent to Mister Wes's land. The two men didn't get along. Mister Martin owned his own farm, a tiny one compared to Mister Wes's. Mister Martin often said that Mister Wes treated the folks on his land like they did in slavery time. Mister Martin had a wife and son but, everyone said, due to the husband's contrariness, she took the boy and left. He and Mister Wes were always disagreeing about something, and everything, until, following one of their heated disputes, Mister Martin apparently threatened Mister Wes to the point where Mister Wes had the law come out and get Mister Martin and take him back to town to jail. One night, wearing only his straw hat and long johns, Mister Martin escaped from jail and went back to his farm. Recaptured, he was declared "crazy" and sent to the asylum down at Milledgeville, where he eventually died.

Mister Martin always liked Mama and us children, whom he invited to help work his farm, and nobody else.

❦

One day Benny told me that he and I were going to run away from home. Up until that moment I hadn't thought anything about leaving home, but Benny had. He led me deep into the woods in back of Mister Jim's house to a small clearing where he had dug three shallow holes for the foundation of the house we were going to build to live in once we ran away from home. At the site were several pieces of lumber Benny had dragged from a nearby sawmill after working hours. Benny said we would get the house built before the sawmill moved, which would solve our lumber problem. Also, he said, the sawmill's slab pile would serve as our firewood supply for the yet-to-be-built house's yet-to-be-built fireplace.

Benny had thought of other necessities as well. The foremost of these was meeting the mailman daily to get the newspaper; then we would read the funnies and return the paper to the box before it was missed. To hear a radio we would sneak up each night outside the window of our house, Aunt Bea's house, or Mister Wes's house and listen (all radios in the community sat in front of windows because of their outside aerials). Our food supply was next in importance. It was to consist of watermelons, cantaloupes, tomatoes, and cucumbers in the summer and sweet potatoes in the winter, all things we liked that did not need to be cooked...and all coming from Mama's garden. In addition, we would eat the wild berries, cherries, locusts, muscadines, persimmons, and plums that grew along roadsides and in the woods. None of these needed cooking either. Then there were apple, crabapple, peach, pear, plum, mulberry, and pecan trees and peanut patches. With all this available food and the funny papers and radios, Benny figured we would be set for life, or at least until we were grown.

Around this time Georgia's number one prison-escaper, Forrest Turner, had broken out again and was leading the bloodhounds and guards on a merry chase around the state. The radio and newspapers were continuously reminding all within range of this chase. Every time one heard dogs barking far off in the woods whenever Forrest, or any convict, escaped, it was assumed the dogs were on the trail of the escapee. One day Benny and I heard dogs barking far off. We didn't go down into the woods that day, or the next...or the next... By the time ol' Forrest was caught, our minds had moved on to things other than running away from home.

About a year later was when I seriously considered running away from home. This happened when I felt I got from Mama "someone else's whipping" (a common childhood feeling in a family of one or more children). Following Mama's major mistake, I ran down into the woods and across several fields crying, with the intention of never going back home. I would show them, especially Mama. But about time I got through crying, and exhausted from running, I couldn't think of anywhere else to go. Besides, I didn't want to see anyone I knew as I didn't want them knowing I had gotten a whipping and had been crying. So I went back home and forgave Mama.

❧

We first heard about THEM in connection with Town School, where the country folks said all the children were bad. And THEY were said to be the baddest of them all.

Then, one early Saturday morning we children stopped playing in our front yard to look up and see THEM walking down the road on the way to see a cousin, Missis Mary Allen, wife of Mister John, brother of Mister Wes. They were the Masseys. Lil' Bubba, Minnie Pearl, Jesse, Pig, Harry, George, and Paul. They came in a pack. At home was R.Z. As a baby R.Z. was tossed over a pigpen fence by one of his older siblings who missed the intended receiver sibling on the other side, thereby crippling R.Z.'s legs for life. But talk was R.Z. was still a Massey, having such upper body strength that if he didn't like you and got close enough to you he could, and would, tear you up.

That Saturday morning without uttering a word we just knew that on their return the Masseys were going to stop by our house.

Meanwhile, we kept playing close to the house...and waiting. Mama and Daddy went off to town, leaving Harvey in charge of us younger five. I continued to play, wondering why Mama and Daddy had deserted us with the Masseys loose in the neighborhood. Yet I was old enough to know that parents didn't fight their children's fights. We had to fight our own fight. The Masseys. So we six children played on...and waited.

Then, sometime in the early afternoon when all the adults were doing their Saturday-in-town business, we children all looked up from our playing in the front yard at the same time to see coming around the bend of the road THEM! The Masseys were coming back!

Harvey herded us all into the house. Sister, Shirley, and Joe got under Mama and Daddy's bed (earth's safest hiding place for children). Harvey, Benny, and I hooked all three screen doors from the inside and closed and latched the lone back door and one of the two front doors. Then just inside the open doorway, and behind the kitchen screen door, Harvey, Benny, and I stood...awaiting the Masseys.

By now the Masseys had turned off the front road and were heading for our front yard. They came walking toward our house so spread out behind their big brother, Lil' Bubba, that to me, peering out between Harvey and Benny, the Masseys looked like they covered our whole front yard. They were walking slowly now, their overall pockets bulging with rocks for throwing at things and folks. Stopping at the front porch, Lil' Bubba started talking first, about something which quickly led to an argument with Harvey. Harvey's advantage at that moment was having the screen door between him and Lil' Bubba. Lil' Bubba, two years older than Harvey, had the advantage of being able to cuss. While Lil' Bubba was cussing him to his face, Harvey had Sister at his back hollering from under the bed that she would "tell" Daddy and Mama if he said a "bad word."

What I remember most about this Andrews-Massey confrontation was the battle of the screen door. The Masseys were trying desperately to pull open the hooked door, while Harvey and Benny pulled the door toward us. Benny, an accurate spitter, was spitting through the screen and hitting his insulted targets. One of the Masseys was pressing his face against the screen and Harvey quickly grabbed a needle from Mama's sewing machine drawer and stuck it through the screen and deep into the pressed lip. The victim's screams from Harvey's acupuncture sent the Masseys off the porch and back into the yard to regroup. Then they returned to the porch and came straight for the screen door with a rock in each hand, only to meet Harvey...standing on the other side of the screen and pointing at them Daddy's double-barreled shotgun. The Masseys, led by Lil' Bubba, left our front porch and front yard running.

The shotgun wasn't loaded (Daddy kept all the shells locked up) but the Masseys didn't know that.

We were destined to meet the Masseys again...and again...

Soon. Not many months following this Saturday afternoon confrontation the word went out. The Masseys were moving to Plainview! This meant that rather than waiting until they came to visit their cousin, Missis Mary, we could now on practically a daily basis see...and fight...the Masseys. Each school morning the children living on our end of the community would meet at the crossroads and walk to school together. One morning waiting at the crossroads were the Masseys. Minnie Pearl, six years my senior, pushed me off the road into the water-filled ditch. Older brothers always came to the rescue of a younger brother...except if the latter was being attacked by a girl. Then the younger brother was on his own, unless his sister intervened, but this would be the height of embarrassment...a boy's sister saving him from being "picked on" by a girl. But Sister, never one to let awakened dogs stop barking, instantly jumped to my rescue. In words only. Sister got Minnie Pearl "told," and then some, about picking on me while the big Massey girl kept shoving me back into the ditch with each Sister sound. So as Sister talked and Minnie Pearl shoved, I walked the muddy ditch the entire two miles to school.

It wasn't me who told the teacher why I came to school so muddy. Sister told. (I had not wanted to walk the muddy ditch home along the other side of the road.)

At recess, with a fist in the mouth Minnie Pearl hushed Sister...temporarily. The Code of the Schoolyard sent me, a brother, up against Minnie Pearl to save Sister's honor...for which I got from Minnie Pearl a whack in the back that brought up breakfast. But with a bleeding mouth...and out of roundhouse range...Sister got Minnie Pearl "told," and then some, for picking on me.

(During her first week of school, Shirley, accompanied by Sister and en route from school one day, took the Minnie Pearl test...a fist in the face. Landing in the ditch she was immediately joined by Sister. But in defending her younger sibling, Sister kept crawling out of, and getting knocked back into, the ditch to tell off Minnie Pearl, who as usual wasn't listening, just hitting. Meanwhile, Shirley stayed put, thus learning early that whoever was knocked down by Minnie Pearl best stayed down.)

VIII. Mama's Folks

After finding out Grandmama had once been a girl my next big surprise in life came upon learning that our Mama had a grandmama! It was at the age of eight that I first remember hearing about Greatgrandmama Polly...the day she died. This is when Mama first began telling us children about her folks.

Polly Walton's maternal grandfather was white, her grandmother black. This made Polly's mother a mulatto. She mated with a white man to produce Polly, circa 1858, in Eatonton, Georgia. Polly's father was "Mister Walton." Polly's mother died when Polly was very young and Mister Walton took her into his home and raised her with his other children—Polly's white half brothers and sisters. One of these children, a boy, whom Polly was very close to, died before reaching the age of ten.

Mister Walton's wife didn't like the idea of her husband bringing his child by a mulatto into their home but, having no choice, she lived with it. This didn't mean she had to like Polly, whom she punished often.

Once Missis Walton was missing an important set of keys and she immediately blamed, and for days scolded, Polly for losing them. Polly was saved from more scolding when one night in a dream, or a vision, her young half brother, the Waltons' dead son, came and told her the keys were on top of his mother's chiffonier in a room that Polly wasn't permitted to enter. The next morning Polly told Missis Walton where to find the keys, and sure enough they were there, which ended Polly's punishment, temporarily.

During the Civil War when the Yankees came through Eatonton, rumors spread that the soldiers were taking all mulatto children and sending them North where—word went—they'd be white. Missis Walton assisted her husband in hiding his mulatto (quadroon?) child in a trunk until the Yankee soldiers had passed through.

Polly didn't have to work in the field but worked around the house much harder than did her half brothers and sisters. Polly rode on horseback over the farm, carrying messages between the Big House and the fields. She was also in charge of rounding up the milking cows and herding them back to the barn each evening. Often during heavy rains the creek would rise up to her horse's belly, but come rain, shine, sleet, or slime, Polly and her horse brought the cows home every day.

At about age twenty, Polly met and, with the approval of her father, married Harrison Allison, a black man about twenty-five years old. The couple moved north from Putnam County to adjoining Morgan County. There they settled on the land of a white family named Harris, for whom Polly cooked and Harrison did yard work. Harrison also helped with the cooking, especially when the family was entertaining guests, since barbecue was his specialty.

Following the death of Mister Harris, whom Harrison nursed until the end, the couple moved within the county to a place near Buckhead called Baldwin Hill. Meanwhile, between 1880 and 1902, Polly and Harrison had thirteen children, including one who died at birth. Polly had milky white skin, blue eyes and long, straight black hair which, in the style of the day, she wore in a huge ball atop her head. All 13 of their children had her complexion except one, Ruby, who was tan like her father. Slender during an era when fat was fashionable, Harrison had a sister, Nan, just as thin as he, causing everyone to feel sorry for these two skinny, starving critters who were believed to have worms.

Along with her skinniness, Nan was well known for her unsweet cookies, which she never failed to bring to family gatherings. There everyone politely tasted a cookie, praised it, and while Nan wasn't watching, disposed of the alien cookie, preferring to return to more familiar, sweeter foods.

Polly's mother had another child, Sam, but not by Mister Walton. Sam, Polly's half brother, was a short, dark, red man with pointed features and straight black hair. Some said he was part Indian. (Back then if one—black or white—was not sure of his or her ancestry, it was blamed on the Indians.) After Polly got married Sam came to visit her family with his wife, Julia. Julia was a regular churchgoer, and she was a shouting addict. She would begin to shout the moment the preacher started the sermon, even before he had had a chance to warm up to the Word. She shouted until the sisters in the congregation determined she'd felt the spirit long enough. Then they would lead her outside the church building for some fresh air where they would try to keep her as long as possible because the moment she returned to her seat the Holy Spirit would immediately strike again and send her off into another shouting fit. Back out for fresh air she would be taken. With Julia, no matter who the preacher was, he was guaranteed a sure shout.

While the Allison family lived on Baldwin Hill, two of the sons, Cleveland and Hobson, were drafted during World War One and went on "over there" to France. While they were away their youngest brother, Gassett, died at age sixteen. Less than a month later, Harrison died, at approximately age sixty-five. Death was not due to worms.

When Mama's father John Crawford Perryman was born in Putnam County in 1871 his mother, Mary Perryman, was in her forties and his father, William Henry Perryman, whom it was said was pure African, was in his fifties. Besides John, who came to be known by his middle name, Crawford, there were nine other children. Hard-working farmers who owned their own land, the Putnam Perrymans (not to be confused with the Morgan County Perrymans) kept to themselves. As a young man, Crawford, tall, dark of skin, and hefty, with a thick mustache, left home for Morgan County where, in the community of Barrows Grove, he met, married, and had a child by the sister of Eddie Andrews, husband of one Jessie Rose Lee Wildcat Tennessee. Both the wife and child died during the birth.

Then, Lord, at the turn of the century the widower John Crawford Perryman met and married Lula Allison, the eldest daughter of Harrison and Polly Allison. Born in 1880, Lula, with the light skin and long, straight black hair of her mother, bore a slight resemblance to Jessie Rose Lee Wildcat Tennessee. But in appearance only. There was nothing fast, sassy or, heaven help, "jazzy" about Lula. Lula, Lord, was a "lady." And over the years Jazzy Jessie came to envy Lady Lula her beautiful manners.

Meanwhile, the Putnam Perrymans, led by the father William Henry, disowned Crawford, accusing him of marrying "that white woman," or a "Plantation Nigger."

Quite a number of blacks in the pre-boll weevil South owned their own land. Those who did or who were not directly dependent upon whites for their living, referred to those blacks (sharecroppers, day hands, et al.) who lived on or directly from the white man's land as "Plantation Niggers," a group felt to be too close to and too dependent upon whites to be trusted by other blacks. And any light-skinned or "tainted" Negro was automatically labeled a Plantation Nigger by these independent blacks, whether the contaminated one was any longer associated with the plantation or not. And by the rules of these proud blacks, the Lady Lula was "tainted." Thus the old, proud, African William Henry and his Perryman family disowned their own John Crawford for marrying a contaminated Plantation Nigger.

Crawford's younger sister, Lucy, later married a fair-skinned man, Howard Perryman of the Morgan County Perrymans, and suffered the same fate as her brother, being ostracized by the family. Crawford and Lucy spent their lives comforting each other, since the Putnam Perrymans had cut off all ties with these two family traitors.

Unlike Lucy, who had a childless marriage, Crawford and Lula had nine children: John Crawford, Junior, Lula, Polly, Soncie, Mary, Viola, Harrison, William Henry, and Junie. All lived to adulthood except Mary, who died at seventeen, William Henry, who died at one, and Junie, who died at age two.

The Crawford Perryman family lived in the bottom half of Morgan County, some six to eight miles outside Madison in Barrows Grove near the black farming community of Springfield. In this area blacks either owned their own land or rented farms, often from other blacks. No sharecropping went on there. Crawford rented a large farm with a beautiful, roomy, sturdy house from the white family Adams with the understanding between him and the landlady (Doctor Adams's widow) that he would eventually buy the house and farm.

Thanks to his Perryman background, Crawford had a strong belief in education and made sure that all his children went to and remained in school while living under his roof. A fervent admirer of Booker T. Washington and George Washington Carver, Crawford dreamed of sending his oldest son, John Junior, to Tuskegee Institute in Alabama. Crawford also read a great deal, and he encouraged his children to read by keeping as much reading matter as possible available in the home. He followed closely local, state, national, and world news. Crawford also kept close tabs on the day-to-day price of cotton, his farm's staple, through the daily newspaper from Atlanta to which he subscribed. And when the time came, Crawford was wise enough to let a white neighbor friend sell his cotton since it was well known that black farmers didn't get top prices when trying to sell their cotton themselves to white buyers.

While Crawford grilled education and racial pride into his children, Lula was the teacher of religion and manners, in addition to cooking, baking, sewing, having babies, and handling the many domestic chores expected of a farm wife. Lula had fine tastes in clothes and household furnishings. And she showed a keen interest in the studies of astronomy and astrology, both of which she closely followed in the yearly almanac.

Members of Crawford's family were, besides readers, avid school and church goers; none of them were ever known to be troublemakers. In addition to being a good family man and farmer, Crawford, known to take an occasional drink, was an avid follower of politics, which he often discussed in the morning with the mailman who delivered the newspaper.

Then, Lord, came that lil' bitty bug. From Mexico to Texas on across to, first, south Georgia, the boll weevil hit Morgan County in 1922 like the locust, devastating all the cotton fields. Crawford had been saving to buy the farm but during that year the land didn't produce enough cotton to pay the rent or support his family. Thus the savings had to be tapped...and retapped...Crawford found work at a local sawmill to make ends meet. (His oldest son went as far north as the coal mines of Matewan, West Virginia, to find work.) Shortly after starting the job, he took sick from an illness that local doctors were never able to correctly diagnose. He was soon unable to walk, or work, and was confined to a chair, then bed, as his big body began losing weight.

Because of the boll weevil and illness, Crawford and his family were unable to maintain the rent payments. With their savings gone, the Crawfords were forced to leave their beautiful house and farm and their community in 1924. They moved up the road a few miles to the white-owned Barnett Farm, next to the Orr Place, to sharecrop—Plantation-Nigger style—thus bringing on a boll-weevil cultural clash.

In the words of Crawford's youngest daughter, Viola, twelve years old at the time of her family move:

"The neighbors visited us. Among them was the Andrews family, Missis Jessie and her three children, Freddy, George Cleveland, and Beatrice. They lived in a nice house, painted white, similar to the one we moved out of. They had everything and no one worked. We children thought they were white, but with a closer look at their mother, we saw that she looked like ours (fair skin and long, straight black hair). We accepted the statement that she was colored but I could not accept the statement that the children were colored. Freddy had red hair, Beatrice's hair was sandy brown and George, they called him "G," had blond hair and they all looked as white as any white folks.

"Missis Jessie and Jim Orr lived together. He was white and owned the plantation that joined the Barnett Plantation which we lived on. Missis Jessie cooked for him; they did not admit that they lived together but it was a known fact. The Andrews children had various kinds of art material in abundance, plenty of paper, crayons, watercolors, etc., and they did a lot of drawing. They also had a lot of books which they let us borrow to read. They had financial support to go to school and great potential to learn but had no one to encourage them.

"We two families were friends but our philosophies were poles apart. I will never forget the time that Jim Orr visited us and spent a while talking with Papa and Mama. When he got ready to leave he assured Papa and Mama that he would not take advantage of their daughters. He realized that we were a nice family and Papa and Mama wanted the girls to marry. During this time if a white man desired a colored girl and could not get to her he would ask her parents for her and if they consented he would furnish them with mules, farm tools, whatever they needed so that they could rent rather than sharecrop. He would give the girl what she wanted and in due time the family or girl, through his support, would own their own land. I witnessed white men furnishing colored families because of their daughters.

"Missis Jessie was a very lovely person; all the young people and children loved her. She could adjust to any age group, giving children parties at her house and furnishing everything herself. She could, and did, entertain children without tiring. Maybe partially because she had never really worked hard and had no worries about where the next meal, shoes, or garments were coming from. However, we loved her and as time passed G and I were considered to be sweethearts."

Unaccustomed to the life of sharecropping, and hoping to improve their lot, Crawford and family moved the following year to another plantation in the area. There they would remain for only one crop year because the plantation owner offered Crawford and Lula the opportunity to once again rent their own farm as they'd done originally...in exchange for one of their daughters, Soncie, who was too voluptous for her sixteen years. The offer was refused by both parents, which meant another move...to yet another plantation...

Now completely bedridden, Crawford continued to fail and, in 1926, died. (Years later it was thought he had polio.) His sister Lucy, with her husband, was the only member of his Perryman family to attend his funeral.

Through the years, very little came out of Putnam about the Perrymans. What little was learned was that when the mother, Mary, died, she was in her nineties and William Henry, who died close to or over a hundred years old, spent most of the last year of his life sitting beside his wife's grave. Also Willie, the youngest child, fought in World War One in France and returned safely to his home, eventually settling in Atlanta. Much of the rest of the family scattered gradually, many going North. But the ties of Putnam Perrymans to Crawford and Lucy and their families had been long ago cut...and for good.

IX. THE LAST MONTHS ON MISTER JIM'S PLACE

Late one Sunday afternoon not long before Christmas, Daddy came home, turned on the radio, and listened for a few moments before turning around and saying to the rest of us in the room,

"Well, they went and did it. Started a war. The Japs just bombed Pearl Harbor."

Daddy looked mad. Mama looked sad. Thirteen-year-old Harvey said, "I can join the Navy at seventeen!" Benny said, "I'm gonna be an aviator!"

I wondered, Why would anybody go to all the trouble just to drop bombs on a lady named Pearl? Unless it was Minnie Pearl.

෪

Uncle Bubba and Aunt Bea had always lived with Grandmama on Mister Jim's place. Then in late 1940, Uncle Bubba took Aunt Marie and June and moved from Grandmama's house onto Mister Sid Moore's land, about a mile up the road from Mister Jim's place and closer to town. Mama and Daddy said (where we children weren't supposed to hear) that Uncle Bubba and Mister Jim didn't get along.

Less than two years later, Uncle Toodney moved Aunt Bea, Betty Jean (no longer a bald-headed girl baby) and Grandmama off Mister Jim's place onto Moore land, just across the field from Uncle Bubba. Mama and Daddy said (where we children weren't supposed to hear) that Grandmama and Mister Jim weren't getting along.

Soon Mama and Daddy started talking about moving off Mister Jim's place, even going around the area to look at other houses. To move to another house on other land sounded exciting to me.

෪

Between the ages of six and eight, my eyes and ears began opening to "other" things. Like the first time I recall hearing Mama saying we were "poor." Other than being barefoot and ragged, never getting more than one toy each Christmas, and having little money to buy ice cream, candy, or funny books or to go to the picture show with, I thought we were rich. Then to learn we were "poor"! God, what a shock!

෪

Pauline Allen, a distant cousin, was the first girl I ever fell in love with. I was six years old at the time and she was in high school but this made no difference to me. I would've married Pauline then even if I didn't have a job or a bed to sleep in by myself. I never told anyone that I was courting Pauline, not even her, but she knew since she was the one who first told her family—with me present—that I was her "little" boyfriend. I eventually forgave her for calling me little...just so long as she didn't notice my short pants. June would sometimes go with me around to Mister Wes's during my courtship of Pauline but he was still young and wasn't yet interested in courting.

§

I don't remember who brought it to school but the football was only there for one day. To the best of my recollection it was owned by the cousin of one of the male students who was visiting from Atlanta. On this day he had allowed his country relative to bring the football to Plainview Elementary School to show off. Baseball was Plainview's main game but on this special day everybody spent the recess hour kicking the football, or watching it being kicked. Even the young and pretty teacher, Miss Johnson. (Pauline was the prettiest girl in the world and Miss Johnson was the prettiest woman in the world. I was torn between the two.) Missis Bertha Douglas, who was neither young nor pretty, was the other head teacher.

When Miss Johnson was asked to kick the football, and accepted, everybody, particularly the older boys, stood watching. (Nobody asked Missis Douglas to kick the football.) Miss Johnson didn't kick the football worth a hoot but the ball was quickly retrieved by one of the older boys, who ran right back and handed it to her to kick again. She declined a second kick but for some reason, unknown to me, the older boys were excited over her first kick. They were grinning and whispering among themselves, led by Big Boy Mapp's loudest whisper, "Did you see all that 'pussy' under her dress?!" I was watching to see how far Miss Johnson could kick the football—which was not far at all—and I didn't understand why in the world anyone would want to see her kick it again.

When I got home that afternoon, I asked Mama, "What's a pussy?"
"A cat."
Miss Johnson had a cat under her dress? How? Why? The way Big Boy had looked, and sounded, when he said that didn't seem to me like he was talking about a cat. I had never heard anybody talking like

that about any cat before. I went out on the front porch to call our cat.

"Pussy! Pussy! Pussy!"

"What're you hollering, boy?" Daddy was sitting on the porch.

"I'm calling the cat."

"You don't call the cat that."

"Mama said 'pussy' is a cat."

"I don't care what your Mama said, you don't call the cat that anymore. You hear me, boy?"

"Yessir."

The cat didn't know its name anyway. Only the dog came running.

೫

Aunt Polly's only child, Geraldine, was just as pretty as her mother. Each year Geraldine came down from Atlanta, where she and Aunt Polly lived, to spend the summer with us. All of us children looked forward to this visit every year. All, that is, but Sister, who got her thunder stolen by her city cousin each summer.

Country children loved showing off their city relatives to their peers. Geraldine was a year older than Harvey and when she came to visit she took charge, to the chagrin of Sister. Instead of playing with Sister and her playmates, Geraldine played with the boys. When it came to playing "Cowboys and Crooks" we were always at a loss about what to do with this girl, who didn't want to play a cowgirl (whom she said never did anything except sing) but did want to play a cowboy. She didn't even fit as a crook. So she always ended up playing the Indian scout.

Once she even followed us boys deep down into the woods to the spot where no girls, even girl Indian scouts, were allowed—the boys' swimming hole. We boys jumped into the water without bothering to take our pants off. Meanwhile, Geraldine, with all of us turned watching her up on the bank, took off her dress and stood there wearing only her bloomers! Lord, we all saw! Geraldine, our cousin, an Indian Scout, had titties! Then she jumped into the water with the rest of us boys.

Later, when we all got out of the water and stood on the bank, the devil made me run up behind Geraldine and pull down her bloomers. Before she could yank them back up I saw that from behind she looked normal, just like us boys. But when scooting in front of her I got a quick glimpse of something else! Hair! While being hollered at and chased through the woods by her for my bit of devilment all I remember thinking was that Geraldine had no pee-pee!

❧

Nearly a quarter of a mile from the crossroads, heading away from town, ran the main road, straight up a hill and past a big, pretty white house that, everyone said, Mister Jim once owned and lived in long ago. No one lived there when Harvey, Benny, and I would go to pick figs in season from the big tree in back of the house. We also went there before the fruit was ready to eat and learned that unripe figs sure could put a burn on your lips.

Eventually, Mister and Missis Clarence McIntire moved into this house and over the years turned the once cotton-growing land into pasture for the grazing of Herefords. The family McIntire also owned a 1942 Buick (it and the Ford were the only two automobile models that I knew of for 1942, as no more new cars were released until the war was over). Missis McIntire was seen mostly speeding back and forth to town in this big cream-colored car. She never stopped to give anyone a ride—only red dust or mud in the face. Often in the car with her was her young daughter, Roxie Ruth. About Joe's age, Roxie Ruth sat in the back on the lap of her nurse, Missis Susie Slack, while the mother drove. While Missis Susie and her husband Mister Charlie (who also worked for the McIntires) had no children of their own, they did raise Eura, or "Nookie," Missis Susie's niece and one of Sister's best friends. But Missis Susie treated and talked about Roxie Ruth like she was her own child, fussing about her in the presence of others even more than she fussed over Nookie, who was a year older than I.

Among us community children, the real "Roxie Ruth Watcher" was our playmate, Margaret, who was Sister's age and was the daughter of Mister John and Missis Mary Allen. From standing on the side of the road (or in the ditch, since Missis McIntire drove as fast as Odessa and almost as fast as Uncle Bubba), catching fleeting glimpses of the child shooting by in the big Buick, along with keeping constant watch on the McIntire house, Margaret became a Roxie Ruth expert. This plus listening to Missis Susie kept Margaret abreast of what the littler girl wore, ate, and looked like, as well as all the three-year-old's important thoughts and sayings.

Margaret also knew about other people of the neighborhood. One day I followed her and Sister to a place on the far side of the main road up from the crossroads towards town where the large Hall family lived.

Whitefolks. Daily we sat on the bank across the road watching the doings of the Halls, all of whom Margaret knew on sight. They were more interesting to watch on late Saturday afternoons when the daddy would be home and, according to Margaret, drinking. Then there would be a lot of fussing, cussing, door slamming, hollering, running in and out of and around the house, and guitar picking and singing. They were almost as much fun to watch on Saturday as Uncle Bubba. Margaret said the Halls were "po' white trash." I wondered if that was the same as being "poor."

One day I had to stay home from school to take care of Shirley and Joe while Mama went to town and Daddy worked. That day I made the decision to cheat on Pauline. I would go to see Roxie Ruth. (I'd lost Miss Johnson, who had gotten married to Carl Moore and then gone away to teach at another school.) Greasing my hair down with vaseline and washing my hands and face, I took Harvey's bicycle (given to him by Geraldine) and pedaled off to see Roxie Ruth. Five-year-old Shirley and three-year-old Joe ran along behind. Reaching the top of the hill, I stopped on the main road in front of the driveway leading to the big white house to wait on Shirley and Joe, who were huffing and puffing their way uphill from the crossroads. At that same moment, just turning off the road to the driveway on his mule came Mister Sid Moore, a colored man who did occasional work for the white McIntires. I figured if Mister Sid could go up the driveway, so could we. Shirley and Joe ascended the hill with tongues hanging and followed me as I biked up the driveway to see Roxie Ruth. I had nothing special to say to Roxie Ruth, I just wanted to see close up a child who lived in such a big, pretty, white house and whose daddy and mama owned a 1942 Buick. So we followed Mister Sid up the driveway to see. At that end of the driveway, alongside the house, stood Missis McIntire. She let Mister Sid pass, making me feel a little better since Mister Sid knew us children. Then Missis McIntire—the only thing standing between me and Roxie Ruth—stood waiting for us.

"What do you all want?" She didn't sound at all like she knew I had greased my hair and washed my hands and face just to see Roxie Ruth.

"Nothing." Greased hair and washed hands and face notwithstanding, I could think of absolutely nothing else to say. And Shirley and Joe were no help either.

"What do you see out at that road?" Pointing, sending our three heads swirling following her finger.

"Nothing."

"Then go back out there and get it."

We did.

Pedaling as fast as I could, I didn't stop until I reached the cross-roads, where I waited for the running-like-scared-rabbits Shirley and Joe to catch up. Reaching me, Shirley, between gasps, hollered, "I'm gonna tell Mama and Daddy on you!" Knowing that going too near to white folks was worse than going to hell when you died, I figured if I was going to get a whipping for popping in on the McIntires, then I might as well make the whipping worth it. That's when I shot out, up the road, pedaling for the house of the Halls, just ahead of Shirley's "I'm gonna tell!" as she and Joe followed behind running.

The Halls had no long driveway, just a rutted road leading into the big dirt front yard of a shotgun shack. There were several young children playing in the yard. They didn't seem to have to go to school like Mama always made us.

"Y'all niggers?" The oldest boy, about my age, asked me as I hopped off the bike in their yard.

"Naw." Mama had always told us that we were Negroes. "Y'all Crackers?" Mama also told us never to call anyone else "names." But today I knew I was going to get the whipping of my life so I was going for broke.

"Naw." His mother must've talked to him too.

Once the air was cleared as to who we weren't, we children began to play. We continued playing up until it was parents-descending-time, whereupon I pedaled for home. Running behind me were Joe and Shirley, she hollering all the way, "I'm gonna tell!"

Shortly after we got home, Mama arrived from town. Her only question about our doings while she was away was to ask me, "What's that in your hair?" To my surprise and relief, neither Shirley nor Joe told our parents about our doings that day. But for many months (years?) afterward, whenever I did or said anything she didn't like (or sometimes just for the hell of it), Shirley would threaten to "tell" about the day we went visiting the whitefolks.

❦

Over the hill from us lived the family Mapp, who eventually became our next door neighbors. Reverend Melvin Mapp was a preacher-farmer with a great singing voice. He and his wife, Essie Mae, had four sons, Isaac, or "Cootney," Mance, John, and Josette, and one daughter, Jessie Ruth, all of whom we played with as children. Often down from

Atlanta to visit the Mapps came their two cousins, Junior and Yank. Yank, the younger, was about my age, and we played together—or rather, most of the time, fought. Especially on that day he said to me,

"Your daddy's a white man."

"My daddy ain't white!" A stunned me didn't understand why Yank would say such a thing!

"Then your granddaddy is white."

"My granddaddy is dead!"

"Mister Jim is your grandaddy."

"Mister Jim ain't my granddaddy! Mister Jim is a white man!" Then Yank and I fought until Missis Essie Mae came out and broke us apart, sending me home mad at Yank. Nobody had ever said anything like that to me before. I didn't think Yank liked me or my family.

That year we moved from Mister Jim's place.

Mason's:
1943-1949

X. THE MOVE

During the winter Mister Sid Moore possum hunted at night and slept during the day. To those working for someone else this meant Mister Sid was "doing nothing." So whenever someone in Plainview had to move, they looked to Mister Sid to help them. The day we moved from Mister Jim's place Daddy was working at the sawmill, "doing something," so he naturally got the "doing nothing" Mister Sid to move us. Mister Sid had help, and hindrance, from Mama and us children and the Mapp children. All the community adults were busy doing something on this day, except, of course, for Mister Sid.

Mama and Daddy were born and grew up on farms and longed to go back to the soil. Since we owned no land, Mama had wanted us to rent a farm like her daddy had done for many years. But renting a farm would have required that we own farm animals and equipment, which we did not. This automatically sent us to the only type of farming available to our "po' folk" kind.

Sharecropping. Thus in 1943, on the birthday of Abraham Lincoln, the man who freed the slaves, we moved across the hill from Mister Jim's place to the old Barnett Farm to become sharecroppers. Barnett Farm was now rented by one C. R. (Charley) Mason. This same Mason would speed about his vast acreage (owned and rented) in, and out of, Morgan County in his brown, mud-splattered, 1941 Plymouth sedan, and it was talk of the time that all he wanted to see of "his niggers" bent over working in the fields was their "elbows and assholes." We were now, officially, "Mason Niggers." Amen.

Most of my growing-up years occurred between February 12, 1943, and December 4, 1949, the period during which I lived on the old Barnett Farm (where Mama's family Perryman experienced its first sharecropping cultural shock) or, as my generation knew the land, "Mason." This was a period of less than seven years but during the time I thought I was living through the longest and most "unimportant" years of my life. It seemed to me that I was spending much too much precious time growing up—years I felt would have been better spent already grown up. Sharing with me this, not quite, seven-year lifetime were:

XI. MY FAMILY

Daddy:

Shortly following the bombing of, not Minnie but Pearl Harbor, saw-mills opened in the area and Daddy left the WPA's weekly five dollars for the big-time sawmill money which, before the war ended, went as high as $30.00 a week. But once we moved to Mason's, Daddy became a full-time farmer, only working at other jobs when there was little or no farm work to be done.

Like his mother, Daddy was a "grasshopper," having no long-range plans for himself or his family. He just played life by ear day by day. Also, like Grandmama, Daddy was a social soul, more concerned with the goings-on of others than his own family. Daddy loved being with his friends, giving to others, and, especially, being given to. He never could receive enough gifts. What ruled Daddy was what "others" thought. What the community thought of him and his family was of the utmost importance to Daddy, who never wanted to be thought of as being "different."

Playing a big—maybe the biggest—part in this bowing to please at all cost was the fact that Daddy was overly conscious of his skin color, which was light, as in white, and his blond hair, which was light...as in white. But few saw his blond hair because he began cutting it himself as a young man to keep his head shaved of these "unnatural"-for-a-colored-man strands. Daddy never wanted *anyone* thinking that because of his light skin and "good" hair he considered himself better than any other colored person, no matter how low down or under the socioeconomic ladder they could get. A colored person of that time accused of thinking himself or herself "better" than another colored person was committing one of the deadliest of sins in the colored community.

Another colored community deadliest of sins: calling a male "boy." To whites, all coloreds, regardless of age, were either "boy, girl, gal, Uncle, A'nt, " or "A'nty." *Never* "Mister, Missis, Miss, man," or "woman." This is the reason why today blacks are never heard referring to each other as "boy," not even boys among boys. It's *always* "Man." In the South when a white male turned twenty-one he automatically became "Mister," a man. Not so the black male. Even after turning twenty-one and for as long as he lived he, to whites, was still "boy," or, if he knew his place, he was "Uncle" when he got old. But *never* "Mister." That's why today he's "Man." Perhaps the deadliest sin of all, though, was to call a colored person "black." In these years, long before black became beautiful, calling a colored, a Negro (the then-proper term, which is Spanish for "black") *black* no matter how dark his or her skin, could get the caller killed, especially if the caller had a fairer complexion than the called. Self-consciousness about one's complexion and hair texture—"nappy" hair was out—was prevalent. When I was growing up blacks were "colored.")

To be certain that *nobody* could possibly accuse him of holding an "I'm better than thou" attitude, Daddy carried humility in his shirt pocket, constantly bringing, or, as Mama said, "dragging" home many of life's low-lifers, usually filled with liquor Daddy had bought.

Daddy wanted Mama and us children to conform to his "I know I ain't no better than nobody else" way of thinking. This philosophy, unfortunately, meant showing little or no interest in formal education—a no-no for coloreds among many of their own. To the white man an educated colored meant a forever lost worker and a newly found "up-pity nigger." Colored thinking often was, I don't send my children to school, so you shouldn't send yours or they'll start thinking they're better than mine and acting "too proper," or "putting on airs." But Mama was a great believer in school and she made sure her children went no matter what color were the toes she stepped on to do so. Not conforming to his way of thinking and forbidding her children to, Mama made Daddy extremely frustrated. This caused him to continuously lash out at his family in the privacy of his home (never where the neighbors could see or hear). Daddy accused Mama of thinking herself "too good" for his friends and teaching us children the same. (Mama always told us to treat everyone equally...even Daddy's friends.)

Everybody loved the public face of "Good Ol' G," thinking him the sweetest of souls, which toward outsiders he was. Nothing was ever too much or too precious to give to others. Daddy wanted to get along with *everybody, all* the time about *everything.* A tough row to hoe...especially for a colored blond in a black world. Regardless of the cost to his family, Daddy kept right on hoeing down that row. This was the only person he knew how to be—a community person, like his mama. Daddy loved his mama more than anyone, but Grandmama always put him on the back burner of her affections behind Uncle Bubba and Aunt Bea...seems she was too busy with her public to spend much time with her son.

Daddy had another face. He was a hard worker. He never let us go hungry, providing the best he knew how, though it was obtained living by ear, day to day. Also, when he and Mama weren't arguing and he wasn't disciplining us children by mouth or hand, Daddy could be very entertaining, telling us stories, especially about his life as a child. No matter how many times Mama told us a story, it *always* had the same ending, making it a dull story on second telling. We loved to hear Daddy's stories because even a familiar one had a different ending. The great anticipation was, How will it end this time? Thus even the "true" stories, with their different endings at each telling, never became dull. Mama's stories suffered by her being hung up on the truth, the ruination of many a good story. Daddy had no problems with the truth.

I often wished Daddy would spend more time telling us children stories.

Daddy read a lot—the newspaper, detective and western maga-zines, and novels and comic books. He was Plainview's "closet" reader, since reading wasn't "manly." As a child, Daddy had learned to play the violin, or "fiddle," and guitar. He also learned to draw and "paint" pictures. But by the time he had reached adulthood Daddy had aban-doned these "unmanly" habits in order to be accepted into the world of "real" men who didn't indulge in, or even acknowledge, such sissy activites. Real-men duties, or burdens, were to drink too much, fight too much, sire too many children, and get too deep into debt with the boss-man. Real men had *real* responsibilities.

Daddy was also gifted in other ways. Around whites he could "out-Tom" the original Uncle, but would refuse many of their offered favors. Whites, perhaps because he looked so much like them, were always favoring Daddy over other coloreds, which embarrassed him, with his not-wanting-to-be-thought-better-than-anybody-else philosophy.

Of the ten of us children, Daddy favored Harvey, the oldest, and, years later, Veronica, number eight down the birth line, because of their darker complexions. He wanted the public to see that in spite of his light skin and blond hair, he was colored enough to produce "natural" colored children.

Mama:
Her early childhood was a happy one. Growing up on a big farm with plenty of food and love, Mama learned to appreciate toiling the soil, idolized her older siblings, and was surrounded by many self-sufficient relatives. But, most importantly, she saw her parents, apart from loving their children, loving one another. She especially loved her "Papa" who, in addition to being an intelligent man, was one whose family came first. Even after her Papa took ill his family still came first, and

from his sickbed he yet made all important family decisions. Mama was fourteen years old when her Papa died but from him she'd already gotten his feeling for family (which, ironically, he inherited from his papa, who disowned him for breaking family tradition by marrying a Plantation Nigger). From the time she was a little girl, Mama wanted to grow up to live on a big farm (her family's own) with a big, close family and, like her Papa had been to her mama, a loving husband. Then, Lord, she met Daddy.

To Mama, Daddy was, besides good-looking, most importantly, "so nice" (that charming public facade rearing its face from the beginning). He was a boy (sixteen years old when they started courting) nice enough to grow up in the mold of her Papa who would love family and farming. So Mama believed. She got one right—Daddy did love farming. Thus it came to pass that the "sweethearts," Mother Jessie's and Mister Jim's son, George Cleveland Andrews, and Lady Lula's and Crawford's daughter, Viola Perryman, granddaughter of the Ol' African, got married as teenagers (a common pastime of the day). From that day onward their marriage became the battle of the public person (Daddy, raised by a mama whose first allegiance was to the community rather than to her family) and the family female (Mama, raised by a daddy who felt that without the family there could be no community).

At some point in their marriage Mama eventually realized she was not going to change Daddy. She realized that Daddy loved his own mama and her grasshopper ways as much as Mama loved her now-dead Papa and his ant-like ways. Until that moment of realization, we children went to bed and awoke listening to our parents arguing, piling argument atop argument down through the years. Daddy tended to be the loser in these verbal confrontations. When feeling himself sliding toward defeat, Daddy would quickly accuse Mama of getting "too proper" by throwing "big words" into their simple argument. During those rare times when Daddy thought he was getting the best of Mama he would start laughing until she, a devout Christian opposed to his unbaptized soul, would counterattack by breaking out in a religious hymn, which would shut up Daddy, fearer of deadly lightning bolts.

Early in their marriage, when he was losing one of these arguments badly, Daddy would resort to the "man's" way out of such husband-wife confrontations with an occasional fist in Mama's face. (When and where I grew up, wife hitting or beating wasn't uncommon. In fact, such behavior was expected of males, otherwise it was said that within your family or house, "the wife wore the pants," apparel *real* mean didn't tolerate on their wives.)

It was also early in her marriage that Mama decided that her children and their futures took priority over everything else. In the process she continuously reminded us children, "I'm taking care of you and when you grow up and have your own children make sure *you* take care of them." We did.

Harvey:

The ideal big brother. Harvey looked out for all of us under him, protecting us particularly from the Masseys. For example, he was the first one in Plainview to take on, and best, Lil' Bubba, and to fight and beat Minnie Pearl (no easy feat even for males, believe me). Harvey, though never one himself, had no fear of bullies.

Before finishing, Harvey dropped out of Plainview Elementary School, which went as high as the seventh grade (to further one's education one had to go on to the colored high school in Madison—Burney Street—which we country people called "Town School" and which went as high as the eleventh grade). From there Harvey went to work alongside several of his peers cutting and hauling pulpwood. It was while hanging out with the pulpwood crowd that the teenage Harvey got himself a pistol. I never saw it but Reverend Mapp's son, John, a good buddy of Harvey's, told me he had one and that he kept it in the loft of our house, where nobody went but the bats. I never heard any more about the pistol but not too long after this, Harvey did the unthinkable, for a teenager, by "dropping out" of work to go back to school. Instead of going back to Plainview, Harvey entered Burney Street.

Then in the summer of 1945, Harvey, dressed in his zoot suit and knob shoes, left home for Atlanta. With him were several former pulpwood buddies, and they all moved into Atlanta's Butler Street YMCA. After a short stay, most of Harvey's buddies returned to the pulpwood world and cotton field but Harvey stayed on. At a cost: his wardrobe. Associating with his new Atlanta friends, he quickly discovered that his old zoot suit and knob shoes were *passé*, and sent them all back home to Benny. Meanwhile, he enrolled at Booker T. Washington evening high school.

Harvey brought the family many gifts from Atlanta. Besides Benny's zoots, I especially remember the sports books and magazines, and the football and softball. But most of all, I recall his visits home when he would tell us about the many wonders of Atlanta.

Harvey lived just off an avenue he called "Auburn." He would tell us about things colored folks owned and did there, as well as in a few other spots around Atlanta, that we children found hard to believe. What I most clearly remember him telling was that Atlanta had all-colored picture shows, where the colored sat downstairs, and colored drugstores. In these drugstores, the colored could order milkshakes and sit down at the tables inside and eat, rather than taking what they bought and eating it outside in the street like we had to do in Madison. In fact, in Madison the colored couldn't even buy milkshakes, only ice cream cones, and once you paid for one you had better be gone. I wanted to go to Atlanta. Harvey promised me that someday he would help me get there.

Yes, Lord, as far as we Andrews children were concerned, Atlanta wasn't discovered by Scarlett O'Hara or Andrew Young. Altlanta, on July 22, 1945, was discovered by Harvey Christopher (Columbus?) Andrews. Amen.

Benny:

Knowing from birth exactly what he wanted to do—draw—Benny was also *always* doing those things everybody said, or felt, he shouldn't be doing. Things "different." It started when he was a baby and almost burned down the house. Later he learned to pour water from bottle to bottle without spilling a drop (a true sign of the moonshiner, mourned Mama, who claimed he got this talent from his Daddy's side of the family). While other boys his age extolled the virtues of plowing mules, driving tractors, and hunting, Benny was always drawing pictures. But he learned to plow along with other farm chores and when it came to testing his skills against his peers at boxing, baseball, basketball, running, swimming, climbing trees, or other competitive games, Benny was better than most. He loved to compete, and he hated losing in any effort. In fact, he was a bad loser. Even at girls.

In his preteen years, Benny fell madly in love with Louvina Parks (this was around the same time I was courting the much older Pauline). One day she broke his heart by saying to him that she could never bring herself to love him because he looked "too white." Benny turned red. Knowing that being a blue-eyed blond with pink skin and freckles didn't necessarily make one white, Benny took a cue from me and Pauline and went out and got himself more female security, an older girlfriend. (Benny was such a bad loser that sometimes in playing games with him you'd hope he would win so you two would still be friends afterwards. Yet if Benny thought you weren't playing your best against him he'd also get mad—though he was a good winner, never rubbing it in, sometimes acting like he wished there could've been two winners. But since there could only be one winner he always tried to be that one.)

The vast majority of country children never went to school beyond the seventh grade, much less continued on to the town high school. But Benny went on to Burney Street and there his world was expanded while he continued to draw. Yes, Burney Street opened up a new world for Benny...and a can of worms for Daddy. Those days when Benny wasn't working in the field and was allowed to go to school, he was told by Daddy to hurry home after classes to help with the farm chores before dark. Many times Benny returned home in time to help out, but when a basketball game or some other after-class activity was scheduled that caught Benny's fancy, he would stay to attend and not get home until after sundown. By that time Sister and I would have done Benny's work (instead of being annoyed, we envied Benny and his Town School status) and Daddy would be pitching a fit, or two...or more.

Having just joined the church, at about age ten, Benny was the first soul I ever heard describe heaven in finite detail. One day while walking through the wilderness (blackberry picking) with Sister, Shirley, and myself, Benny took it unto himself to explain heaven to us young heathens. He explained going to heaven so beautifully, especially the part about all the grapes you could eat, that I wanted to go *right* that moment. The only thing that cooled me down was his telling me that I had to die first.

Benny's explanation of heaven on that day was so complete that he included the answer to the mystery of where we all came from: heaven, Benny told us. For years afterwards I told many of my peers about my days in heaven before I was born. But as hard as I tried I never could remember being up there.

Benny was *always* doing something. He never stopped to watch the grass grow or the creek flow. He didn't have the time, or the inclination, being always too busy listening for and following the drum beat only he heard. There was, for instance, the Savannah trip.

In the summer of 1944 Benny went to Savannah for a 4-H Club convention. A couple of summers later, still a 4-H Club member (purely for the travel), he got the chance to go to Savannah again. But this summer Daddy didn't feel he could spare Benny for a week away from the farm. Mama, considering this trip an extension of her son's education, felt we could. Benny, whose topic of discussion at the convention would be the chicken egg, naturally thought so too. Daddy, firmly con-

BENNY ANDREWS
DEC 29, 1989

vinced that the chopping of cotton was of much more importance than traveling all the way to Savannah just to talk about a chicken egg, argued the matter with Benny. They even wrestled over it. Daddy won the wrestling match, but Benny won the title. He ran away from home. He returned late that night, but only to get the clothes he needed for Savannah, not to beg back bed. Sister and I knew he would return, she knowing he would need clothing and I knowing he couldn't get far in the world without his Boy Scout knife. Both of us were lying awake in the dark with everything he would need awaiting him. Around midnight, while the rest of the house slept, Benny knocked softly at the window next to our beds. Taking the clean flour sack filled with his belongings, he exchanged a few hurried whispers with us before disappearing back into the dark of the night. That night, with his Boy Scout knife by his side, Benny slept in an abandoned house about a mile from home, and the next day left for Savannah, where he told them all about the chicken egg.

When Benny returned home, Grandmama mediated a peace treaty (meaning no "whipping") between him and Daddy. Not too long afterward, Benny broke the treaty by running away to Atlanta, where for two nights he slept in the bus station (he always talked about wanting to be a hobo in order to travel). Returning from Atlanta, he stayed home long enough to finish high school, whereupon he won a 4-H Club college scholarship (the chicken egg hatched) and went, in the fall of 1948, to Fort Valley State College in Georgia. Benny's departure took away much of the excitement from our home—Mama and Daddy didn't argue as much and Sister and I felt less adventurous having no one around to cover for.

Sister:
Sister got folks told. "Blessed" them out, honey. Even at the expense of a universal war, if Sister felt it, Lord, Sister said it. Like Daddy, Sister was a social soul who loved folks and giving and yet, like Mama, she loved the family. She spent her entire childhood defending (with her mouth, of course, as she was always too busy talking, or "telling," to bother with something as unimportant as fists) her siblings and *all* those she thought were being wronged. Sister loved us, *and* her friends, and wanted to protects us *all* from *all* harm *all* the time. Well, with Minnie Pearl on the map, that was always a challenge for Sister.

Also, Sister didn't bite her tongue when feeling the need to put one, or all, of her brothers and sisters in their respective places. No, Lord, Sister's tongue sported no scars. Like those Saturdays when she would accompany Harvey, Benny, and me into town. Each of us were carrying fifteen cents from Daddy's WPA pay. We boys would pay a dime apiece for the picture show to see a double feature (a cowboy movie and "another" picture), a chapter from a serial, a cartoon, and previews of shows for the whole next week. Following the show and with our remaining nickels, Harvey would buy a bag of marbles while Benny and I would put our nickels together to buy a comic, or "funny," book. Sister, a much more practical soul, would spend her fifteen cents every time on a loaf of white, or "light," bread and a jar of peanut butter. With these she made sandwiches which she ate herself during our long walk home while berating us (who could hardly hear her over our growling bellies) for spending our money so foolishly. Sister's Saturday afternoon lessons came through so well to us that we stopped taking her to town, keeping our hungry march home to ourselves.

The perfect oldest sister, Sister was always in charge. She carried the lunch bag, or "sack," to school where, during recess, she would dole out our biscuit and fried Irish or sweet potato sandwiches. She took charge, seeing the younger of us to school, church, town, or elsewhere. (As for myself, after the age of eight I was either going places with Harvey and Benny or was alone since I felt I was too big of a boy to come under the jurisdiction of a sister). Sister was in charge, defending, disciplining, and, except for her peanut butter sandwiches, feeding us all.

At night Sister dreamed a lot, and the next morning would tell us her dreams scene by scene. One pitch dark night we didn't have to wait until the next morning to find out what she had dreamed for she woke up screaming, "There's a black snake on the ceiling!!!" Jumping out of bed she ran into Mama's and Daddy's room. At the urging of Mama, a now awakened and grumbling Daddy came into the room where we older children slept. He flashed his flashlight on the ceiling and all over the room without finding Sister's black snake. Convinced that no snake could hang on the ceiling, much less be seen—a black one at that—in the dark, Daddy went back to bed, only to get up a few minutes later to threaten me with a whipping if I didn't stop laughing. I laughed till I cried (and cried again when Daddy got up a second time to deliver his threat) at Sister and her hanging-on-the- ceiling-in-the-dark black snake. I still haven't stopped laughing.

Ever busy, Sister, besides working harder in the field than any of us other children, each day after work or school would sweep the yard and clean up both outside and inside the house. She also put up we children's first family Christmas tree. One morning shortly before Christmas she took us younger children down into the woods where we found and brought back a small cedar tree. Having no Christmas tree decorations, Sister sprinkled flour over the little tree. It looked like it had snowed. I'd never before seen a more beautiful Christmas tree, nor have I since.

Shirley:
"Oh, she's sooo pretty." That's all the grown folks could ever think to say when they saw little Shirley (some going so far as to even call her "Shirley Temple"). For the rest of us children she was not fun to be taken any place with because she got *all* the attention, unless you made a monkey out of yourself, which was still no guarantee you'd divert everyone's gaze from Shirley. Besides, it wasn't advisable to monkey around in the marketplace with Mama or Daddy standing by ("acting up" in public always got you a bigger whipping when you got back home than performing regular domestic terror). Even when Aunt Soncie and Uncle Corris took Shirley all the way up North, Aunt Lula's expression when she saw Shirley for the first time was said to have been, "Oh, she's sooo pretty."

Shirley was also good at getting you whippings. Like the time Shirley wouldn't come out to play with us so I decided to fix her. Several old women (Shirley's biggest fans) had come by to see Mama and Shirley, who rather than come outdoors and play with the rest of us, just sat, without even saying a single word, in the house by the fire while the old folks just oozed, "Oh, she's sooo pretty." Going inside the house I sat down next to her...to await my chance. None of the old women had seemed to notice that I had even entered the room. All eyes were aimed on Shirley. They didn't see me, that is, until Shirley stood up (probably to take a bow) and I jerked the chair from under her, whereupon she sat back down on the floor with an oh-not-so-pretty bang. I broke up. The old women didn't break up, just shook their heads at me. Shirley cried. Later, after the old women went home, I cried too...following the whipping Mama gave me.

Shirley, of course, never got any whippings. But to be honest, she never did anything interesting enough to deserve a whipping. She was a little doll, always put on display the instant folks came round. And being Daddy's favorite was another reason she didn't get any whippings.

Until, Lord, that rainy day when "Oh, she's sooo pretty" Shirley, about seven or eight years old at the time, stood up on a chair to reach the mantelpiece while searching for something, perhaps a pencil. She never found what she was looking for. While groping around, Shirley's little fingers bumped into a big bottle of cod-liver oil and knocked it off the mantel, smashing it on the hearthstone below, sending glass, oil, and its smell all over the room. Frightened, Shirley jumped down and ran into the kitchen screaming, "Mama, Mama, I broke the cod-liver oil!!!" (Tells you how little she knew about getting into trouble. One *always* ran away from—even out into the pouring rain—*not to* one's parents when something fell or broke, and one admitted to *nothing,* even after being whipped.) That big bottle of cod-liver oil (we children's annual storebought winter medicine) cost money and, with this in mind, Daddy, who was inside the house that day the bottle kissed the hearthstone, administered unto lil' "Oh, she's sooo pretty" Shirley her *first* ever whipping. That was one of the highlights of my young life. Not only did I savor Shirley's first whipping but, thanks to her, gone was a year's supply of detestable cod-liver oil. God works in mysterious ways.

From that day forward, with switchmarks on her soul and a broken bottle of cod-liver oil to her credit, Shirley officially became one of us children. Amen.

Harold:
Our "Joe Louis" spent much of his life before ten being sick, or feeling "puny." Something was always wrong with him. He even broke his collarbone. You'd think with a name like Joe Louis he would at least know how to box, but he couldn't even beat boys smaller than himself. I, of course, beat him all the time. Joe was important in my life since I had spent much of it getting whipped by Harvey and Benny and I was badly in need of a little brother of my own to whip upon, and having one with the name of Joe Louis only made the whippings sweeter.

Joe liked playing sports even though he couldn't catch a ball. Whenever a ball was thrown to him he would spread both of his hands too widely apart, close his eyes, and miss the catch. Then, Lord, came the time when our Joe Louis, upon seeing all of Shirley's, wanted a doll! Daddy hit the ceiling. Mama bought a little Robin Hood doll for Joe and he played with it for awhile until he tired of the indoor sport and then returned outdoors to miscatch balls.

Despite my beating on him, Joe and I had fun together. We both started following sports closely at early ages and about whose teams were better we never got through arguing. (He liked baseball's New York Yankees and Giants and football's Chicago Bears and San Francisco Forty-Niners, while my teams were the Boston Red Sox, Brooklyn Dodgers, Chicago Cardinals, and Cleveland Browns.) When I left home Joe was only eleven. I got to know and love him much better after I left Madison.

Johnny:
Before dawn on the morning of August 28, 1942, I was awakened by a loud cry. My first thought was, I hope it's not another baby. It was. Johnny. I should have recognized the situation sooner because Grandmama had been at our house late the night before, and anytime Grandmama stayed late at anybody's house you could almost be sure there was a baby coming to that house soon. Sometimes I thought Grandmama must have been the stork, taking babies around in her apron pocket to give to folks.

During the first year of our farming I came to appreciate Johnny, the baby, whom I was allowed to stay home from the field to care for. I didn't miss working in the fields at all, nor was I missed, since early on I earned the distinction of being the family's, and the community's, *slowest* field worker.

The problem was that whenever I was working in the field my mind was elsewhere (usually in places like World War II, Hollywood, New York City, sports arenas, and other exotic settings) rather than focusing on the task at hand, usually cotton.

Caring for Johnny required that I spend much of my time in the rocking chair singing, and daydreaming, him to sleep. He probably only fell asleep not to have to hear more of my singing. Once he was asleep, I would put him to bed and catch up on reading, and rereading, my ever-growing collection of funny papers and funny books. If Johnny and I were outside, I would sit him facing the sun so he would have to close his eyes and, hopefully, fall asleep. As soon as he awoke it was right back to the rocking chair of song and hoped-for sleep. Asleep was where I figured all babies belonged.

Starting with Johnny, Joe (who now had someone of his own to beat up on) was to take on the role of "big brother" to this tail end of the Andrews children.

Veronica:
"Ronnie" was a real surprise, at least to me. After almost six years of no babies, Ronnie was the first, and only, one of us born on Mason's. Ronnie was a happy baby. Or maybe by this time Mama and Daddy had mellowed (having lost most of their energies on the first seven of

us) so that they allowed Ronnie to get away with things we older children would have gotten whipped for just thinking about at her age. Even more so than "Oh, she's sooo pretty" Shirley, Ronnie got away with everything. Ronnie, I'm sure, could have broken the cod-liver oil bottle, *even* the castor oil bottle, without getting a whipping. Unimpressed by babies as I was, even I accepted Ronnie. And I named her after the movie star, Veronica Lake (to this day Sister argues over which one of us named Ronnie). Another reason for my acceptance of Ronnie was that she was born in 1948, the year Babe Ruth died. I envied her that distinction.

Deloris ("Cookie") and *Gregory ("Greg")* were born after I left home and did not have any in(or out)put on my behavior, or nonbehavior, during those less-than-seven, l-o-n-g, years of my growing up on Mason's.

XII. HOUSE OF HOARDERS

I came from a home of hoarders. We all had our boxes full of personal stuff kept under our respective beds, starting with Daddy, who kept beneath his and Mama's bed a big wooden box he built himself to store his personal things, mostly books and magazines (plus the non-operative first Plainview radio). Daddy kept this box locked but when no one was about, I often got the key from where he thought it was hidden and looked through these periodicals. Many of these were "art" books and magazines, showing a lot of bare-chested (and bare-behinded) females.

Mama also saved many things, mostly pictures and stuff about the family. Included was seemingly everything we children ever drew. All of us children drew and were constantly in need of something, anything, to draw a picture on, from a sheet of paper "clean on one side" to a brown paper sack. (We also drew in the dirt of the yard, finding a solid, or "hard spot" and using either a nail, stick, or finger to draw in the dirt. Our hand served as our eraser—that is, unless Sister was sweeping the yard, when her brushbroom would be our unwanted eraser. Sister never let art stand in the way of cleanliness.)

Shirley collected dolls and their clothing, mostly rags she dressed them with which were given to her by Mama, who saved such to make, or "piece," quilts.

Sister was more concerned with neatness and orderliness than hoarding—with keeping things clean rather than keeping them. Once, though, she suddenly decided she too wanted to save the Sunday funny papers like I did. When she announced this before a shocked me, saying in front of Daddy and Mama that she had just as much right to save the Sunday funnies as I did, I saw red. Mama told Sister she could share saving the funny pages with me—we each taking every other Sunday—but, like me, she had to *save* them, and not throw them out. I still saw red. But after one Sunday of these funnies cluttering up her life, Sister, to my delight, decided against opening a new hoarding harem and gave me her young Sunday collection before going back to concentrating on keeping the house and yard cleared of all the clutter.

Meanwhile, under our bed Benny and I kept cardboard boxes filled with our "savings." Besides daily clipping out and saving from the newspaper the war cartoon "Up Front," Benny started a scrapbook on boxing and another one mostly on baseball, with some football. Then there were the few toy soldiers he could afford to buy from the town's Five and Ten Cents store. But most of all, the saved things of Benny's were those things he did himself, with sheets of his work between tacked or sewn on covers taken from 4-H Club and other periodicals. In these homemade books he drew his own comic strips, movies, and movie stars, military men, and countless other figures. (Like Daddy, Benny could also tell good stories, but he preferred drawing his stories over telling them.)

Under my side of the bed my cardboard boxes over the years were kept filled with the funnies, the movie, sport, and radio sections of the newspapers, funny books, movie, radio, and sport magazines, football scrapbooks, and detective, mystery, and western (predominantly paperback) novels. (By age nine I had no interest in toys, only the printed word, film, and radio.)

A day wouldn't go by when Benny and I didn't pull out our cardboard boxes from under the bed and "go to work" on them. Benny in his drawing would often need a comic strip incident for inspiration, and all he had to do was say what he had in mind, and from among my vast collection I would pull out and hand him exactly, or near to, what he needed. (This working, or "thinking" together planted the seed of my telling Benny that when I wrote my first book he could "draw" the cover, which he did.)

Daily Benny drew and I reread and "straightened out" my boxes of collectibles. Yet what I enjoyed best was sitting in the room alone, straightening out my boxes while listening on the radio to a football or baseball game. Often on a Saturday afternoon during lay-by time or late fall, rather than go into town I would stay home just for this reason. It was my favorite time of all—listening to the radio while straightening out all my boxes.

XIII. THE FARM

In our first year of sharecropping we had what was called a "one-horse" farm. That is, we used one mule (Ol' Churchill) to work twenty acres of land (fifteen acres of cotton and five assorted acres of corn and vegetable gardens). To get two mules one had to work at least thirty acres. Daddy and Mama, though themselves "dirt daubers" with a houseful of soil-untested children, wanted to enter sharecropping one mule at a time. All the mules and farm equipment for all the Barnett Farm's sharecropping families (averaging between ten and fifteen each crop year) were kept up at the "Big House," occupied by Mason's white overseer, James, or "Mister" Brown.

Mister Brown and his large family were mountain folks, or "hillbillies," but were considered unusual for the breed, as it was often said that folks from up in the hills had no use for lowlanders, particularly colored folks. But Mister Brown's entire family was to become known to us as "good white folks," for they were never known to cause any trouble for colored folks. For hillbillies, we thought the Browns, unlike the Halls, were low key. Except for the oldest son, Winfred.

It was said by those knowing him that Winfred, who had his own family plus some sharecropping acreage, wanted to do everything but farm. He was always trying his hand at something else, which never seemed to work. For instance, he opened up a little store in back of the Big House but soon went out of business because most of the business he got was "on credit," which was the easiest and most expensive kind to get. He then went into Madison and opened up a little diner known as the "Snack Shack." Out of it he sneaked and sold bootleg liquor until he was caught and the place was closed down. Winfred came back to his farm, which his wife and father had been running in his absence, and for a while he continued selling illegal liquor (Daddy even helped him sell it).

Winfred loved singing and picking his guitar most of all. Often he went on the road singing, and sometimes he appeared on the radio, during the hours when most folks were asleep. Everybody liked Winfred because he was always quick to laugh, even at himself.

Sharecropping meant sharing half of your yearly crop with the landowner who supplied the land, mules, and all the equipment necessary to farm—all except the sweat. The sharecropper's seed and fertilizer had to be bought from the landlord from the sharecropper's half of the crop's earnings. Everything was bought on credit, or "time," and paid for at the end of harvest. If all debts couldn't be paid (which was mostly the case) then they would automatically go into "the book" and carry over onto the next year's crop.

In our second year of farming, we began sharecropping on thirty acres, of which twenty were cotton. This meant farming with two mules ("Red" and "Clyde"). Of seven harvest years of sharecropping, only in one year did we show a profit. That year came in 1945, when we harvested twenty bales of cotton, ten belonging to us. (One bale per acre was considered a good crop.) We were able to pay off Mason and have three hundred dollars left over. Daddy and Mama used the money to buy winter clothing for us, then six, children (Harvey had gone to Atlanta and Ronnie was still on hold) and whatever else had to be bought until the next year's harvest. When Daddy brought the three hundred dollars home that day and showed it to Mama and us children, I had never seen so many dollar bills at once before. I wondered, Did Daddy leave Mister Mason any money?

On Mason's, the only other thing we sharecropped was corn. Of our non-cotton acreage, about six or seven were planted in corn. We would take our share to the mill for cornbread and feed the livestock. After pulling the corn, we cut the dried stalks for fodder to feed our cows over the winter. All the farm's livestock (cows, pigs, chickens, dogs, and cats), belonged to us, except the mules.

The first week of December was hog-killing time, a yearly ritual when neighbor helped neighbor. Most families had either one or two hogs to slaughter for winter meat. The exceptions were farmers like Mister Wes, who had several hogs to kill and who sold most of his meat. Hog-killing was always a bloody mess. I imagined that it must have been like the French Revolution with its guillotine. I liked pigs and felt sorry for all animals put here solely to be killed and eaten. The pig would only be a few months old when castrated, or "cut," and put in a too-small-to-turn-around-in pen to be fattened for death. On hog-killing day, the colder the weather the better. Everybody worked quickly, enduring all the blood and guts because the meat had to be eaten, salted, or smoked immediately since there was no refrigeration. For weeks afterwards I smelled pig.

During the summer we ate vegetables and fruits almost exclusively, thanks mostly to Mama, who also had her flower garden. On three to four acres we grew most of the vegetables congenial to local soil. What we and the animals didn't eat, Mama canned, down to the watermelon rinds, which she pickled. *Nothing* edible went to waste in our house. Mama canned fruit, (mostly peaches, berries, pears, apples,

and crabapples) and made jellies and jams. These canned goods, the hog meat, which we ate only on Sunday, Irish and sweet potatoes, which we kept hilled, and dried black-eyed peas, plus the rabbits, squirrels, and possums that hunting brought to the table, fed us through the winter. There was never money to buy anything other than staples, like flour, sugar, salt, grits, and rice. In dire emergencies, money could be borrowed from Mister Mason, who would put the debt in the book against the next year's crop.

Our only hungry time came in early spring when the garden was being planted and the long hours of plowing in the field were at hand and most, if not all, of the winter's food had been eaten. This is when the females took to the woods and pastures to pick poke salad, and rabbits were running in their sleep trying to dodge the hunter and his hungry hound because folks badly needed food while awaiting their garden's first vegetables.

From late winter, with the cutting of the dead stalks left from the previous crop, to the spring plowing, or "breaking up" of the land, cotton, being the area's chief crop, demanded, and got, most of the farmer's attention. After spring plowing came "middle busting" or lining off the rows. This was considered the most difficult of all plowing because a straight row had to be "lined." The rows were fertilized with Guano brand just a mule ahead of the cotton seeds being planted into them. But custom called for nothing to be planted before Easter. Later, we helped the baby cotton shoots shoot up faster by running a mule-drawn device called a "scratcher" up and down each row to break up the clods of dirt surrounding the young plants. Then came the thinning or "chopping" out of the cotton plants with a hoe. To grow faster the plants then had to be "sodaed," which involved sprinkling a sulfur type of fertilizer locally called "soda" by hand around the base of each plant. This soda is remembered mostly for burning the skin.

There were always the boll weevils, which the small farmer kept under control by "mopping." (The big farmers had their cotton "dusted" by tractor or, in a few cases, airplane.) Mopping entailed dipping a cloth tied to the end of a hand-held stick into a bucket, which you carried in your other hand. In the bucket was poison-laced, black strap molasses which you dabbed on the leaves of each cotton stalk while walking up and down between the rows. A sticky mess.

Back came the hoe to "hoe," or "bunch" the last bit of grass from around the plant before lay-by time. Lay-by usually started during the first half of July when the farmers began the wait for the cotton bolls to begin popping open by late August to be ready for picking on the first of September. But during much of lay-by time we Mason sharecroppers had something else to occupy our time besides sitting in the shade of the porch eating watermelon waiting for the cotton to open. The peach orchards.

Mister Mason owned many acres of peach orchards. At the height of the peach-picking season—June and July—he would pull his sharecroppers from the cotton fields to work alongside the regular peach pickers, who lived in houses scattered about the orchards. The farmers and the peach pickers didn't always get along and often had to work in separate parts of the orchards because of it. The orchards, owned by Mister C. R. Mason, were located near the border of Putnam County, and those owned by his son, C. L. Mason, were just on the other side of Madison. We picked peaches from seven in the morning until six in the evening, with one hour for lunch. The men were paid two dollars per day, the women one dollar and fifty cents, and the children one dollar.

The most memorable event of my years in the orchards occurred during my first peach-picking summer, 1945, in the orchards near Putnam County. One lunch hour appeared this very pretty young colored girl of about fifteen or sixteen years old to dance alone before—shortly—a large surrounding crowd of hand-clapping workers (sharecroppers and peach pickers side by side) beneath the hot sun there in the dusty big backyard of the overseer's white house on the hill overlooking the orchards. Following this introduction, each day she appeared at lunch to dance, sometimes alone and sometimes with males, one at a time, from the crowd. There was no music for her dancing, just hand-clapping, finger-popping, and humming from the always big crowd surrounding her. One day following her dance, while walking past on her way back into the orchards, she looked me right in the eye and smiled. Not just with her lips but with her eyes. I fell instantly, and madly, in love with her. She did not dance again that summer...nor the next four summers that I worked in the orchards. I never saw her again. Talk was she was from around the town of Eatonton over in Putnam County, but I never met anyone who knew her. I've never stopped seeing her smile...nor have I ever fallen out of love with her.

Another big peach man in the county was a Mister J. A. Nolan who, supposedly, owned as many orchards as, or more than, Mister Mason. Each Saturday night on the back street of Madison this matter of which of the two white men owned the bigger and better peach orchards was debated with fists, and oftentimes knives, by "Mason Niggers" and "Nolan Niggers."

One main reason Mama wanted to move from Mister Jim's place was to get more room, a larger house. On Mason's place we had a three-room house and now no one had to sleep in the kitchen, exept the cats. Mama and Daddy had their own room while we children slept in the other, bigger room. Harvey, Benny, and I continued to sleep in the same bed and on winter nights we would sit in front of the fireplace keeping our knees and faces hot and our backs cool until it was time to go to bed. Harvey and Benny sent me first to warm up a spot under the covers. When they came to bed they would push me off that spot and fight, or push, over it themselves while I lay in the cold, eventually warming up a new spot that would then be taken away by the loser of the first warm spot. I was allowed to keep the third spot I'd warmed for the night. Both rooms had fireplaces and during the winter, Daddy, a before-sunup riser even on Sundays, awoke the household each morning building a roaring fire that he was always so proud of.

The farm was full of chores year round. Any time I went anywhere, whether to town or just visiting the neighbors, I had to be back home before sundown to bring the cows up from the pasture to the stable to milk, to slop the hogs, to feed the dogs and cats, to bring buckets of water from the spring to the kitchen for the night and morning, to tote firewood for the fireplace and cooking stove, and, once a week, to fill the six to eight reading lamps with kerosene. This work was never finished—it was enough to drive you to daydreaming about being somewhere else.

Learning how to plow so late in life—at age 13—made me somewhat of a local retard. And to top matters off I was a slow worker. I didn't so much mind plowing (just so as long as no one from town saw me doing it) since the mules, unlike working folks, took their time up and down the rows, and I never hurried them. (While plowing I loved singing. Once while following the mules' tails up and down hot, sweaty and dusty row after row of "middle busting" I—no doubt to the annoyance of the mules—spent the entire day in the field singing over and over the one line, "There's a long, long trail a-winding." Little did I suspect *how* long.) But picking cotton was something else.

To pick anywhere between 125 and 150 pounds of cotton a day was considered average. Many people picked two hundred pounds and more. My daily average was seventy-five pounds. Or less. In all my years of picking (my first boll was plucked at age five before we started farming, when we picked other people's cotton "by the day"), only once did I break the one-hundred-pound barrier. I reached that lofty plateau in October of 1948 with two pounds to spare, having picked 102 mighty proud pounds of cotton! And this without Sister slipping me some of her cotton, which she often did to keep Daddy from fussing at me for being so slow, or "lazy"—the same difference in the field of cotton. Never again did I pick as much as a hundred pounds (though I did break the ninety-pound barrier twice) but having done it once put me for one day in "tall cotton," cotton's Hall of Fame.

In our own fields, Daddy could better tolerate my slowness, a "problem" kept in the family. But when we went picking other people's cotton by the day, when one got a dollar per hundred pounds (by the end of the war the rate had soared up to two dollars per hundred), I became a public problem. Slow *and* lazy. All pickers starting out together, regardless of age or sex, everyone would instantly leave me behind, meet me on their way back picking on new rows and then pass me again (some picking two rows at a time on each trip up and down the field) before I'd finally finish my first row. A *retard*, a slow and lazy one at that, if Mister Mason's sharecroppers ever saw one. My picking, or non-picking, cotton in public was a constant embarrassment for Daddy (a two-row picker), who spent most of the cotton picking season fussing at me. But, I must add, to no avail.

Daddy, Mama, Harvey, Sister, and Shirley were fast in all facets of the field while Benny, Joe, and, of course, I always brought up the rear. I did have the distinction of being faster than Johnny, seven years old when I left home, and Ronnie, one-and-a-half at the time of my departure. As a baby, Johnny developed a defense I would never have dreamed of against picking cotton. He became afraid of it—a fact, phobia, or fib that scared Daddy more than Johnny. After the family stopped sharecropping, Johnny's fear of cotton suddenly disappeared.

As I mentioned before, the chief reason for my slowness afield was that my mind was never there with me. Whether following behind a mule, holding a hoe, or carrying a cotton sack, I'd be daydreaming about being a pilot, a private detective, a movie star, an athlete, or whoever my reverie felt I should be that particular day, or moment. My daydreaming made Walter Mitty appear unimaginative by comparison.

Oh, I'll add that I might have picked cotton slowly, but the bolls I did pluck were the cleanest in the field. I made sure of that by taking off all the dried leaves and all other specks of trash and dirt before dropping the cotton in my sack. Daddy, in that way of his, kept reminding me that he paid the cotton gin to clean the cotton, but I wanted to clean my own.

When not daydreaming, and ginning my own cotton, I kept busy chasing, catching, killing, and burying all the grasshoppers I could find.

Local supersititon had it that if one killed and buried a grasshopper it would rain the next day, and if that happened, it meant no work in the field, so I could either go to school or stay home and read, and reread, my funny papers and funny books, and my movie and sports magazines. My row was *always* a grasshopper graveyard.

Besides farmland, Mister Mason owned sawmills and the town of Madison's cotton gin, planer mill, cotton seed oil mill, and fertilizer plant. During the winter when his sharecroppers weren't tilling soil, or his peach pickers weren't tending the trees, they had to work for daily wages at one of these places, mainly at the "back cracker" of the lot, the fertilizer plant. Mister Mason also owned the Madison peach shed, where his peaches were sorted for the market. But only the whites worked there, no colored workers being allowed other than to haul the peaches from the orchards to the shed.

During those days there was a thick line separating town and country folks, a fact felt very strongly among the young. Most town folks, particularly Town School children, figured that the deeper one lived in the country the dumber one was. And we lived four long, *dumb* miles into the country from town. We Andrews children felt pretty deep into dumb.

Saturday was "country day in town." Folks poured in from the county's surrounding farm communities: Barrows Grove, Bethel, Bethlehem, Bostwick, Brownwood, Buckhead, Ebenezer, Flat Rock, Godfrey, Holland Spring, Indian Creek, Mars Hill, Mount Zion, Plainview, Rutledge, Saint Paul, Smyrna, Stanton Grove, Sweet Home, Swords, Thankful, and Walkers Chapel. Into Madison they came by car, truck, wagon, buggy and foot. Owning no car, we were among the walkers. On occasion we would get a ride into town. But if that ride came on a wagon, Harvey, Benny, and I would ride to the edge of the pavement leading into Madison before hopping off and walking the rest of the way, a distance behind or in front of the wagon, into town. Sister would *never* even get on the wagon as, Lord knows, *no* self-respecting country children would *ever* let themselves be seen by the town children riding aboard, or even near, a lowly wagon, pulled by that ultimate symbol of deep-down country dumb—the mule.

Lord, I truly hope that up there in mule heaven the Main Mule can find a spot somewhere in His heart to forgive, especially, Benny and me for what we thought of His kind down here on earth back during the 1940s. Yes, Benny and I were convinced God put the mule here on earth solely to personally embarrass the two of us. Our first year of sharecropping, when we had just one mule, Churchill, Daddy spent most of the time plowing himself. When we went to a two-horse farm the following year, Churchill, too old and ornery, had to be retired (to hanging around the Big House barn eating, sleeping, and waiting to feed the buzzards). Churchill was replaced by two younger mules, Red and Clyde. Then, Lord, came that day when Harvey left home for Atlanta and not too long afterwards Daddy's health went bad for a spell, which meant *all* the mule work fell upon Benny and me. A conspiracy from on high! Besides not liking farm work of *any* type, Benny and I shared a greatest fear in life: being *seen* by the Town School children while working in the field, especially plowing a mule. Lord, God! The thought of God *and* the Main Mule up in heaven figuring out ways *together* to catch us in the act of field work for the Town School children to see haunted our minds constantly. So much so that when we were plowing in the field near the main road and saw the dust from a car approaching, we would instantly "hit the dirt," falling flat out on our faces on the ground and lying deathly still until the car passed and was well out of sight. Then, with a mouthful of dirt, we would jump up and run to catch up with the mule, who went right on pulling the plow down the row alone in full view of the passing car. For some reason mules weren't ashamed of being seen with themselves.

To buy food staples during the winter, or anytime, Daddy (who for some odd reason *loved* mules) always drove the wagon—alone, of course— into town. But during the winter of 1947-1948 when his health was poor, guess *who* had to drive the MULE AND WAGON into Madison to be seen and laughed at by all the Town School children? Yup. Benny and me. God and the Main Mule seemingly worked overtime that winter making Daddy sick just to "get" Benny and me. They got us.

But just as God and the Main Mule spent <u>all</u> of their waking hours scheming to get us, we spent all of our time planning how not to be gotten so badly. In the wagon a cotton sheet was always kept—used in the field to tie up and weigh in cotton—for covering whatever was being hauled in case of rain. Now the instant we reached the edge of the pavement, beginning about a quarter of a mile outside the heart of town, on this demeaning trip into Madison, Benny and I, he yet holding onto the mule reins, laid face down flat on the floor of the wagon, *under* the cotton sheet, and rode right up into town. All the folks on the street, or in their vehicles, saw these two mules pulling an empty

Daddy, a lover of the Blues, as a child learned to play the guitar and violin (fiddle), plus he could draw. Yet he lived a life apologetic for, or "ashamed" of, his talents.

Mama didn't like those who made fun of colored folks, people like Amos 'n Andy and Al Jolson.

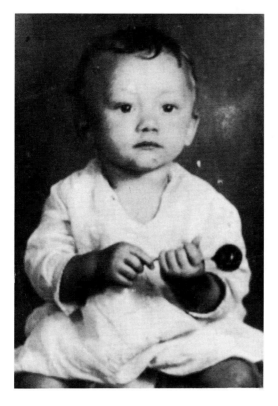

The only way they could get six-month-old me to sit still and shut up for this picture was to take away Harvey's lollipop and give it to me. Following the click of the camera, Harvey got his candy back and I went back to crying.

Mister Jim lived in a two-room log cabin across the spring back into the woods where he read and hunted. Years earlier he was ostracized by his peers and made open game for the KKK for keeping a "colored" family.

When Grandmama Jessie told us on her 69th birthday about once having been a young girl, 7-year-old me was shocked. I wondered who back then had been our Grandmama.

Grandaddy Crawford. A Putnam County Perryman who was ostracized by his family for marrying a "white looking" woman, or a "plantation nigger."

Grandmama Lula, or "Lady Lula," who was just the opposite of Grandmama Jessie, or "Jazzy Jessie." Always quiet, like her mind was forever elsewhere.

With new jacket, or "jumper," and hunting cap bib kicked up, 12-year-old me being cool while standing beside Aunt Bea's house in town.

Dew Boy was the photographer, and 13-year-old me had the dime to pay for this one made in front of Grand-mama Jessie's house in town.

SCHOOL DAYS 1949-50
B.S.H.S.

I am standing third from left on the last row in the Burney Street High School Freshman Class, 1947-48. This was "Town School," where daily I wore my corduroy pants, Army shirt and Army combat boots. High school cool. Second from right on third row is Sister. (Insert) My first high school crush was on Yvonne (here a junior) in the eighth grade. The first of many "one-sided" love affairs.

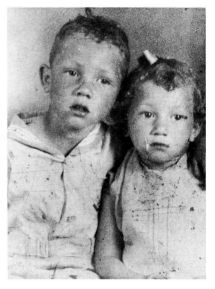

Atlanta wasn't discovered by Scarlett, nor Andrew Young, but by our oldest brother, Harvey, in 1945.

Benny was always "doing" things and "going" places that folks, especially Daddy, thought he oughtn't. Sister started early getting folks "told."

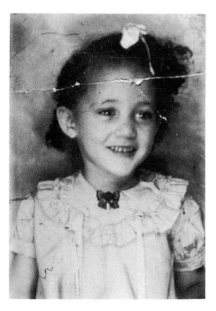

Shirley, Daddy's pet. We never forgave her for going to the World's Fair. She didn't become one of us until she broke the bottle of codliver oil.

*Joe (right) wasn't the "real" Joe Louis. Nor was his playmate and cousin, T.J., here the **real** Thomas Jefferson.*

Johnny early on solved the problem of picking cotton. He became afraid of it . . . until we stopped farming.

Ronnie was born the year Babe Ruth died. I envied her that.

Deloris and Gregory were born lucky—after I left home; thus they were in no way responsible for helping mold The Last Radio Baby.

Left to right: Daddy, Aunt Bea, Virginia (Uncle Bubba's young and pretty second wife), Uncle Bubba and his car (filled with neighborhood children) in Atlanta in about 1947.

Aunt Bea smoked cigarettes, danced (even on Sunday), went to the picture show, among other things. But most of all, she loved all of us children.

*I envied Uncle Toodney, Aunt Bea's husband. Besides driving a taxicab, he went to the picture show **every night.***

Uncle Johnny, Mama's oldest brother. The boll weevil sent him to work in the West Virginia coal mines before he went on to Chicago.

Aunt Lula, Mama's oldest sister, sent us boxes of clothing (all too big for me) from New Jersey.

Aunt Polly, the family's "Jet (Greyhound) Setter," and Uncle Few, who came back from World War II shell-shocked.

Aunt Soncie, who lived in "town," in 1948 voted against the party of FDR.

Geraldine, our Atlanta
cousin. Every summer she
came to visit us, stole Sister's
thunder and climbed trees,
played cowboys . . . and one
day swam with us boys.

Everybody was sad-faced on this Saturday, April 14, 1945,
in town, including Aunt Bea (left) and Shirley. Two days
earlier, President Franklin D. Roosevelt had died. As far as
most Southern colored felt at the time, Roosevelt had been
America's first **real** President since Abraham Lincoln.

wagon right through the heart of town. Those close enough might've heard giggling coming from beneath the cotton sheet over how God and the Main Mule hadn't counted on the ol' "empty wagon" trick.

All of our staples were bought from the Rock Store, the town's biggest general store, located on Main Street, where most of the country folks got credit and bought their supplies. The farmers shopping there would drive their wagons in the back of the Rock Store and load up. Not Benny and I. To be seen back there with a whole passel of overall-wearing, tobacco chewing farmers talking crops while standing alongside their mules, a public admission to the whole world of being "country," was not Benny's and my style. No, no, no!... Instead we parked the mules and wagon all the way down in back of the Mapp's Funeral Home, several blocks away from the Rock Store, where we felt no Town School children were likely to be hanging out. Folks in and around the Rock Store thought we two were a bit "tetched" in the heads toting those heavy bags of flour, for example, on our backs God knew how far (we never let on to anyone we had a wagon, much less where it was hidden). We might've been tetched, not to mention exhausted from the long and heavy hauling, but we weren't "country." We thought.

Dug in under the cotton sheet for the ride back through the middle of enemy territory, we passed the oldtimers sitting on the empty crates on the corner of the main drag chawing, spitting and talking and then staring speechless at two mules pulling a driverless, giggling wagon right down through the heart of town, its invisible pilot and co-pilot feeling as discreet as a heartbeat 'neath a cotton sheet. The driverless wagon having completed its mysterious mission into Madison drove right on through a red light and all sorts of horn-honking and brakes screeching traffic as it giggled its way right on out of town. Amen.

XIV. THE COMMUNITY

The many small colored farming communities scattered throughout Morgan County were not officially recorded under the names given
them by their inhabitants (such as Plainview, Smyrna, etc.), nor were
there boundary lines, except in the minds of the people living there.
Each community was named after its church, the center or "soul" of the
community. We, of course, lived in Plainview and during the 1940s the
population must have averaged three hundred people, counting babies. During this time Mister Jim, the McIntires, and the Browns were
the only stationary whites in Plainview (some four other white families,
including the Halls, all stayed for short durations before moving on).
Mister Mason lived in town.

Ol' Barnett Farm was the biggest single-owned tract of land in
Plainview, which Mason rented. Including the overseer's, there were
thirteen houses, in which twenty-one sharecropping families lived at
one point or another between 1943 and 1949. These Mason sharecroppers were the only ones in Plainview. Mister McIntire rented some land
to a colored family or two or more (the Masseys being one of these
families), and the rest of the farmers in the community owned their
own land, with Mister Wes being the biggest of these colored landhold-
ers.

The center of activity on Mason's was the overseer's Big House, a
fat two-story white (looking more whitewashed than painted) frame
structure standing back behind several oak and pecan trees just off the
dirt main road running to Madison. But back of the Big House was
where everything was at. Back here was "the Yard," a sprawling area
lined with sheds that housed all of the farm equipment, including the
big green and yellow John Deere tractor, wagons, and a blacksmith
shop. (We Barnett farmers would often argue, and sometimes fight,
with the Masseys [who else?] over which was the superior tractor, Mister
Mason's John Deere [our choice, naturally] or Mister McIntire's Farmall.)
At the end of the Yard began the vast fenced-in lot that ended in a
pasture extending far into the woods. Here were kept the thirty-odd
mules used to farm this Mason land. At the top of the Yard, toward the
end of this huge lot, were several wood structures—barns, stables (where
the mules ate and slept and where their food of corn and hay was
stored) and a gear house. Each spring and summer morning from
Monday through Saturday, weather permitting, the farmer rose at dawn
to go up to the Yard, enter the lot, bridle or "catch" and gear up his

mule (or mules) for a long day in a field of hot sun and, believe me, no fun. It is because of the farm that I do not to this date seek opportunity to be out in the sun, a symbol for me of work in the field. I loved awaking in the morning to the sound of rain beating on our tin roof, which meant it was a day to stay inside and read or to get away from the farm altogether by going to school.

But the Yard was more than a place lined with sheds full of farm equipment tools. The Yard was *the* meeting place. Here everyone met in the mornings with their mules, greeted one another, and briefly discussed crops and the weather before they marched off to the fields with their animals. When it rained, most males, rather than hang around the house with the womenfolk (and reading children), would walk up to the Yard and sit under the shed just out from the lot. Here they could watch the mules and talk crops and weather. They also spent much of their winters here talking, watching the mules, and awaiting spring plowing.

It was also up to the Yard before the crack of dawn that we crowd of sharecroppers went those summer mornings to await the tall-bodied truck that came to haul us to work in the peach orchards. Yes, Lord, everything went on up at the Yard...

1. THE NEIGHBORS

The family Mapp lived close by and the children helped us fight the Masseys. In one of these on-the-way-home-from-school fights, John and Mance Mapp and Benny were attacked by the Masseys. This was the time Minnie Pearl caught John's neck in the crook of her arm beneath her armpit in a tight bear hug while with a rock in her free hand she beat it against the top of his head. The next day, John, his head full of knots, didn't go to school.

The day of the Masseys' massacre of the Mapps and Benny was unusual in that Mance was involved. Mance was rarely ever in a fight, even though the Masseys made sure every male child, plus Sister, ate their quota of Massey Knuckle Sandwich each school year. Mance was not afraid to fight, he just did not want to fight and would let no one provoke him into doing so (except, on occasion, Minnie Pearl). Mance was considered "good" and wasn't ashamed of it. Even the Masseys, most of the time, respected him for this. Eager to learn, Mance followed Benny by a year to Town School; the two of them were for a time the only Plainviewans in high school. Many felt that Mance, like his father, was going to be a minister someday. (He became one.)

Every weekend for a period during the summer of '43, I'd sneak cigarettes from Daddy's pack of Camel's "ready rolls" (as opposed to his can of "roll your own" Prince Albert tobacco) to take down into the woods where John and I would smoke them. John was younger than Mance and about two years older than I. This sneaking and smoking went on until Daddy bought a pack of Lucky Strikes and I stole one and sneaked away to the woods to puff alone. I had only to inhale once to become so dizzy and nauseous from this potent cigarette that I thought I was dying, and this was enough to make me kick the nicotine habit at the ripe old age of nine.

Many nights the Mapps sat out on their porch and, led by Mister Melvin and sometimes Mance, sang spirituals. Their voices carried beautifully over the neighborhood. Often some of us Andrews children joined in the singing and, fortunately, our voices couldn't be heard. Not even Sister's, which was the only time I recall her voice being drowned out.

Then there were those times of summer when down from Atlanta would come Yank.

The Mapps, who came to Mason's a few years before we did, moved to Atlanta following the 1945 crop year. They settled in a section of the city called "Summer Hill," where lived the family of Yank.

Moving from the north end of Barnett Farm into the house vacated by the Mapps, in a change of home but not landlord, came the family Roland.

Mister Will, the father of the Roland family, and his wife, Missis Minnie, had ten children (the oldest three, all girls, Ada, Anna, and Ruth, were among the area's prettiest). Mister Will, along with Mister Ed Brown, who lived with his wife and six children and sometimes some of their children on Barnett Farm's west end, had lived on this land longer than any other of us sharecroppers, or the overseer. The two men, both about sixty, were in constant competition with one another for the unofficial title of "King of the Yard." The two old-timers rarely had anything, and nothing ever good, to say to one another. This despite the fact that their children got along well together.

Mister Will lived closer to the Big House than Mister Ed and was the first one up at the Yard every morning. Nobody, including Mister Ed, would ever try to beat Mister Will up to the Yard (even the overseer, Mister Brown, didn't walk out his back door in the morning until he looked out to see Mister Will there to awaken the Yard). Also he was

the last one to leave at night. These were duties, or privileges, Mister Will felt he'd earned from his longevity on Mason land.

Mister Ed's claim to the throne was being a carpenter who was hired to do all of the carpentry work for Mason's Barnett Farm. That is, all except the for carpentry work on Mister Will's house, which he, not wanting any "jackleg" messing up where he lived, did himself.

Mister Will's answer to Mister Ed's role as Barnett Farm's Carpenter-in-Residence was his son, Will Junior. "Junior," as all called him, became the first Barnett Farm colored to drive the tractor, a job previously performed only by the overseer's son-in-law and three oldest sons. Junior started driving when Mister Brown's three sons became interested in other things: Winfred wouldn't let tractor driving drive out his dream of singing; Bobby married a town girl and moved to Madison; Ezra was more interested in hunting and trapping than farming. Thus, Junior and Mister Joe Irving, Mister Brown's son-in-law, became the Barnett Farm's two main tractor drivers, which involved mostly plowing and working Mister Mason's own personal fields of cotton, corn, wheat, and oats, and the overseers' cotton. We sharecroppers with our trusty mules didn't use a tractor. Junior learned to drive the tractor at a very young age by hanging around up at the Yard with Winfred and Bobby. He loved driving so well that he, in the same grade with me, dropped out of school to drive more. I, too, wanted to drive tractor, and when I asked Mama if I could drop out of school to learn to drive to make some money, she said I could quit if I wanted to but if I did I would have to stay home and work on our own farm, which meant mules and picking cotton. I stayed in school. Mamas!

What catapulted Mister Will into being the "real" King of the Yard came right after the war ended. Mister Ed's youngest son, Bonny, came home from the Army (all five of Mister Ed's sons served in the war) driving a big, black, shiny Lincoln-Zephyr. This was an unheard of car for a sharecropper's son—a colored one at that—to own. While Mister Will's son was driving tractor for Mister Mason, Mister Ed's son was riding around in a Lincoln-Zephyr. Well, he didn't ride around in it for long. Soon after Bonny came driving home from the war, whenever you passed the Brown's house you'd see this big, shiny black Lincoln-Zephyr sitting out in the front yard with a pair of legs sticking out from underneath or a bending butt whose head was stuck beneath the car's open hood. Next, the car was sitting on blocks. True, it never ran again, just sat there beautifully polished and shined up on those blocks, but no one else in Plainview, including Mister Will, had a Lincoln-Zephyr in their front yard like Mister Ed did.

Mister Will had served in the Army in France during World War I. Mister Ed hadn't served in the Army at all. Our Uncle Corris had also been in the Great War. Serving in France with him and Mister Will had been Mister Walter Few, or "Speck" (so called because of his face full of freckles), who married Uncle Corris's sister, Anna Rose. Mister Walter came home from the war in 1919, drunk. Most everybody thought at the time that the effects of the war and whiskey would kill the then twenty-one-year-old veteran before he was twenty-five. Well, during the 1940's Mister Walter was yet alive, working with Uncle Corris at Mapp's Undertakers (no relation to our neighbors) and chauffering for one of Madison's leading white families...while still drinking. (Mister Walter was to work, and drink, up to his death at age eighty-four, outliving Uncle Corris by more than thirty years and Mister Will by nearly as many.)

Up at the Yard, Mister Will told many World War I stories. The stories I remember most were not about the fighting in France (or the women—talk he tried, sometimes unsuccessfully, to keep away from the ears of children). I remember Mister Will telling about meeting a bunch of colored soldiers from Mississippi. After talking to these men and listening to their stories about their home state, Mister Will said he came away from the war in France thanking God he didn't have to come back to a home like Mississippi. Mister Will talked about Mississippi as if World War I had been fought, and was still going on, there. He even talked around the white overseer, Mister Brown, about how bad the coloreds were treated in Mississippi.

Mister Will also talked about boxing. He liked Joe Louis a lot, but his main man had been the first colored Heavyweight Boxing Champion, Jack Johnson. When Johnson was killed in an automobile accident in the spring of 1946, Mister Will was deeply saddened.

The game of baseball was another sport Mister Will kept up with. In 1947 when Jackie Robinson started playing baseball for Brooklyn, thus becoming the first colored man in the white Major Leagues this century, Mister Will (like most coloreds throughout America) instantly became a Dodger fan. Mister Will, at least for me, was more interesting than all the other farmers because he talked about something other than crops, the weather, and religion. (Mister Will read the Bible, along with the newspapers, but wasn't much on going to church). He was also known for tying a tight hame string, the knot that held the mule's harness in place. He often tied one for me since I wasn't known up at the Yard for my hame string knots. (Some thought Mister Ed could tie a tighter knot than Mister Will.) For some reason Mister Will liked

Benny and me. When Benny went away to college to become the first colored male in Plainview ever to do so, Mister Will acted more proud of him than Daddy did.

Mister Ed had never been in a war, nor had he met anyone from Mississippi, and he did not follow boxing or baseball, which made his talk mostly about crops and the weather. Some said Mister Ed could talk better with the overseer because he listened. Mister Will didn't listen to anybody, white or colored, because he was always talking. That's why, they also said, the overseer was always quicker to make the listening Mister Ed a strawboss in the fields, woods, and orchards than he was the talking Mister Will. Besides listening, Mister Ed, everyone agreed, talked "sensible" talk—crops, weather, and religion. And, it was also thought, because the overseer was able to talk to Mister Ed (while only being able to listen to Mister Will) that Mister Ed could have been, hands down, the unofficial "King of the Yard," if it were not for that Lincoln-Zephyr sitting up in Mister Ed's front yard on them blocks.

Both Mister Ed and Mister Will claimed to be Mister Mason's favorite sharecropper, each proudly proclaiming that the rich white landowner promised them a home on his land for as long as they lived.

But such an understanding was, apparently, never put in writing. Following the 1948 crop, Mister Will moved, in his own words, "up to the country," a few miles past Madison. Mister Ed, after his five sons returned home from World War II, showed little to no interest in continuing sharecropping and then moved out of the house, giving up his large house and two-horse farm to a new, larger family and moving with his wife into a house too small to hold all of his pride. The Kings of the Yard were dead. Amen.

The family who moved into Mister Ed's old house was named Mitchell, headed by Mister Henry, the father. A thin, short, pigeon-toed man, Mister Henry could with one hand paper, roll, lick, and light a cigarette in a windstorm. But he was no King of the Yard. What Mister Henry was most known for was being the daddy of "Doll Baby," the siren of Barnett Farm in 1949.

Mister Oscar Allen had a wife and only one child, Oscar Junior, not yet ten years old when the family lived just down the road beyond the Rolands. Mister Oscar was slow. Slower than me. One morning he took his wife and son into town to buy groceries, only to find all of the stores closed that day...Sunday. He came back home and kept on to church, getting there just as services were turning out. After that Mister

Oscar always checked with someone when he felt Saturday ought to be near.

Living just behind us atop a small rise in a two-room house was Mister Lonzie Broadnax, with his wife, Anna, and their little girl, Doris Ruth. The wife was not there long before she took the daughter and went back home, the next rise over, to her folks, the Rolands. Mister Lonzie stayed on alone in the house, his only company being the pig he had bought his family for fattening up to kill for their winter meat. After his wife left, Mister Lonzie didn't bother building a fattening pen for the pig, nor did he have him cut, He just let the pig run around the regular pen until he finally rooted his way out and began running wild. The neighborhood didn't like the pig running loose because it rooted up gardens, but sympathized with Mister Lonzie, a young man whose wife had left him, and so would just run the animal off whenever it showed up to root. The pig, a "streak of lean" with no fat on him whatsoever, soon took up with the neighborhood dogs, and when Mister Lonzie called him at feeding time he would come home with a whole bunch of these dogs and they would all eat from his feeding trough together. Mister Lonzie never killed that pig; it eventually died of old age, possible a South "first."

Mister Lonzie, an outgoing, quick-to-laugh sort, didn't remember the month of his birthday, only the year, 1913, so he celebrated December 31st as his birthday. He was amazed by my memory for dates, like the date he moved into the house back of us on Saturday, October 2, 1943 (also the day Yank and I got into our last fight). He couldn't fathom how, over the years, I kept this and other dates memorized. Because of this he was always predicting that great things would come my way in the future. Mister Lonzie, thank you, but I'm still waiting.

Scott, Mister Lonzie's cousin, lived by herself in the little two-room shack just up from the big acorn tree in back of the Rolands. Mister Raymond, the quiet, Indian-looking man who married Aunt Cora, had lived there together with an older, all-gray man before Scott. Scott had had a husband at one time and somewhere there was a son. Scott was never seen in a dress, only man's overalls or pants. She was considered a good worker. Working in the peach orchards, she always let June and me pick with her on her row of trees. Although she worked fast, she didn't talk to June and me like most grownups talked to children. She talked like us and was fun to work with. Scott liked children. But grownups didn't seem so sure about Scott.

We neighborhood children visited her house from time to time.

What I remember most about her house was the horse shoe that hung just above the front door inside…to keep the haints out. Folks said Scott "worked roots." But she was always good to us children.

One day she was gone…some said, sent down to the crazy house in Milledgeville.

He said he was from Texas. Where, he said, he rode a horse on a ranch. In Plainview he was always seen walking. He was, I believe, Missis Mattie Allen's cousin. Old (about fifty), with some front teeth missing from his fox-like smile, he had delicate, pointed features with beady, twinkling eyes, and was always the gentleman around women. The men didn't quite know how to react to him—he was always talking about Texas, where none of them had ever been; a ranch, which none of them had ever seen; his horse, an animal few, if any, of them had ever ridden (though most had ridden mules), and he wore a tall, wide-brimmed black hat like, he said, they did in Texas. Behind his back the menfolk laughed at him. He was an outsider.

One day he came walking past Plainview School beneath his tall, wide-brimmed black hat and stopped to ask Missis Bertha if he could talk to the students. Succumbing to his Texas charm, Missis Bertha relented. All I can remember about his talk that day, besides Texas, ranches, and his horse, was that he told us he had always loved hunting coons and possums. From that day onward we children called him "Mister Coon and Possum." I don't remember his real name. He left the school that day wearing that fox-like smile, eyes twinkling under the tall, black, wide-brimmed hat—walking.

I never saw Mister Coon and Possum again. He had only been in Plainview less than a year when, somebody said, he returned to Texas to his horse and ranch, walking.

There were five of them, Jim, Doll, Gully, Sid, and Bub—the Moore Boys—called this from the time they were youngsters. They all owned their own farms, land inherited from their parents. Talk was that when their mother was alive she was one of the world's cleaningest souls, spending most of her life in her kitchen. A light sleeper, after her husband died she supposedly spent her sleeping hours sitting in a chair in the kitchen to be closer to her work when she awoke the next morning. "Too much cleaning to be done," she was often heard to say, "to waste time sleeping." As little of her time as she could spare was spent outdoors, where the sight of untidiness, and dirt, was too much for her to bear so she stayed inside all the day sweeping, scouring, and scrubbing.

The widow Moore was wooed and won by a railroad man whose traveling permitted him only a week or two out of each month to dirty up her house. It was assumed that on these visits by her railroad man, the kitchen chair she slept in was moved to the bedroom at night. While spending one of these weeks at her house, the couple was abruptly interrupted one day by a woman, a stranger to the area, who hauled the railroad man off, never to be seen again in Plainview. The Moore Boys' mother brought her chair from the bedroom back to the kitchen, where she went back to sweeping, scouring, and scrubbing. She died sitting up in her chair in the kitchen with an apron on and a broom in her hand.

All five of the Moore Boys had one significant thing in common. They all were "stingy." The Moore Boys didn't give out nickels, or even pennies, to children. Also, they spent all or most of their lives as bachelors or living alone. Two of the brothers, Mister Doll and Mister Gully (as in bully), lived in town and commuted to the country to work their farms. Mister Gully got married late in life but, not wanting to change his living style after the wedding, chose not to live in the same house as his wife. She came to his house to cook for him, and perform other wifely duties, before returning to her home. He never brought her out to Plainview to see his farm. Mister Bub, the youngest of the five brothers, was a playboy. He left Plainview as a young man and went North, returning home many years later sick with tuberculosis. He lived with his older, bachelor brother, Mister Jim (not Granddaddy) in the family house, where over the years came several women to attend the sick, unmarried youngest of the Moore Boys. As the years passed, some of these women died young, but the sick and still handsome Mister Bub kept right on living.

Said to be the stingiest of the brothers was Mister Sid. In a Moore Boy oddity, Mister Sid got married as a young man and he and his wife had three children before she left him to go live in town. Their two sons, Crawford and John Wesley, she left with Mister Sid, but they too, before reaching adulthood, went to town to stay with their mother and sister, leaving Mister Sid to live alone.

Mister Sid was well known for his blind mules. Early every spring he'd go to town to the mule auction at the livery stable and for five dollars would intercept one of these, always blind, animals on its way to the glue factory and bring it back home with him. Mister Sid was an expert at picking a mule that had one more crop left in it. At the end of harvest, the mule would lay down and die before being dragged down into the woods back of Mister Sid's house for the buzzards' fall feed. Early the next spring, Mister Sid, with five dollars in his pocket, would head for town to the livery stable and the mule auction.

Mister Sid was perhaps the last adult seen on the streets of Madison barefoot. For years during barefoot season he, like many children, went to town without shoes. Then, some time during the late 1940s, when it was felt that all grown folks in the area could afford shoes, Mister Sid was told by a policeman one day not to come back to town again wearing his bare feet.

Uncle Bubba in 1940 began renting a house on Mister Sid's land, and June and I often visited the landlord, who lived some five minutes by bare feet away. We went to pay our respects quite often during the watermelon and pecan seasons. Yet despite all our thoughtfulness, Mister Sid never once gave June or me a slice of watermelon or even a pecan in appreciation. He took all these goodies to town aboard his wagon, pulled by his blind mule, and sold them. Once when he wasn't home, June and I went down to his house and climbed the big pecan tree in his back yard and shook it until the ground was covered with pecans. Jumping down, we started filling our pockets with the nuts. But before our pockets were full we heard a creaky wagon creaking on down the side road leading to the front of the house. Panicking, we ran, but not fast enough. Mister Sid, unlike his mule, saw us. He made us turn all our pockets inside out and drop all of the pecans back to the ground beneath the tree before he sent us on our way with, "I'm gonna tell y'all's daddies on both of y'all!"—always the worst part of getting caught. After all of that shaking work up in the tree we didn't get to eat a single pecan. In fact, we saved Mister Sid the trouble of going up the tree himself. Maybe that's why he never told our daddies.

But Mister Sid was always fair. He never promised you anything and so you never expected, or got, anything. But you always had hope. Considering that we never shared his watermelons and pecans and pennies, we children got along well with Mister Sid, a tall, slender, easy-going sort who called everybody "sir" or "ma'am" no matter their race or age.

Mister Sid loved possum hunting. Possum hunting was solely a night-time operation since the animal slept during the day and came out at night to seek its food (and often ended up as a meal). "Real" hunting in Plainview was rabbit and squirrel hunting with a gun. (As a child I saw no deer or wild turkeys.) One needed no gun to possum hunt, only a stick with which to hit the possum over the head after shaking it out of the tree, and a croker sack to put it in. "Real" farmers didn't believe in possum hunting, which to these early-to-bedders meant roaming the woods all night and sleeping late the next day—the doings of "lazy men." But Mister Sid loved possum hunting so much that often he went alone.

The possum-hunting season was in the fall and winter, those months between Mister Sid's blind mules. When I reached my teens, Mama and Daddy felt I was old enough to be trusted to spend the night roaming the woods, but only when there was no work in the field and no school the next day. This meant Friday and Saturday nights were big possum-hunting nights. Ezra Brown, the overseer's son, who was about my age and was a true woodsman and hunter, would sometimes go possum hunting with me and Mister Sid, who supplied the dogs, croker sack, lantern, and axe (the woods provided the stick).

Now there was, for me at least, one big drawback to possum hunting, and that was coming upon the dogs who had treed a possum in a tree too big for the three of us to shake (dogs didn't do any shaking, only barking). This meant the tree had to be cut down because the possum wasn't about to volunteer to climb down through a pack of barking dogs to get hit over the head with a stick and put into our croker sack. I was always in favor of passing over these cowardly possums and progressing to the next, shakable tree. In fact, I did not mind if we never caught any possum; I just loved being out in the woods at night. But the dogs, Mister Sid, and Ezra never passed up a possum, no matter how big or tall a tree it was in. So down would come the tree with the three of us sharing the axe (dogs didn't cut down trees either, only barked up them). It definitely was no fun cutting down a tree in the middle of the woods in the middle of the night. Fortunately, having to cut down a tree was the exception, since most possums were sporting and obliged us by climbing shakable trees.

More so than the hunt, I loved the woods, mysteriously outlined against the night's sky. When there was a full moon it lit up the landscape so beautifully that night's earth seemed not to be the same as the one the sun shone upon.

Down in the woods in back of the Moore Boys' family house was their fishing pond, dug by them and also used for swimming. Most of the neighborhood boys swam there, with permission. Jumping from the peach orchard truck during the picking season, we boys would race from the Yard to Moore's Pond, about a half-mile away, to wash off all the sticky peach fuzz. (The girls, as far as we boys knew, had no such place to cool off, or "let go.")

Came July 4th, 1946. We got home early from the orchards after working only a half-day due to the holiday (Independence Day, Thanksgiving, Christmas, and New Year's were the only holidays Plainview observed.) On this particular day, Benny and I were the only two to race straight from the peach truck to the pond. The other boys were going home either to eat, to play baseball, or to get ready to go into town to attend Madison's annual July 4th baseball double-header and picnic. Once within sight of the water, Benny and I saw two of the neighborhood's old women sitting on the bank with their poles, fishing in the pond. Sacreligious! We boys didn't like anyone fishing down there while we swam, or waded. Those fishing, mostly the old, felt the same about our swimming in "their" fishing pond. Determined—and full of peach fuzz—Benny and I jumped into the water with our pants on (normally all of us boys swam naked).

Benny and I had our baseball with us (*our* baseball was a tennis ball) and we played with it in the water by throwing it from the shallow to the deep end and racing one another to retrieve it. This was a fun game, only I did not swim. But by running into the water I would get off to a faster start than a swimming Benny and I would continue running until the water reached my nose before I turned back. Occasionally I could reach the ball before it floated beyond nose-touching water. But most of the time the ball floated too far out for me...out to the deep part.

On this day while race-wading and reaching out for the ball I felt my foot go off a cliff. Suddenly both feet were churning, trying to touch back down on mud bottom. But there was no ground under them now, only water, and I couldn't turn back...and *couldn't* swim. My feet lost no time relaying up to my brain the cold-water fact that I, all of me, was drowning, my brain in turn alerting my mouth to immediately start hollering for help. Meanwhile, my arms were busy doing their share by flailing about above the water just as fast and as helplessly as were my feet, yet churning down below. With all of this commotion going on around it, my mind started doing flashbacks to things I'd long forgotten about or never thought important enough to have remembered. What impressed me most about my mind that day was it reminding me of that old saying about drowning after going down for the third time, like striking out in baseball. Well, I counted myself popping up and down seventy-five times on this day. During these pops to the top I could see the two old women still fishing, not bothering to look my way and count with me. But, most important, I saw Benny swimming toward me, looking very much like he was laughing and not taking my popping up and down and hollering for help as seriously as I was.

Then I remembered going under the water (the seventy-sixth, and last time?) and Benny's arm tight around my waist. The next thing I knew we were standing in shallow water and instead of counting I was coughing, and my ears were full of water. Quickly checking to see if I still had my pants on, which I did, I then looked over and saw the two old women with their eyes glued to the ends of their poles, still fishing. Benny's first comment was, "You were choking me," something I didn't realize I had been doing and was not too concerned about right then. I was thinking that of all the days in the year to pick to almost drown, I had picked this one day when there were two grownup witnesses. We quickly left the pond, hoping they would not tell Mama and Daddy. Perhaps they were just as happy we left because Mama and Daddy never found out.

2. RECREATION

There were plenty of children in the neighborhood and we spent much time playing together, practically living outdoors. Plainview was generously filled with forests and we would roam them, experiencing whatever adventures the woods offered, such as playing cowboys and crooks through the trees, searching for bee honey, finding and eating wild fruit, chasing birds, challenging snakes, climbing the tallest trees, and swimming, diving...and wading...in whatever waters we found. We especially loved walking Sugar Creek for miles at a time until the water got deeper and deeper and the current stronger and scarier. Harvey was always there to add to the scare by telling us that Sugar Creek would take us all the way to the big Mississippi River, on to the even bigger Pacific Ocean...then to the Land of the Rising Run, Japan, where the warlord Tojo lived. That's when we would turn back for home.

Out-of-the-woods games were baseball, boxing, wrestling, running, throwing rocks, playing jacks or "jackstones" (played with tiny rocks), and shooting marbles. There were several "mixed" games where boys and girls played together, like hide and seek, tag, and other "sissy" stuff ("Po' Miss Liza Jane" and "London Bridge Is Falling Down" were others). These games were always conducted by girls, and the boys who played them were always the youngest, those who didn't know better, and the older boys, who knew better but for some strange reason suddenly *wanted* to leave the boys to go play with the girls. The "real" boys, that middle group, didn't play with girls.

Unable to buy many, if any, toys, we made most of our own. Our wagons, slingshots (or "flips"), bows and arrows, guns, spears, fishing poles, and, of course, baseball bats, were all homemade from wood, wire, string, or rubber (inner tube and tire). Playing cowboys and crooks, we used long sticks for horses. The chinaberry tree made the best horse because its bark is easy to peel. For an all-black horse we left the dark bark intact; when we wanted an all-white horse, the bark came off, leaving a gleaming (off) white steed (or stick). For a spotted horse, the bark was partially peeled.

Baseball was the most popular team sport in Plainview. The town of Madison had a colored baseball team that played other colored teams from the surrounding towns of Greensboro, Covington, Conyers, Social Circle, Eatonton, Monroe, and as far away as Athens. Games, all double-headers, were played on spring, summer, and early fall Sundays, holidays, and May Day, the first day of May each year, when all the county school children and teachers met at a selected site, usually some farmer's cow pasture, for a full day of picnicking and games. The Madison team was comprised mostly of grown men who played with a hard ball, uniforms, gloves, and storebought bats. The real stuff. We Plainview youngsters played a different brand of baseball. Our bats were home-made—sticks, poles, boards, planks, slats—the only requirement being that they be made of wood. We had no gloves or uniforms. And our baseball was a ragball or, if we were prosperous, a storebought tennis ball that cost ten cents.

The rules were a combination of American baseball and British rounders, the way it always had been played in Plainview for as long as anyone remembered. Whenever a ball was hit and not caught, the hitter would take off running for all the bases he could reach because rather than being thrown out at a base the runner could only be put out by being hit, or tagged, with the ball *between* bases by the defense. We had no basemen, just a pitcher, catcher, and several freelance fielders. Thus a routine grounder could be turned into a homerun if the runner could avoid getting hit (even on the way to first) by "dodging" the ball being thrown at him while rounding the bases. Thus Plainview's brand of baseball called for both the art of dodging the ball and being able to throw and hit these running dodgers. (Years later, when we first heard about a team called the Brooklyn Dodgers, we naturally thought they were so called because of their ability to "dodge" throws while running the bases.) Also, there were no walks, only strikes, but only if you swung at the ball—no called strikes. The batter could take an unlimited number of pitches until he got the one he wanted. With no called balls or strikes and few plays right at the bases (most of the action occurring on the base paths), there was no need for umpires, whom we had never heard of anyway. Too, *every* foul ball, or "tip," was a half-strike, meaning one could strike out on foul balls.

We played baseball year round, taking the game for granted. But during the BJR (Before Jackie Robinson) years, when we had no national colored baseball hero, the game never quite held that special spot in space with the Plainview of my youth that boxing did, since it had *our* (the "real") Joe Louis.

In the spring of 1942, our Atlanta cousin Geraldine gave Harvey her bicycle. Aunt Soncie and Uncle Corris brought it back in their car after a visit to Atlanta and delivered it out to our house one late Saturday afternoon. By that Sunday after church virtually every boy in Plainview came to our house to see, or try to learn to ride, Harvey's "bike"—Plainview's only one at the time.

But soon many young boys began saving their pennies, nickels, and dimes to buy bikes. In those days of the very popular "balloon" tire bike, Uncle Bubba up and bought June a "po' tire" bicycle. Because he was the son of Uncle Bubba, June's skinny-tire bike was quickly accepted among the fat-tire crowd. Then when Uncle Bubba bought from Mister Francis Fears, the owner of Madison's Rock Store, a used, almost new, balloon-tire bike, everybody felt better. All but me. From Uncle Bubba, Daddy bought the "po' tire" for Sister and me. Now not only did I own a suddenly unpopular skinny tire bike, but shared the critter with my sister! Everybody laughed at the underfed bicycle. Still, this didn't stop me from riding it, which I did much more than did Sister.

Benny was the next to buy a bike. For six dollars he bought a used bike (walking it all the way home from town) which was only in need of tires, a near impossible buy during the war (except on the black market). Before the war ended, Benny sold the bicycle for eight dollars...it still needed only tires.

In 1944, Uncle Bubba went looking for a driving job, going away as far as Atlanta (sixty-eight miles northwest of Madison) before finally finding one. Driving the garbage truck. Uncle Bubba only worked there for a short time. He didn't like Atlanta, or its garbage. He went up on the Greyhound bus but returned driving his own 1936 Ford V-8. More important to us children, though, Uncle Bubba brought home a pair of boxing gloves he had found in Atlanta's garbage, which we kids didn't believe was as bad as Uncle Bubba claimed.

He came back home on a Saturday and word lost no time at all in finding its way to every crook and corner of Plainview, so by that Sunday afternoon (after church, of course) every child, and many grown-ups, crowded the yard of Uncle Bubba's house to see the boxing gloves he went all the way to Atlanta to get especially for his son June. In the eyes of most there that day, June suddenly moved past President Roosevelt in life hierarchy and sat down right next to Joe Louis himself. On that historic day in Plainview pugilism, bare knuckles were replaced by boxing gloves. One boxing glove per boxer. For that day I lost my title of fight arranger, promoter, and referee to June, who also made all of the rules. He owned the boxing gloves.

JUNE'S RULES:

1. Only the gloved fist could be used (the ungloved hand had to be held behind the back at all times).
2. No hitting below the belt (we all wore overalls).
3. No hitting in the face.
4. No hitting in the stomach.
5. No hitting in the back.
6. A round ended only when June said so (especially when he was one of the boxers and got tired...or was losing).

Breaking any one of these rules resulted in the relinquishing of your boxing glove, along with losing the match. JUNE'S RULES applied to *all*. Except June. As owner of Plainview's only pair of boxing gloves, June reserved the right, as a righthander, to get the right-handed glove, to use his ungloved hand in emergencies, and to hit below the belt and in the face, stomach, and back when he was smaller than the opponent. When in trouble, he would turn his back to his opponent and back in close before turning around and swinging with his best punch, a roundhouse right, aimed for the head. June and I, who were both ten, I a bit taller and he a bit stouter, were evenly matched in boxing.

On this Sunday, he and I had just started boxing when he suddenly turned his back on me—a half inch taller than he, therefore technically "bigger"—and commenced to back pedal, then quickly turned and swung that roundhouse right. I didn't quite duck, so it caught me smack in the mouth. I saw red—my blood—at the exact instant I saw June's nose. Then *it* was suddenly red. Red with his blood from my right, ungloved, hand. Disqualified! And without ever having thrown a punch with the left boxing glove! Once again I took too personally a punch in the puss.

On that day when the boxing glove stole Plainview's stage from the bareknuckle, June, backed up by JUNE'S RULES, became a sudden giant-killer, whipping not just me and all the other little boys but the bigger and older boys too. Being taller, they would inadvertently land a punch on the shorter boxing-gloved owner's head or face (June's rule #3) or be unable to pull back a fist when his back abruptly turned on them, fouls automatically eliminating and declaring one a loser. Plainview's first gloved boxing championship was won by the gloves owner that historic Sunday, and when the rest of us youngsters left for our homes shortly before sundown, we were all confused by the boxing gloves, with all their many and strange rules.

But that very next day at Plainview Elementary School's Recess Fistic Tournament of Elimination, we quickly forgot all about JUNE'S RULES as I went back to arranging, promoting, and refereeing (and staying out of) bareknuckle boxing matches, where a round ended when Missis Bertha rang the bell ending recess...or one of the boxers started crying and started a fight.

To us country children, Santa Claus was more real than God. When the Plainview school pupil Herschel Pastor chalked up the drawing of Santa on the blackboard at the beginning of each December, along with the scent of hog killing, the spirit, *and* smell, of Christmas officially hit the community air. Yes, Santa Claus was more Christmas than Christ (though you never dared utter such). Living outside town, we country children were a cinch for our parents to fool about Santa Claus. There was an unwritten local law ruling that no child yet believing in Santa Claus could go into town during the month of December (unless one went solely to the picture show and then came straight back home without visiting any of the stores where Santa kept his Christmas goodies).

Sister, at about age eight or nine, became suspicious of Santa's actions long before a country child was supposed to. One Christmas morning she went and looked up the fireplace chimney and asked Mama how did big fat Santa Claus come down our small chimney, and with a fire in the fireplace? Mama said he didn't; he came through the back door when we were all asleep. The next Christmas morning, Sister asked Mama how come Santa's reindeer could fly while other deer couldn't? Mama told her the modern Santa came by car. Sister immediately jumped up and went out in the yard to look for tire tracks and came back saying she had found none. Mama told her it must've rained early that morning, washing out the tracks. Before Sister could say she hadn't heard any car (a sound country children never slept through) or rain, Mama shut her up by calling us all to eat breakfast. (I always felt that breakfast on a Christmas morning was life's most senseless meal.) Surprisingly, the next year Sister didn't conduct her early Christmas morning investigation of Santa's night-before doings...or even the Christmas after...

Then, Lord, came the fall of '46, the fall my world fell. On a bright, hot day in the cotton field, Benny and Sister TOLD me. Told me that there was NO Santa Claus! Twelve-year-old me didn't want to believe them. (I suppose they were put up to this by Mama and Daddy, who probably didn't want me to get drafted into the Army and go off to war and die still believing in Santa Claus.) Junior Roland had told me a couple of years earlier that there was no Santa Claus but I wasn't about to take his word over Mama's and Daddy's. In fact, the picture of Santa Claus was everywhere to be seen. Why tell me *now?* Why didn't they just let me go on believing in Santa Claus the rest of my life? God, what a disappointment! All those years and all those lies! Then I got mad for having been fooled all this time. Without Santa Claus how could there be a Christmas? But a few days later, I started looking forward to Christmas so I could help fool Shirley, Joe, and Johnny.

3. RELATIVES

After leaving Mister Jim's place in 1942, Uncle Toodney moved Aunt Bea, Betty Jean, and Grandmama to a rented house on Mister Jim Moore's land, a bit up and across the road from Mason's overseer's house. In early 1943, the week we moved to Mason's, Uncle Toodney got a job in town driving a taxi (wheeling the county's only 1942 Ford) for Mister Renfroe Spears. Besides housekeeping (most of it done by Grandmama), Aunt Bea was kept busy selling on commission candies (a lot of peppermint and peanut brittle bars) and soda pops (Double-Cola, Pepsi-Cola, Red Rock-Cola, Royal Crown-Cola, et al.), delivered to her by salesmen. But, talk was, Aunt Bea was kept busier with her boyfriends.

Three years after getting the taxi job, Uncle Toodney moved the family to town, living for a short spell in Canaan, the colored neighborhood in back of Burney Street School, before moving into a house Mister Spears had built for them across town in the "Horse Branch" section.

I envied Uncle Toodney his taxi-driving job—not so much the car-driving itself as the job permiting him the opportunity to go to the picture show *every* night. From Monday through Friday the picture show lasted from seven to eleven, hours when nobody was on the street needing a taxi, as most taxicab riders were inside watching the picture show, including the cab driver himself, Uncle Toodney. After the first show ended at nine, Uncle Toodney would hurriedly haul home all those after-show folks needing a taxi, then rush back to catch, for the second, third, fourth or more time, the last of the night's picture, and afterwards take care of what fares there were. Most folks went to the first show. On Saturday, with town crowded, Uncle Toodney was busy all day, yet he always made sure he saw that night's last show. In over ten years of driving Spears' Taxi, Uncle Toodney *never* missed a movie at the Madison picture show, seeing many of them as many as four times or more. I wanted to drive a taxicab so I could see all of the movies, too.

Betty Jean, though an only child, didn't spend all her years growing up without a playmate at home. While still on Moore's land, Grandmama, following a death in her family then living in Atlanta, went up to the city and brought back a young relative orphaned by the death. He was T. (Thomas) J. (Jefferson), a year or two older than his cousin Betty Jean, and his home was now with her and her family.

Grandmama had not liked Atlanta one bit. She said that the folks on the streets there would not even speak to you. Everybody just shook their heads in disgust upon hearing this.

The move from Plainview to Madison seemed to change Grandmama. She appeared lost. In Plainview she'd been a big fish in a little pond...always in charge. But in the big town pond she was just one of its many old folks, or minnows. Powerless. Maybe that's why she

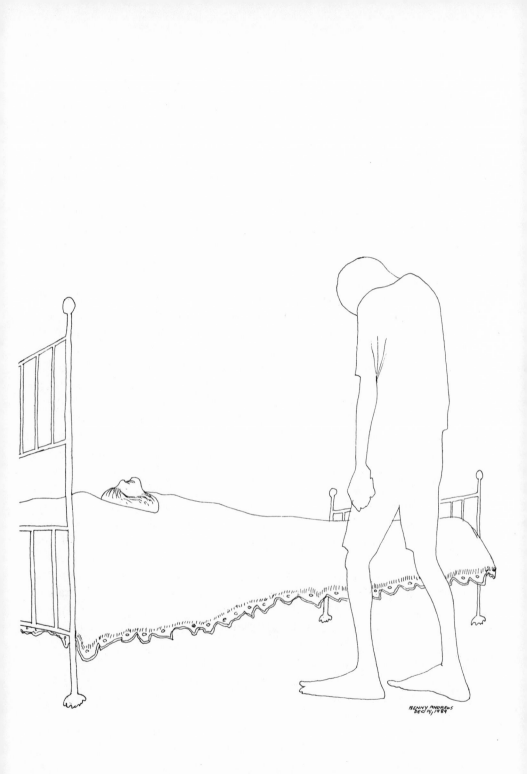

continued to come back to Plainview to church every meeting Sunday.

Once moving to town, which she loved, Aunt Bea gave up selling candy and soda pop...but, talk was, kept her boyfriends.

Aunt Marie was the local high priestess of superstition. For example, according to her, it was bad luck to step over a seated person's foot or (if seated on the floor or ground) leg. If the victim was a child, then his or her growth would be stunted, unless the wrongdoer restepped backwards over the cursed foot or leg. (The statute of limitations on such a misstep remained just as long as the growing one could grow.) Aunt Marie was also down on folks who "split poles." If two or more people were walking together and came upon something like a pole, tree, or fire hydrant, they should walk around the *same* side of it, the left or the right side not mattering so long as they did not "split" up while passing the object. Folks who failed to obey these laws of nature were, in Aunt Marie's view, doomed to bad luck for the remainder of their lives.

According to Aunt Marie, two dietary don'ts were eating watermelon sprinkled with baking soda and drinking liquor while eating bananas. These two cross-my-heart-and-hope-to-die beliefs were, in the words of Aunt Marie and many other localites, "sure killers." Watermelons were plentiful in Plainview so, instead of the deadly soda, many folks seasoned their melons with salt. Liquor was also, most churchfolks felt, too plentiful but bananas weren't, so no one locally was ever known to die from mixing this particular potion (though many claimed to have "heard" of such deaths, mostly among town and city folks who, apparently, didn't know better...or had enough money to buy bananas). On the other hand, I never knew of anyone dying from eating soda and watermelon (cantaloupe, apparently, didn't count)...though I heard...

Aunt Marie also believed in ghosts, or "haints," and knew all of the haint hangouts in Plainview. It was through Aunt Marie that I found out haints weren't good "mudders," hating to haint when it was raining. There was another thing funnny about haints—regardless of a person's skin color alive, he or she returned as a "white" haint. I never heard of anyone who saw a "colored" haint. Death bleached.

I spent so much time visiting at June's, where the two of us played with his many toys, that folks mistook us for brothers. Even Aunt Marie treated me like her son, always trying to coax me into dining with them. But local protocol dictated that all children eat at home and not hang around other folks' kitchens, even those of relatives. This rule, of course, did not apply when ice cream, cake, watermelon, and other "real" food was being offered.

Uncle Bubba, like Daddy, went from the WPA to the sawmill—the same one. While Daddy worked in the woods sawing down trees with the crosscut saw, Uncle Bubba drove the truck hauling the freshly sawed lumber from the woods to town. It was about this time that Uncle Bubba, to everyone's surprise, quit drinking. Now, they all said, he could concentrate more on "playing the field"—that mythical game we children never saw him play.

Known as one of the best drivers, if not the best driver in the area, Uncle Bubba accepted jobs only when he could drive. These jobs were rare, which meant he was often in competition with white men for such esoteric positions. And, Lord knows, from the sawmills to the peach orchards to the cotton fields and to everyplace in between and beyond, it was an accepted fact of the day that the white, competent or not, automatically got the top job over the colored. And driving *anything* was always considered a top job. Thus, Uncle Bubba eventually, and inevitably, lost his sawmill-truck-driving job to a white man. The day after this happened I was up at June's and remember hearing Uncle Bubba in a very unhappy voice saying to Aunt Marie, "Not only did I lose my job to somebody who can't drive half as good as me but I'm suppose to call the son of a bitch 'Mister' to boot!" Uncle Bubba was mad. The next day he quit that job.

Uncle Bubba always kept a car, and his legs were often seen sticking out from under his vehicle or his back was seen bent with head under hood. You could also find him floating an inner tube in a tub of water as he searched for an air leak in the rubber. (Since we were unable to buy new car tires due to the war's rubber rationing, the inner tube, no matter how many times blown, had to be patched, repatched… and repatched…until there were patches atop patches. A hole in the tire itself would be sealed with a cut piece from another tire, called a "boot." Riding in a car whose tire, or tires, had one or more boots could be very bumpy—or "bootie.")

Uncle Bubba and family eventually moved to town, in 1946, but while still living on Mister Sid's land, Aunt Marie had two babies that lived, Garland (born in 1943) and Herman (1945). June, for years an only child who got tons of toys every Christmas and special attention the rest of the year, suddenly had to start sharing all of these luxuries. Served him right—G's and Viola's seven children agreed.

Uncle Bubba had two other, "outside," sons by two different women, James (born in 1931), and Robert Lee, or R.L. (born in 1933).

After the war, Uncle Bubba got a job alongside Uncle Toodney, driving a Spears taxicab.   This was shortly before he got married to the young and pretty Virginia Brown (Mister Ed's granddaughter) while still married to Aunt Marie (everyone started talking even more about how much she must have loved Uncle Bubba).   This getting another wife while already having one convinced me and my peers that Uncle Bubba *must* have been playing *some* kind of game on *somebody's* field *somewhere.*

   Mama's mama, Grandmama Lula, visited us a few times.   Most of her time was spent living with Aunt Lula in New Jersey.   When visiting us, Grandmama Lula always stayed a few days and seemed to have very little to say.   She just sat on the porch or inside by the fire looking like she was thinking about someone or something somewhere else. Even when Grandmama Jessie came by our house to visit with her, Grandmama Jessie did all of the talking while Grandmama Lula sat and mostly listened.   But she was always very nice to us children, smiling more around us than when around others.   We saw very little of Grand-mama Lula, mainly hearing about her from Mama, who wrote often and received letters from her.   To me, Grandmama Lula always seemed much more serious, or sadder, than Grandmama Jessie, who laughed a lot.
   Then in early September of 1944, just at the start of cotton picking when Benny was entering Burney Street, Grandmama Lula died, at age sixty-four.   Her body was sent back to be buried in the Barrow's Grove graveyard.   This was to be my first time attending a funeral.
   When Grandmama Lula, who hadn't been to visit us for about a year, died, we children weren't too surprised since in Plainview old folks and babies died all the time.   Just that past year, Mister Frank Allen had died without us neighborhood boys ever seeing the hole where the bullet was said to still be in his leg.   Only when a young person died did we take real notice, like the time when Sugar Boy Carter, the young husband of the pretty young schoolteacher Missis Nina Mae, got killed in a car wreck.
   It was raining hard the Sunday Grandmama Lula was buried.   Uncle Bubba drove Mama and six of us children (Daddy stayed home taking care of Johnny, the baby) to the funeral in his 1936 Ford V-8.   I sat up front.   The body was on display in town at Mapp's Funeral Home, whose parlor on this day was crowded partly because it was raining too hard for anyone to stand outside, there being no front porch.   The crowd spoke with hushed voices, as if afraid they might wake Grand-mama Lula.   Many said about Grandmama Lula lying in the casket, "She

looks so peaceful—just like she's sleeping." She didn't look like she was sleeping to me; she looked dead.

At the church, far into the country below Plainview, many people, mostly men, rose to talk, read, preach, and sing about how good Grandmama Lula had been. In the front row of the church right out from where the open casket stood sat Grandmama Lula's children, brothers and sisters. The women, even Mama, were crying, while all the men looked solemn and sad. I couldn't get over seeing Aunt Polly cry; I thought anybody who had killed a fox with their bare hands was tougher than that. Even Geraldine, our old Indian scout, was crying. She was sitting with the rest of us children on the second row bench. Well into the services, Aunt Polly's husband, Uncle Few, whom Benny and I instantly judged the best-dressed man at the funeral in his Army uniform, got up and walked out of the church into the rain. Everyone understood he had just returned home from the war and was said to be something called "shell-shocked." With everyone now mostly crying, I suddenly felt like I wanted to. But I didn't cry because I was a boy.

Outside at the grave it was still raining and muddy and folks were still crying. I stood thinking Grandmama Lula was the only one out there dry.

There came a lot of relatives for the funeral from far away, many needing a place to stay. Our cousins, Geraldine and Lois, stayed with us. Geraldine was too big to play with us now, looking more like a grown woman than an Indian scout. At the funeral she wore silk stockings. Lois was the daughter of Grandmama Lula's sister, Aunt Rosie, who lived in Knoxville, Tennessee, and was married to Uncle Freeman Alford. The two girls spent only one night (the Saturday before the funeral) with us but stayed long enough for me to fall madly in love with Lois. (By this time Pauline had finished high school and had deserted me for college.) I never saw Lois again after the funeral, but for years I kept alive the memory of that one Saturday night when she belonged solely to me, in mind.

Three years later, Geraldine came back to visit us, married. Her husband was Almore Yancey, a slender, sharp-featured, well-dressed young man who right off met the approval of us children for having married our favorite cousin. He must have given us something. But on this trip to the country, our old Indian scout Geraldine took little time with us children, talking instead to Mama and Daddy—the grown folks. It was hard to accept the fact Geraldine was now grown, no longer one of us children, but soon after this visit she had her first baby, Larry, and this proved to us she was now a grown woman. The women liked

Almore because he was well-mannered and good-looking. The men liked him because he took a drink with them and, like them, was born in the country and loved to hunt and fish. Everybody said he was much older than Geraldine.

In late winter of 1946, Aunt Cora suddenly died. Everybody said she died young at age sixty. Sixty sounded very old to then-not-quite-twelve-years-old me. Meanwhile, quiet talk (spoken where the children weren't supposed to hear but somehow usually did) was that Aunt Cora died because someone was "working roots" on her. She had no children but everyone figured Aunt Cora spent her life too busy finding and changing boyfriends to have time to bother with a family. Her last boyfriend she did marry just a few years before she died. He was a quiet, good-looking, part-Indian man whom I remember only as "Mister Raymond." But, it was whispered, somewhere along the line Aunt Cora had gotten on the bad side of the wrong person and got roots worked on her to cause such a sudden, unexpected death. It could have been most anyone since Aunt Cora, known to party and steal other women's men, had a wide circle of acquaintances. And, like Sister, Aunt Cora spoke her mind. (No, no one from Savannah was suspected of being involved in her death.)

By now I was an old hand at funerals, this being my second one. It was held at Plainview Church and we children walked the two miles' distance to the church. At the time, Mama was visiting Aunt Polly in Atlanta and Daddy had no interest at all in anybody dead, even Aunt Cora. So we children went to see Aunt Cora off to her Savannah-beyond-the-clouds. But more than the funeral itself, I recall a night or so following. Mama was still in Atlanta, Daddy and some of the neighborhood men were out somewhere, Harvey had left home the year before, and Benny was attending a high school party and staying in town with a friend overnight. That left Sister, Shirley, Joe, Johnny, and me at home on this rainy and stormy night right after Aunt Cora had just been buried.

Our three-room frame house was L-shaped. Daddy's and Mama's room was at the top of the letter and the kitchen on the back of the house jutted out at the bottom. On this night we five children sat in our middle room (facing onto the front porch as did Mama's and Daddy's room) around the big table in the room's center where, when company came, we ate (at other times, we ate at the kitchen table), but which otherwise we used for schoolwork, to read, and draw, and where Mama wrote her letters. With spring approaching the night was windy but warm enough not to have a fire in the fireplace. A big kerosene lamp provided light from the center of the table while we sat around, partly studying and mostly talking.

Outside the rain beat heavily on the tin roof and against the windows, and the wind howled around and around the house. Sister and Shirley were arguing against me on some forgotten subject when a flash of lightning suddenly lit up the room's lone window.

My eyes were on the window when this happened and in a desperate effort to divert attention from my losing the argument, I pointed at the glass and hollered, "There's Aunt Cora!" The instant these scary words cleared my lips, from Mama's and Daddy's dark and empty room came the sound of a door flying open. A sound loud and eerie enough to send us all jumping up simultaneously from the table and scrambling under it. This wild scramble to secure the deepest, most protected spot under the table caused the lamp's chimney to fall off (and miraculously not break), with a sudden gust of wind from Mama's and Daddy's room blowing out the flame.

Now all of us were huddled up under the table in total darkness, all thinking the same thing. Aunt Cora's haint was in the house! From Mama's and Daddy's room we could hear the front door banging back and forth against the wall while outside the rain poured and the wind roared. Johnny started to cry. Now, I hadn't seen Aunt Cora's face looking in the window—at least, I didn't think I had; I had been looking for a way to save my own face in losing a silly argument. But, Lord, when the door in the other room suddenly flew open, that scared the living hell out of me too. Now here I was under the table, scared, with my sisters and the little children. I *knew*, scared or no scared, I'd better get out from under that table and go in the other room and close that door and come back in here and calm everybody down because if any of the children told Daddy when he came home that I, man of the house for the moment, tried to scare them then I would get the whipping of my life...even if Aunt Cora's haint showed up to be my witness.

More willing to confront Aunt Cora's haint than Daddy's belt (his whipping weapon), I crept from under the table and tiptoed nervously through the darkness into the other room where, against a strong wind, I managed to push the door closed. Finding Daddy's flashlight, I turned it on to find matches to light another lamp. Reentering the middle room, I then tried to convince everyone, including myself, that Aunt Cora's haint wasn't in the house. That didn't budge them one inch. I wanted desperately to get under there with them. But the mere thought of Daddy suddenly coming home and finding us all under the table because I scared us all under there was enough to keep me begging them to please come out...and to keep me from running under. It was my fault they were all scared and now I had to unscare them.

Johnny was still crying while being shushed by an unusually quiet Sister, whom I kept waiting on to come to my aid by coming out from under the table and blessing out Aunt Cora's haint. But Sister stayed under there shushing Johnny. Meanwhile, my cause wasn't being helped at all by the outside sounds of rain, wind, thunder, and especially the flashing of lightning which, when illuminating the window, would lead Shirley and Joe to holler, "Aunt Cora!" This would make Johnny cry louder for "Mama and Daddy!" and right then I would have gladly accepted Aunt Cora's entrance over theirs. Even when I tried reassuring all by reminding them that Aunt Marie *herself* said haints didn't haint in the rain, they still stayed under the table.

Only when the storm abated somewhat, finally, with the help of Sister, did everyone come out from under. Then I went about trying to get everyone to bed before Daddy got home and I got told on. I accepted the fact that early that next morning, just as soon as the first "teller" woke up, I was going to the gallows, but I definitely didn't want to take those final steps up to the whipping block before dawn.

The children's room had three beds crammed in it but on this night with Aunt Cora's haint on the loose in the house *nobody* wanted to sleep alone. So all five of us climbed into the same bed. As soon as the lamp was out, Johnny started to cry again and Sister got busy trying to shush him to sleep. Meanwhile Joe, who was trying his best to be a big boy and not cry, and Shirley, deathly scared of any empty, dark room, at every distant thunderclap continued to holler out, "Aunt Cora!"—which made Johnny cry louder and Sister shush harder. While I was busy trying to hush them all, the bed suddenly broke down. "AUNT CORA!!!" They *all* hollered. With flashlight and the rearranging of slats, Sister and I managed to get the old cotton tick sleepable again. By this time it was getting late (every bit nine o'clock) and following a few more Johnny sobs, Sister shushes, and Shirley and Joe "Aunt Cora!" hollers, sleep crept in beneath the storm and took them all away. Yet awake and lying there relieved, I suddenly heard coming from Mama's and Daddy's room the front door opening! Before I could hear if it closed I had shot down under the covers, not leaving an ear out to listen if Daddy was coming home...or if Aunt Cora's haint was leaving.

That next morning the sun came out bright, lighting up all the corners and crevices of the house where haints hung out at night, putting all but me in a jovial mood. But to my surprise, no one told on me, they all acting as if the night before had been nothing more than an adventure that we all had to repeat soon. It might've helped too that Daddy went to work before any teller awoke. Also, since Mama and Daddy didn't believe in haints, the statute of limitations for "scaring with haint talk" ran out much quicker than hitting, breaking, or, Lord have mercy, using a "bad word."

When living, Aunt Cora, unlike Grandmama, never got too much attention from us children. But following that night she must have gone back to the graveyard a proud haint.

4. MISTER JIM

Mister Jim was now left all alone on his place, about a mile across the hill and beyond Mason's hundred-acre field from us. From time to time I overheard Mama and Daddy talking about Mister Jim—about how he and Grandmama no longer got along (the reason behind her moving) and also about how he and Uncle Bubba had never gotten along and how Daddy, fully on Grandmama's side, didn't want to be around Mister Jim. Mister Jim was said to be particular and fussy about all of his belongings, outdoors and indoors, from rocks in his garden to the manner in which all of his old newspapers were stacked—neatly— in the storage area in the back of his two-room cabin. The older he got, the "whiter" he got, according to Mama. Mister Wes, who now lived the closest to him, took care of most of Mister Jim's requests, which consisted of items needed in town that he didn't grow in his garden or didn't hunt in his woods—woods of over fifty acres, the last family-owned land from the old Orr Place. When anything had to be taken to Mister Jim from our house it was I who did the taking (for a brief period after we moved from his place he continued reading our newspaper, but now after we finished reading it; finally he ordered his own subscription). I didn't mind it at all. I liked visiting Mister Jim's house because of the old newspapers. After all three houses had finished reading Daddy's *Atlanta Constitution* newspaper when we lived on Mister Jim's place with Grandmama, it had automatically gone to Mister Jim and he saved it, each and every one. It was said that Mister Jim threw away nothing but the rocks from his garden...and not even them if they could be read.

After Miz Babe died, Mister Jim had started coming up the hill to Grandmama's to eat his three daily meals. He came for each meal at the same time every day. When Aunt Bea bought her radio he would come up a bit earlier in order to hear the morning, noon and evening news before eating. Grandmama would fix his food and close the kitchen door when she was finished, and no one, not even one of Aunt Bea's cats, was allowed in there until Mister Jim had finished eating and had gone out through the back door and down the hill. Then everyone else would come into the kitchen to eat. After Grandmama moved away, Mister Jim started to cook for himself, and that's when I started hanging around his cabin regularly. Not for his cooking, but for his old newspapers. (The first time I ate food that he had prepared at his house I finished everything on my plate except some too-hard biscuits which I tried to sneak to his dog, Brownie, who wouldn't eat them either.)

When I visited Mister Jim he, naturally, did most of the talking. But by the end of each visit I would eventually be back where the old newspapers were stored. Once back there I'd spend hours reading, and rereading, the old funny papers. Mister Jim did not object to me reading the newspapers as long as I "put them back the way I found them."

After we moved I didn't get over to see Mister Jim and his newspapers as often. By then, my craving for the funny papers had grown and I began daily saving the funnies section from our paper for myself. Being familiar with Mister Jim's old newspapers, I wanted his funnies to add to my newly started collection. (Mister Wes subscribed to the *Constitution* too but he didn't save his papers; instead he used them to wrap things in, sometimes even using the funny paper pages.) One day, figuring Mister Jim wouldn't miss this small part of each of his papers, I began pulling out the funnies sections and stacking them in a separate pile. I didn't tell Mister Jim what I was doing, thinking that when I had removed all the funnies, I'd sneak them out the back door of the storage area a few each visit and he'd never miss them since he didn't read them anyway.

I didn't want to ask Mister Jim for the funnies because I was too afraid he might say no. My plan was to pile all of the funnies sections separately near the back, ever unlatched, door of the storage room. When ending a visit I would bid him "bye," leaving from the front, where he sat most of the time reading or smoking on the screened-in porch. Rather than return home straight down the lane leading from his house, I would casually walk along the side of the house (he wouldn't notice through the screen door) and around to the rear of the cabin, where I would quietly open the back door and take a few papers off the funnies stack, then quickly disappear down through the woods for home with no one aware or hurt.

On that summer Saturday afternoon of the first planned "Brother brings home the funnies," everything worked perfectly...up until I quietly opened the back door of the storage room and saw Mister Jim standing there. Too stunned to speak, I turned and ran down through the woods. God! I hadn't counted on being caught! I ran all the way home, crying, while wondering over and over, how did he know? When I got home, still crying, a frightened Mama wanted to know what had happened to me? Had Mister Jim hit or cursed me? I don't remember exactly what I told Mama about what happened (though I know for sure I didn't tell her about the "Brother's Plan"), but I did tell her something to the effect that Mister Jim didn't want me looking through his old newspapers anymore. Satisfied that I hadn't been hurt physically or cursed at, Mama said to me, "Stay away from over there, we've got our own newspaper now." That's exactly what I'll do, a now-stopped-crying me decided. I won't go back! And that next week I didn't. But well into that second week I began thinking about those old funny papers—Terry and the Pirates, Dick Tracy, Smilin' Jack, Superman, et al.—just lying there waiting to be read and reread. I began craving these pages for my collection bad enough to go back and...and ask for them.

That second Saturday I was back over at Mister Jim's. Mama didn't say anything to me about going back across the hill and when I reached his cabin, Mister Jim started right in talking to me like he always did. I felt so guilty about my earlier attempt to steal his funnies that I lost the courage to ask him to give them to me. I just sat out on the front porch listening to him talk, which he appeared to be enjoying. Keeping my visit short, I bid Mister Jim "bye" and took off from his porch straight down the lane leading through the woods, across the branch, and on up the hill past Grandmama's old house. But before I was halfway down the path, I heard Mister Jim calling me back. When I returned to the front porch my mouth dropped open when I saw Mister Jim standing there at the screen door holding out to me several newspaper pages saying, "You can have these." They were funnies! Each following week I would go over and he would give me, from the funnies stack I'd separated, several sections which I would bring back home and happily add to my growing collection. Eventually he gave all of these sections from his old newspapers to me. Shortly thereafter Mister Jim left for Virginia to work for a railroad company where, Mama and Daddy said, he knew somebody and could make the money he needed to live on.

Mister Jim stayed away for almost a year, during which time my interest in the funnies began giving way to an interest in the movie and radio sections, which I started saving daily from our newspaper. Mister Jim had left his dog with Mister Wes when he went to Virginia and had locked up his house, except for the back door to the old newspapers storage room. With him not around to ask and my movie and radio interest growing stronger by the day, and with that unlocked storage room back door, I felt there was only one thing for me to do. One Saturday I went over to the cabin and went through all of the newspapers and took out all of the movie and radio sections (advertising for the pictures playing in Atlanta and programs appearing on local radio) and brought them home to add to my growing collection. I figured I would tell Mister Jim what I did when he returned.

He did return in the fall of 1944, and appeared almost as glad to see me as he was to see his dog, Brownie. In fact, he seemed in such a good mood that I didn't want to chance ruining it by bringing up the fact that his old newspapers stack had shrunk just a little bit more now that the movie and radio sections had joined the funnies section over at my house. He never asked me anything about the movie and radio sections being missing from his old newspapers, so I never told him.

The last time Mister Jim went away, again up to Virginia to work for the railroad, he again locked up his whole house except for the back door to the old newspapers storage room. I wondered why he always forgot to lock that door? By this time, 1946, it so happened that my interest in the movies and radio was sharing time with a new preoccupation of mine—sports. So one Sunday following Sunday school, Benny (at the time compiling a boxing scrapbook) and I entered Mister Jim's storage room through the unlocked door and pulled from his old newspapers all of the sports sections and took them home to add to our growing sports collection. When Mister Jim returned home in the early spring of 1947 he seemed in such a happy mood to be back (though Brownie had died before he left and I was the only one there to witness his return) that I didn't have the heart to tell him that his stack of old newspapers had grown a little smaller while he was away, now that their sports sections had joined their funnies and movie and radio sections over the hill at my house. He never did ask me about why these sports sections were missing, and I just never bothered telling him.

Mister Jim always did a lot of talking about, it seemed, everything whenever I went to see him. I paid little attention to most of what he talked about as my mind was always on his old newspapers. But in the summer of 1947 I started paying attention to some of the things he had to say.

One thing I do remember very well was Mister Jim always asking me what did I want to be when I grew up? During the war years I always told him that I wanted to be a pilot (when Terry Lee of Terry and the Pirates became a pilot I knew I wanted to be one too). Following the war, I changed my wants to wanting to be a private detective (reading the Philip Marlowe detective novels and later seeing Dick Powell play him on screen in *Murder, My Sweet* sold me on this career). Mister Jim asked me why did I always want to do something where I could get shot at or killed? I told him I would be a detective in the movies where they shot blanks. He always laughed whenever I told him what I wanted to be, and I could not understand why he found it so funny.

The summer of '47 during lay-by time, Mister Jim got Daddy's permission to let me help him do some work around his place. It turned out to be a very busy, and interesting, summer. Mister Jim moved from his cabin in the woods over to the house where we had lived near the road. Once he had moved in, Mister Jim closed off the front door leading from the bedroom onto the front porch and built a window there. This left just one door facing toward the front, at the kitchen entrance. Later, he had his cabin hauled from the woods, across the spring, and placed against the back of his new home. With some adjustments, the merging of the two houses worked, and you could walk out the back door of our old house right into the front door of Mister Jim's cabin without having to cross the branch. For these moves, additional help was required besides Mister Jim's and my thirteen-year-old muscles. This extra help included Mister Wes and an outfit that moved houses.

But Mister Jim and I tore down Grandmama's old house; we did this dirty, sweaty job ourselves that summer. I hated to see Grandmama's old house torn down (Mister Jim wanted to plant all of his land in trees) but in tearing it down I came across one of Aunt Bea's old movie star magazines from 1933 with a lot of pictures of Jean Harlow, who had died a few years later. Mister Jim and I also cut down several trees, trimmed them of limbs, and crosscut-sawed them for his cookstove and fireplace. Every day I ate my noontime meal (called "dinner," the evening meal being called "supper") at Mister Jim's, cooked by him.

He was a much better cook now than in those earlier days just after Grandmama had moved—either that or I was hungrier now…although I still didn't try his biscuits.

Mister Jim also hunted a lot. At the time he owned two shotguns, a seven-shot pump and a five-shot automatic, having bought both following his return from Virginia earlier that year. Much of his time was spent roaming the woods hunting rabbits and setting out "rabbit boxes" with which to trap the animals. He never asked me to go hunting with him (and I never asked him to go with Mister Sid, Ezra, and me because I knew possum hunting wasn't his—a shotgun man's-style). But I always felt he wanted Daddy to go hunting with him, which was why he bought the automatic shotgun, for Daddy. In the spring of '47 Mister Jim gave Daddy the automatic shotgun.

Daddy loved hunting too and was very proud of the big, beautiful five-shooter automatic. The men he hunted with had either single-shot or double-barreled shotguns. Daddy even wanted his sons to go hunting with him. Harvey had already left home at the time Daddy got the automatic, so one day he pulled Benny away from his drawing long enough to take him down to the edge of the woods and try to teach him to shoot the big, pretty gun, in the hope that this would awaken an interest in hunting in his son. Benny appeared to enjoy shooting the gun well enough, but as soon as practice ended he went right back in the house to draw while Daddy went down in the woods and shot something. Daddy wanted his sons to be more like the sons of other men in the community—they were interested in hunting, plowing, saw-milling, all *real* men things, not drawing, reading and schoolgoing. "Sissy" stuff. But Daddy's sons never got interested in hunting.

One summer Sunday afternoon, Daddy came home much earlier than usual and laid down on his bed in his room and fell right to snoring. He had been drinking. Benny was in the room listening to the radio (we older children were now trusted to turn on the radio ourselves), and was so engrossed in whatever was playing on the radio that he didn't see Daddy roll off the bed. After hitting the floor, Daddy lay there waiting for his son to help him up and back onto the bed. Benny, with his back to Daddy, kept right on listening. Insulted, a suddenly-no-longer-helpless Daddy jumped up and broke into a wild fuss about "his own flesh and blood son" who could not stop listening to the radio long enough to help him, the father, back up onto the bed. Benny just kept listening to the radio. A yet-"lit" Daddy reached around Benny and turned off the radio. Now with Benny's full attention he continued fussing about his own flesh and blood son having no respect for his own lying helpless on the floor daddy…

By this time Mama had come into the room from the kitchen
(where else?) to see what was going on. Benny, the disrespectful son,
left the room…without being told to do so by his daddy. Now Daddy
and Mama (the Fred Astaire and Ginger Rogers of the argument) went
at it with all four feet and tails. Suddenly, Mama came running out of
the room (I'd never seen her running from Daddy, or anything else,
before), grabbing children and hollering at all of us to "get out of the
house, he's getting his gun!" The house cleared in seconds. Mama had
Johnny, who of course was crying, in her arms, and Sister, Shirley, and
Joe were running ahead of her out the back kitchen door and on up to
the top of the hill to Mister Lonzie's house. I, the world's slowest cotton
picker, was already up there waiting on them. When Mama said "gun!"
I'd dropped my funnies, movies, radio or sports section and hit the
back door and didn't hear the first shot until halfway up the hill. We
were all standing up on the hill when the roar of the next three shots
broke up that quiet, after-church, Sunday afternoon feeling, not to mention what they were doing to the inside of the house.

There was one shell left. I was counting. I was hoping he wouldn't
shoot the radio. Instead of counting shots, Mama was counting heads,
checking to see if we were all there and unhurt. That's when, from
where we stood atop the hill, Sister saw, and hollered, "Benny's under
the house!" Nobody knew why Benny had gone under the house,
where he now lay below the room where Daddy was hollering something about his "own flesh and blood!" and blasting away with the
automatic shotgun. Mama started praying aloud that Daddy wouldn't
discover Benny under the room and start shooting through the floor. I
kept hoping Daddy hadn't shot the radio. Then there was Benny
coming out from under the house and running up the hill toward us
with all of us hollering him on, hoping and (Mama) praying that Daddy
wouldn't look out the rear window and with his last shell shoot the
back of his fleeing, disrespectful son. Would Daddy shoot Benny in the
back. I wondered? But when I saw Benny wearing at his side his
scabbard with Boy Scout knife I felt we on the hill had everything
under control. Then. The last shot sounded, not aimed at Benny but
exploding inside the house. This time I *prayed* it didn't hit the radio.
Here followed a long silence from the house as we all stood up on the
hill waiting.

The neighbor Rolands had all come out on their front porch to
watch what the polite and mild mannered ol' G was up to with his big,

brand-new beautiful, automatic five-shot shotgun and his running-like-scared-rabbits-up-the-hill family. Visiting them that Sunday was Mister Wes (whom some said liked Anna), who came down off the porch and walked the approximately three hundred yards over to our house, calling Daddy's name as he neared the front door. Going slowly into the house, still talking nicely to "good ol' G," Mister Wes disappeared. Just moments later, came the sound. The sound of somebody crying...Daddy! Daddy was crying! *My* daddy?! I thought it was a physical impossibility for a grown man to cry. Besides, I wondered, why was he crying and not Mama? *He* had the gun!

Mister Wes took the now empty shotgun and on his way home later that day stopped off and gave it to Mister Jim. Gun gone we came down off the hill, slowly, and went back into the house to resume whatever we were doing before. Mama, singing a hymn, went back to the kitchen, Benny drew but kept on his Boy Scout knife, Sister quietly put Shirley and Joe straight about something or nothing, Johnny stopped crying, I re-reviewed my funnies, movies, radio and sport sections...and Daddy snored.

All of the shotgun shells had exploded into the wall, all, apparently, aimed at, and hitting, the big mirror that had hung there. The radio, praise the Lord, had been spared. Mama and Daddy didn't argue any more that day.

That next day in the field, Daddy, for a change, had nothing to say at all to any of us...He did not even get after me for being way behind everybody else.

Not too long following the Sunday afternoon shoot-up at the house, Mister Jim saw Daddy and told him that hanging with the wrong crowd and drinking the way he did would bring no good to him and his family. For the next several weekends Daddy stayed home, mostly reading. But this sort of cramped our styles, since with him around we children couldn't get away with as much hitting, breaking, taking, etc., as we could with one lone guard, Mama.

That summer Mister Jim talked to me about some of the things he did when he was young, like attending high school in Madison (not Burney Street) and bicycling, which he apparently loved. He also recalled the land on which we then lived, talking about it in the days before the family Barnett rented it to Mister Mason. He even talked about his own family, referring from time to time to his dead father and his older brother and sister. But he talked mostly about his younger brother, John, who was alive at the time.

Mister Jim had been a sports fan, at one time following baseball closely. He had been a big fan of both Ty Cobb and Babe Ruth but had not been particularly impressed with the New York Yankees' Lou Gehrig, whom Mister Jim said had been a good baseball player statistically but, unlike Cobb and Ruth, had been a colorless individual. Another sport Mister Jim had followed at one time was boxing, with Jack Dempsey having been his favorite fighter. But he never liked the man who beat Dempsey, Gene Tunney, putting him in the same class with Lou Gehrig, as having no "it." (I *never* dared ask Mister Jim his opinion of Joe Louis, and he never gave it, as colored children grew up knowing never to ask a white person—even if your own grandaddy—his thoughts on Jack Johnson, Joe Louis or Jackie Robinson.) Mister Jim's interest in boxing ended when Dempsey retired from the ring and in baseball when Ruth quit playing. These tellings of sports of yore usually ended with Mister Jim telling me that instead of my spending so much time reading the sport pages I should spend more time learning algebra, English, geography, history and my other textbooks. Enough to make you wish your granddaddy still followed sports.

Following the settling of the crop with Mister Mason each year, usually in early December, Daddy would buy a battery for the radio which, without fail, would die early the next November, before the football season ended. In order to get the Saturday afternoon football scores during these dead-battery periods I would cross the hill to Mister Jim's. Here I would listen with him on his radio to the Saturday evening six o'clock news, and at the end of the newscast they would give the football scores. But by this time Mister Jim (who no longer liked football either) would have begun talking to me about what had just been said on the news (a subject he followed closely both over the air and in the newspapers) right through the heart of the score-giving. I quickly learned to teach one ear to listen to the scores and the other one to pay attention to Mister Jim's news recap. After the news went off Mister Jim's radio went off (he listened to nothing else) while he continued to break down the news for me.

In 1948, Mister Jim got electricity for his house and bought himself a new, electric, radio. His old radio, which was much better than Daddy's, he gave to me. Daddy was happy to have this practically new (it had only played the news) radio in the house despite it not belonging to him, a fact Mama had to keep reminding him of. Now I could turn the radio on, turn the volume up and down, or change stations (this radio had *three* buttons) anytime I felt like it. Power! When I left home the next year I gave the radio to all the children yet there.

Despite having his old radio, I continued to go see Mister Jim (besides Mister Wes, who saw him mostly when bringing him things from town, I was his only visitor and I think he was always glad to see me). One reason I kept going back across the hill was that I admired Mister Jim's lifestyle, living alone and doing what <u>he</u> wanted to do. For instance, he didn't have a mama and a daddy always telling him to put aside whatever he was doing to go take the cows to water, or chop wood for the fire, or hurry up and get that row of cotton picked or... Mister Jim had his newspapers, magazines, books and radio and could read and listen to whatever he wanted to for as long as he wanted to without *anyone* bothering him to go do something else. Lord, I wanted to live like that.

5. THE CHURCH

Plainview Baptist Church was the community's center. The community's soul. For many years following the end of slavery this community had no church of its own and most folks attended the church of the bordering community of Smyrna. Then in 1898 the community got its own, Baptist church, Plainview, the same name the community came to be known by. But this church was built on private land and the preacher was the landlord, who was often accused of acting as if this house of worship belonged solely to him rather than to God and the folks. Then in the early part of this century onto the church grounds strode one Jessie Rose Lee Wildcat Tennessee (before she became Grandmama) who was to create Plainview's "Great Schism" when she had her white man, Mister Jim, donate two acres of land for a new church to be built upon, land given to the people for *their* church that has remained theirs ever since. Built in 1916, this new building became known immediately as the Plainview "Upper Church" because of its location, a quarter of a mile *up* the road from the older Plainview, now "Lower" Church.

The Upper Church started out with mostly the community's young, those who dug Jessie Rose Lee Wildcat Tennessee, who was well known for getting along fabulously with young people. The older heads, believing Jessie Rose Lee Wildcat Tennessee too earthy for the spiritual Lord's taste, stayed with the Lower Church. The "real" Christians would, when the sermons ended at one church, mosey on down, or up, to the other church, thereby being the best sources for God's gossip.

When Jessie Rose Lee Wildcat Tennessee turned into Grandmama, the two churches were still split. Mama had us attend both churches but when the meetings coincided we always went to the Upper Church. Monthly meetings for both churches occurred on the third Sunday of each month (when the preachers preached), with Sunday school being held on all Sabbaths. Whenever a month possessed a rare fifth Sunday, about twice a year, local churches in the area would form a program on what was called "Union Sunday." Plainview was in the same area (conference or league) as Barrows Grove, Smyrna and Springfield and on Union Sunday each of these churches would present its respective program held at one of the four churches on a rotating basis. A program consisted of speeches by grownups, individual and choir singing, and children's recitations. Those were frightening times as a child when you had to learn a "speech" and then walk up to the stage and stand in front of everybody, all of whom were looking at you, and give your speech with enough volume for all (especially your mama and your teacher) to hear without missing a word.

Mama *loved* these Sundays. She was always in charge of Plainview's (Upper Church) program. For herself she always took some section from the Bible and would have us children, usually Benny, Sister and me, get on stage with her and follow her lead by speaking individual, memorized parts. Weeks ahead of time we started rehearsing our Biblical roles and, thanks to Mama's firmness, had them down letter perfect come Union Sunday. These performances always put Plainview's program at the top, but I envied the children who only had to learn a few lines to recite instead of the pages we had to memorize. But we children found it much easier to learn our parts than to try to tell Mama we couldn't do it. We were always telling Mama that she always made us do things other children didn't have to do, to which she always replied, "Don't worry about the 'other' children; that's for their folks to worry about." Mama *always* had an answer.

Plainview's pastor, Reverend Love, was probably in his thirties during the 1940s. But, many felt, he was too young and inexperienced to preach that "old-time religion" the way it was meant to be preached. That is, loud and lively enough to make, throughout the church and within the soul of each individual, the spirit "move." To do this, everyone said, the preacher had to have a voice loud enough for God to hear on high and deep enough to scare Satan down below. Yes, Lord, his dissenters felt Reverend Love was a bit too low-key, or "modern" to make the Bible come "alive" for his congregation. These were the men

talking. The women felt fine about the Reverend who was young and good looking and who, many of these same females thought, had a too-fat wife.

One could join the church on any meeting Sunday and get baptized on the following month's meeting Sunday. But nobody worthy of note was ever known to join the church on a meeting Sunday. The time to join the church came at "Revival." In August of every year, during lay-by time, there would be one week, Sunday night through Friday night, of Revival, an old-time religion membership drive that led up to the Third Sunday when all the new members would be baptized. During separate weeks in August a revival was held at both the Lower and Upper churches, thus allowing folks to attend this high holy period at both houses of worship.

To attract as many new members for the church as possible, tradition called for the regular pastor to invite a guest minister to help with the preaching during this special week of the year. Most of these guest preachers were freelancers, those not having their own church or those too old to pastor a church full-time but with plenty enough old-time religion left in their souls to "whup" a week's worth of it on the souls of a congregation. For these younger preachers, the more people they got to join during Revival the bigger grew their own reputations and the better chance they had of getting their own church. Such hungry guest preachers were invited to Revival for one purpose only...to kill the devil in the souls of the congregation. We called them "Hired Guns."

Most everyone in Plainview joined the church as a child, many before the age of twelve, the official local age for becoming a "sinner" if not a member of the church. During Revival all non-church members, starting anywhere from ages six to eight, were required to sit in the front row, on the mourners' bench—the seat of the sinner. From there as the night's meeting drew to an end and as an especially-for-the-occasion hymn, "Old Sinner You Can't Hide," was sung, one stepped forward to join the church by shaking the offered hand of the preacher. In doing so, one left behind forever the mourners' bench and, hopefully, hell. But becoming a Christian consisted of much more than just stepping up and shaking the preacher's extended hand. One first had to get one's soul right with the Lord through constant prayer...and no horsing around during Revival week.

I made my way, or was sent, to the mourners' bench at age seven. Not that I was feeling extraordinarily sinful on that particular night, but

Harvey and Benny, who had just joined the church themselves and didn't want to be seen sitting next to a sinner, sent me up front with the rest of my sinful kind. Up front on the mourners' bench the rest of the church could see you and give thanks to the Lord that their souls had already been snatched from the gates of hell. Sitting here that night, I, for the first time, began feeling sinful, especially whenever someone said a prayer, they all aimed at the mourners' bench (jammed elbow-to-elbow with us sinners this night). During these prayers the rest of the congregation, the saved, just lowered their heads while we sinners had to get down on our knees with backs bent and heads bowed and lean our elbows on the seat of the bench in order to be prayed over. Enough to make one want to join the church just to get up off your knees and out of the spotlight...not to mention saving wear and tear on the knees of your best Sunday pants.

Revival, 1943! After suffering through two years of the mourners' bench blues, I felt I couldn't take being a sinner anymore...and decided to join the church on the very first night of Revival. This meant for the rest of the week I would have to sit in the special "holding" section, the front bench of the sacred (and saved) Amen corner, reserved for those who had just joined the church and were awaiting their baptism on the upcoming Sunday. Over here one was "special," sitting safely among the saved deacons and sisters while looking across (and down) with pity upon those poor souls left behind still wallowing in sin on the mourners' bench, "death row." But in order to join the church and for God to forgive me for my nine years of earthly sin I knew I had a whole lot of praying ahead of me.

That Sunday the Andrews children went, as usual, to Sunday school. Afterward, I went up to June's to play...and pray. All afternoon we played cowboys and crooks, but having definitely decided to join the church that night I, in between shootouts, fistfights, and horseback chases, would quickly recite the Lord's prayer to myself. When there was little time between the action, I would say beneath my breath the shorter child's prayer, "Now I lay me down to sleep..." When the riding, fighting and shooting got fierce, I only had time to mutter to myself the even shorter table blessing, "Lord make us truly thankful for this food..."

I cut my visit short with June on this pious day, realizing that if I was going to join the church that night, I had better get serious about my praying. When I got home before sundown it was such a rare occurrence that Mama thought I was sick. While on my way home, bringing up the cows, toting water from the spring, and even en route to church that night, I kept repeating to myself prayers—the Lord's and some of my own creating. Yet from time to time my mind would wander from prayer to wonder what was on the radio or to think about the pictures playing that coming week at the Madison picture show (don'ts with sin written all over them during Revival week). Catching myself, I would quickly ask God's forgiveness and go back to praying...to the thundering hooves of the silver screen in the background.

An extremely important step in the process of joining the church came at the end of the "Oh Sinner You Can't Hide" hymn, the last chance for the mourners' bench sinners to be saved that night. Now all attention focused on the newly joined—those (or that one) who took the preacher's hand and sat in the special chair placed for the occasion between the pulpit and the mourners' bench, facing the latter. This was when the preacher would ask the new joinee to please stand and tell the congregation in his or her own words why he or she felt they had religion enough to become a member of Plainview Baptist Church. This was the tough part, tougher than praying, since you prayed to yourself while this stand-up confession had to be said in front of everybody. The thought of having to undergo this public confession, I'm sure, kept many glued to the mourners' bench...and sin. Most newly joined who ventured into this public display stood and with heads lowered hurriedly mumbled the old standard, "I prayed and prayed and asked the Lord to forgive me for my sins and I feel he did," before quickly dropping back down in the chair without looking up and around at anybody in the church. Sometimes the girls would just cry and the preacher and congregation felt this was proof enough that God had forgiven them their sins. But boys couldn't, or had better not, cry so they had to think of something to say.

One of the most unforgettable confessions ever spoken in the history of Plainview was delivered one year by Cootney Mapp, our neighbor and Reverend Mapp's oldest son. That historical night Cootney stood up and in a loud voice confessed, "I came to a wall that I couldn't get through. I couldn't go around it, I couldn't climb over it, and I couldn't crawl under it. That's when I knew it was time for me to get myself right with God and that's what I went and did through prayer." This classic confession from such a young person (Cootney was fifteen) drew a long chorus of "Amen!s" and "Bless him Lord's" that had never been experienced before at either an Upper or a Lower Church joining. Unfortunately, following this beautiful confession, Cootney never came back to Plainview Church again, not even to be baptized. But Plainview yet remembered his words.

That night I joined. Mama didn't shout. I was extremely disappointed since I had seen her shout over happenings of much less
importance in the church. Some years earlier I had walked out of a
meeting because the shouting had scared me. On my way back home I
met Mama coming down the road on her way to church (she always
sent us children on ahead). I told her that all of those folks shouting
had scared me. But when she took me by the hand and led me back
into church I felt safe. Then, before the preacher got through with the
congregation that day, Mama shouted. I felt deceived. Not able to trust
my own mama! Now on the eve of my joining the church—something
to shout about—Mama just sat there. I was hoping she would at least
cry. She didn't. Later, while standing to confess and with Cootney's
classic words ringing in my heard, I hurriedly mumbled, "I prayed and
prayed..."

The next morning Mama called me aside and asked me if I truly
felt I had prayed long and sincerely enough to have gotten a true
religion, especially after having spent most of that previous afternoon
playing at June's. Daddy, who was not even a church member, asked
me the same thing. I told them both I had religion. Before the week
was up, Sister had joined the church, and when she stood to confess
she, of all people, couldn't talk. She cried. That next morning she had
to go before Mama and Daddy to explain herself and she too told them
she had religion. Well, Mama would not allow us to be baptized that
following Sunday because she didn't feel our souls were ready, or
"ripe," for God. Back to the mourner's bench.

I was both embarrassed and mad. All of that praying going to
waste! I seriously thought of *never* joining the church, becoming instead a full-time career sinner. Even though Benny had made heaven
sound so wonderful that I just wanted to go without even bothering to
die, now I began thinking seriously of remaining a sinner and dying
unbaptized and going to hell, which I felt would really fix Mama and
Daddy, rather than going through all of that praying again.

But the next year I reran my prayers and, with Sister, I joined the
church again. At confession time I stood up with the fullest intention of
quoting Cootney...chickened out and ended up hurriedly mumbling, "I
prayed and prayed..." Sister cried. This time Sister and I, along with
many others, were baptized on Third Sunday by Reverend Love in a
pond down in the woods in the back of the church. Saved, finally!

Through the years there were a few who always managed to
squeeze through the Revival net and enter adulthood without joining

the church. These grownup, "genuine" sinners rarely came inside the church during Revival, being too embarrassed to walk up front to the mourners' bench and sit among a bunch of youngsters under the lime-light of sin and be stared at, looked down upon, and pitied throughout the sermon by the smug saved. Plainview's three oldest living sinners during the 1940s were Mister Coot Durden, Mister Charley Jackson and Daddy. Mister Coot, approaching his nineties, was getting a bit too old to be out at night, so during Revival he stayed home to reserve his energy for daytime sinning. This left Mister Charley and Daddy to represent sin outside the house of God where each Revival night they stood talking, mostly about crops and the weather. Then, Lord, came Revival 1945.

It was that next to last, Thursday, night of Revival when Mister Charley didn't show up and Daddy stood outside talking to a few saved souls about crops and the weather when a storm suddenly came up. When the rain started coming down, the saved souls ran for the only available cover, inside the church. Daddy, preferring rain over religion, remained outside standing under a tree. Then from out of the sky the Lord sent forth to Earth Daddy's greatest fear, a bolt of lightning. Be-tween the long flash of lightning and a heavy explosion of thunder, Daddy streaked through the door of the church. Not wanting to be noticed, he quickly sat down on a bench on the very last row. Too late! For, Daddy, one of Plainview's Big Three Sinners, not to be noticed entering church—even if he was sent in by a streak of lightning—was like God or, better, Satan walking through the church doors trying not to be seen. The preacher stopped in mid-preach. But Grandmama was the first to react. When she stood up everyone thought she was fixing to shout. Instead, Grandmama, from the women's Amen corner up alongside the pulpit and with a now totally stunned and silent preacher and congregation looking on, walked all the way to the back of the church, took Daddy by the hand, and brought him and his bowed head back down the aisle and sat him up front on the mourners' bench.

All this time the only sounds in the church were Grandmama and Daddy's footsteps and the loud overhead claps of thunder resounding from outside. Yes, the Lord does work in mysterious ways. Daddy seated, Grandmama, on her way back to her pew broke out in the hymn, "I Was Lost but Now I'm Found...," which was immediately picked up by the rest of the congregation. The preacher, realizing he had on *his* mourners' bench one of God's "most wanted" sinners, Daddy, went back to preaching with a hellfire-and-brimstone vengeance. Oh, Lord, the congregation immediately answered back in louder song, shouts, hand-clapping and foot-stomping while the outside wind, rain, thunder and lightning stormed on. Mama cried. Rescued by a year from the mourners' bench, I sat watching Daddy's bowed head, thinking this was the first time I'd ever seen him with his cap off in public. His head was shaved clean of any blond hair.

They didn't get Daddy that night but the feeling ran strong that he was "on the edge." Ripe. And with one more night of Revival to go. Lord, have mercy!

Following the services that night, both Grandmama and Mama went up and had separate private sessions with the preacher. Talking about Daddy. In a controlled voice, I heard the preacher say, "We must show patience..." Yet while saying this over and over to both Grandmama and Mama, the preacher kept wringing his hands as if he was getting his right one in shaking shape for that Friday, and final, Revival, night. All Plainview went home to wait.

All during that next day, everything was quiet around our house. Even Sister. Early that morning, Mama told us children not to bother Daddy because he was deep in thought...prayer. We spent the whole day practically tiptoeing around the house. Mama didn't even argue with Daddy one single time. In fact, when talking to him she spoke softly and would give him kind looks. Having gotten religion twice myself, I knew the hell Daddy must've been going through trying to inwardly pray with only one night left to get saved. And especially while trying to concentrate on those crime magazines he sat reading all day.

All day all of Plainview waited for that night.

With the exception of the white families, everybody in the community, including all the babies, showed up at church that night. All wanted to be there the night of Plainview Revival's biggest sinner catch ever! Honey, hush!

Everybody showed up, that is, except Daddy...who stayed home that Friday, final Revival night reading his *True Detective* magazines.

Daddy never went back to church to stand outside when there were signs of a storm brewing.

Children of the community learned early that church was not meant to be a place of fun. Church was serious. It was the *only* place where *all* the colored, both the good and the bad, met as *one*. Sure, the good went inside church and prayed and the bad (unless they wanted to sit on the mourners' bench) stayed outside and played. Yet after services everybody got right back together. At no other place within, or outside, the community could the entire colored family meet like at church; it was the only place we could rightfully call our own where for a few hours each week we conducted our lives our own way. On occasion, Mister McIntire, the white landowner, would come and sit in the back of the church to listen to, or watch, the proceedings. When this happened, the atmosphere instantly changed and the signal "alien in church!" registered within the soul of the congregation, automatically sending up a guard, or "putting on a face," for outsiders. Perhaps this reflex reaction could be traced back to slavery, when the restrictions on blacks congregating were very severe. Whatever the reason, the church, our *only* possession entirely independent of the white world, we only shared with one another...and God. Amen.

6. THE SCHOOL

When the New England schoolteachers came South after the Civil War to Morgan and other counties to teach the black freedmen (and women and children), they set up school in the local churches. When I started school in 1939, classes in Plainview (as in many other Southern black rural areas) were still being taught in a church building, Plainview Lower Church. Like all country grade (elementary) schools of the day, Plainview included grades one through seven, in addition to the pre-primer and primer grades where beginning pupils learned the alphabet and reading and writing. All text and library books were passed down to us, used, from the white schools (at the height of World War II our geography and history books had been printed before World War I). To continue one's education beyond the seventh grade one had to go to the colored high school in Madison, Burney Street, which, in addition to its own elementary school, offered grades eight through eleven.

Starting during the Depression and continuing throughout the 1940s Plainview's main teacher was Missis Bertha Douglas, or, as her pupils called her, "Missis Bertha." In her fifties (probably, since most adults look about "fifty" when you are in grade school) and plump, Missis Bertha spoke "proper" and had a full face decorated with glasses, a stern glance and, when she wanted it, a warm smile. Up until 1944 she had several assistants but never more than one at a time. The three who taught me were Miss Green, Miss Johnson, and Miss Nina Mae Hampton (Missis Mamie's daughter and J.B.'s sister). They, unlike Missis Bertha, were young and pretty. Missis Bertha was a widow; her husband had been a policeman on the city of Detroit's police force. But this she didn't talk about. What Missis Bertha did talk about all of her days at Plainview (some 20 years) was where she and her husband, whom she called "Mister Douglas," honeymooned, Bermuda, which she called "The Old Country." The honeymoon was about two weeks long but she spent her twenty years at Plainview telling the pupils all about The Old Country. And she didn't even know Aunt Cora...unless, of course, they met later as haints and sat around the graveyard swapping Old Country and Savannah stories.

Practically all of Plainview farmed, which meant most local children, like the rest of the state, and the South, only went to school when there was no work to be done in the fields or the weather didn't permit such work. There were beautiful days when the enrollment read only one (always Nookie, Missis Susie Slack's niece, who lived a ten-minute walk from school and didn't have to do farm work). From late fall to late winter the enrollment on some days reached well beyond fifty.

Shortly after I started to school the state of Georgia began supplying its schools with free lunches. This free food consisted almost entirely of yellow grits, oatmeal, black-eyed peas, an assortment of beans, Irish potatoes, peaches, prunes, raisins, apples and oranges and, oh yes, cornmeal—with every lunch we had cornbread. This meant Sister no longer had to take our greasy paper-sack lunch to school daily. Most children, naturally, came to school during the winter months with many of these coming solely to eat. They came to the right place since the childless Missis Bertha loved cooking for "my children," as she called all of her pupils. In fact, Missis Bertha loved cooking so well that she would turn all of the teaching duties over to her assistant and spend the entire morning preparing her children's lunch of cornbread and something. Cooking in the church meant everything had to be cooked on the elongated stove that sat middle way of the big, airy room and supposedly provided our winter heat, though on cold days it seemed only interested in keeping itself and those hugging it warm. (When the stove would finally get hot you didn't want to get too close to it too early in the morning because the heat coming from it would let you smell who of those sitting around it had wet the bed the night before.)

On the day the old church floor, for decades having withstood the foot-stomping of Christianity and the pitter patter and hobnail hopping of pupils, suddenly gave way with one thunderous WHUMP! No one was hurt but most of us children gladly panicked in order to get to run out of doors and, later, go home early. Classes were able to continue in the building for the rest of that school year, until the community men got together and hurriedly built a log cabin schoolhouse with one large room for teaching and a smaller one for cooking. This marked the end of the line for the Lower Church, the collapsed floor sending all its members up the road to the Upper Church, now Plainview's only, and official, church. Amen.

Meanwhile, in her new kitchen, Missis Bertha was as happy as a freshly slopped pig wallowing in a new mudhole. She now had a real cookstove to sweat over while preparing her children's lunch. Now she rarely came out of the kitchen before lunch time. Even after her last assistant, Miss Hampton, left without being replaced, Missis Bertha continued to spend the entire morning in the kitchen cooking while assigning the teaching duties to the seventh grade students. In the afternoon, in between telling us all about The Old Country, Missis Bertha taught the seventh grade subjects. When Mama heard that students were being taught by other students she became furious. Sister and I (Harvey and Benny were gone from Plainview school at this time), on orders from Missis Bertha, were two who taught grades below ours. But after awhile outspoken Sister (who said she wasn't "getting paid to teach") quit teaching, causing Missis Bertha's time for cooking and The Old Country stories to be deeply cut back. Missis Bertha, who had never liked Sister before, liked her even less now. In fact, Missis Bertha never seemed to care too much for any of us Andrews children. I think it was mainly because of Mama.

Mama made no bones to *anyone* about wanting *all* of her children to finish school. Daddy, a fourth grade dropout, was, like his mama, never big on education. He figured, as did many local folks of the day, that children, especially males, needed only to learn how to read and write their names and do simple arithmetic like adding and subtracting. This old Plantation Nigger mentality called for all young males to start work to make some money for the family as soon as possible. Too much schooling (going on to higher education, beyond the fourth grade) was purely a waste of time because according to the Plantation Nigger Philosophy, no matter how much learning a colored person got (even a seventh-grade education) he, or she, was going to end up working for the white man. White men, most of whom didn't trust education for their own children, certainly had nothing against this colored thinking. In fact, most of the whites preferred the coloreds didn't bother going to school at all, especially the males. Girls were allowed to go to school longer than boys since it was believed all they were going to do was get married eventually, or become school teachers to teach other girls to become school teachers to teach...

Mama finished Burney Street's eighth grade and was looked upon in the community as being educated, or "odd." Besides the Bible, Mama enjoyed reading books, magazines, and the newspaper. Despite her oddness, the community folks looked up to and trusted Mama. Those not knowing how to read or write trusted her enough to bring to her their yet-sealed letters from far-away relatives and friends (and Uncle Sam) to open and read to them. They all knew to bring along a page or more of lined notebook paper and an envelope for Mama to write a reply dictated by them (in her own words). Mama was also secretary for the local "Society," a small body of elected men and women who met in the schoolhouse on the first Monday of each month to take up community issues, like helping the needy, those sick or unable to help themselves and in need of food and clothing or help with their farms or in their homes. Building and maintenance of the new school-house was another of the "Society's" functions. (The church had its own board members, part of whose duties were to see to the upkeep of the building and its grounds.)

Missis Bertha (who, incidentally, adored Grandmama) didn't ex-actly approve of Mama and her "homemade" way of teaching her chil-dren. Every night following school Mama would ask each one of us what homework had we for the next day. After getting the answers, "None," or "I studied it at school," she would make us turn to the page where the next day's lesson began and quiz us and then help us with that we didn't know. Even when we missed school for a day, or weeks, Mama made us study each night as if we were going to class the next day. When school was in, Lord, Mama was no fun. But thanks to her we always went to school prepared in our lessons, something that could not be said of most of the other children. Meanwhile, Missis Bertha was constantly trying to find some pupil in school to outshine an Andrews child in everything.

The best example of this was the artistic battle between Herschel Pastor and Benny. Herschel could draw well, especially Santa Claus, and as a result became Missis Bertha's pet, which meant Herschel's chalk drawing of Santa Claus covered one end of the blackboard from December to April, school closing. Meanwhile Benny, who could, and did, draw any and everything, never got one of his drawings exhibited on the blackboard, Herschel's museum, and had to be content to pass his paper drawings among the children who loved them. But Herschel had the big blackboard where *all* could see *all* the time, thus becoming the school's official drawer.

144

Besides most of the children, Missis Bertha's assistants always liked and praised Benny for his drawings (they also appreciated our being prepared with our schoolwork) but this was not enough to get Benny's art on the blackboard.

Herschel, the only child of Mister Willie and Missis Annie Pastor, besides being a very talented drawer, smart in class, and sensitive, was, with his sculpted features and his soft, beige skin spotted with freckles, extremely good looking...almost pretty. Missis Annie had three other sons and a daughter from a previous marriage to a Williams. There were the twins, Melvin and Elvin, or "Bro'" and "Fat," who were about Harvey's age. The oldest boy, Eddie B, was one school grade above the twins. I always ranked Eddie B in a class with "Wild Bill" Elliott (Eddie B's favorite movie cowboy, who wore his guns backwards, sported black gloves, and would take on and beat an entire barroom of crooks singlehandedly without so much as his hat falling off and walk away with the words, "I'm a peaceful man"). I reasoned Eddie B was part Wild Bill because, on occasion, he would go into town during the week. Even though he would go with his mama, it was still a country oddity to go into town on any day other than Saturday. Only a Wild Bill type could pull this off.

The family Pastor for a long while lived a five-minute walk the other (non-Nookie) side of school. During the school year Missis Bertha, who ordinarily lived in the neighborhood of Canaan in Madison with her sister and her sister's husband, roomed with the Pastors. Everyone loved Herschel (even his blackboard art rival Benny liked him) because he was such a nice child who never gave anyone any trouble. Mister Willie and Missis Annie were proud of him, and showed much love for the gifted, beautiful child, and he was so well protected by his older brothers, Bro', Fat, and (Wild) Eddie (Bill) B that I don't recall him having to defend himself with his fists. Nobody (including the Masseys) fought Herschel. In spite of the fact that he was Missis Bertha's pet, everybody liked, *loved* the sweet, pretty little boy who never caused any trouble.

Herschel could draw more than Santa Claus. He was extremely good at drawing cowboys and, especially, horses and cars. (Benny could draw a better airplane than Herschel.) Also, I remember his subtle humor—he could make us younger boys laugh...whenever we could figure out what he was joking about. Shortly after Benny left Plainview for Burney Street, the Pastors moved to a house and farm equally as close to the school of Smyrna as Plainview. Here I lost track of Herschel. Almost.

It's possible Herschel went on to high school at Burney Street (which Missis Bertha apparently wanted him to do although she never expressed any love—for the school or its teachers—except for Missis Love) but if he did, it wasn't for long. Years later, during my occasional visits back to Madison, to my continual surprise I would see Herschel on the town's back street hanging out with a crowd one never suspected Missis Bertha's pet of even knowing, much less drinking...and getting drunk...with. Herschel had stopped drawing and had gone into the woods to cut pulpwood, a local addiction for too many young colored males of the day, while coming into town with his new friends and drinking away the weekend, another local, deadly, custom.

Then came that Sunday Herschel went visiting the Moore Boys' family house where lived alone the youngest brother, Mister Bub, since the oldest brother, Mister Jim, had died. Mister Bub was the one who had come back home many years earlier to die a young death, but instead all of his brothers died before he did.) The men came to see Mister Bub because he sold liquor. That's why, some said, Herschel went to see him.

That night Herschel didn't come home. When he didn't show up that night, Mister Willie went looking for his only child, ending up at the Moore Boys' family house. Down at the pond the father found all of Herschel's clothes piled on the bank of the water. Here, Mister Willie found his only son in the Moore Boys' pond, drowned. Mister Willie broke down.

Mister Bub said that after Herschel drank the liquor he bought, he said he felt like going swimming and went down into the woods back of the house to the pond. That, Mister Bub said, was the last he saw of Herschel. When he didn't come back past the house, Mister Bub said he figured Herschel had decided to take another way home, which from the pond was possible. Mister Willie didn't believe Mister Bub.

The law reported no foul play in Herschel's drowning but Mister Willie took no stock in what the law said because it was said Mister Bub sold liquor for the Man.

His only child dead, Mister Willie was a broken man. I guess I remember the time so well because Herschel was the first person whom I had gone to school with to die.

From time to time during the school year we had visitors from the county school board, all white except for the colored superintendent of the colored schools. On such special occasions, Missis Bertha would show off her brightest students, the best reader, the best speller, the best reciter of the multiplication table, the best drawer and the pupil with the best handwriting. No Andrews child was ever selected by Missis Bertha to perform before these visiting dignitaries. I was disappointed in never being selected because I loved reading and at the time thought I could read better than anyone in the school and almost as good as Missis Bertha. Despite all of this, the white visitors were only interested in hearing us sing. So when they came we pupils ended up singing them religious hymns.

At school Missis Bertha couldn't get us Andrews children for too much since, thanks to Mama, we had our lessons ready and our manners intact. Oh, behind the teacher's back we acted like children and whenever we got caught she made sure we paid dearly. Missis Bertha got me several times with the razor strop she carried hanging over her shoulder. Once when I was too young to know better after getting "stropped" by Missis Bertha, I came home searching for sympathy and told Mama who replied that if the teacher whipped me then I must've been doing something wrong (I was). That taught me to keep my schoolhouse whippings at school.

Missis Bertha used her strop only on the boys. To punish the girls, she would have them go across the road into the pasture, select and bring back a wooden switch which she would use across their legs. One of Missis Bertha's favorite switch selectors was Sister (along with Minnie Pearl) who was never known to let manners overrule her sense of feeling wronged. Sister and Missis Bertha clashed often—the teacher always winning the battle by sending Sister for a switch. But that never ended the war. As a result of all these clashes, Missis Bertha made Sister repeat the third grade (allowing me to catch her) not because Sister failed her studies but because she was always getting Missis Bertha, or somebody else in school "told."

Most children got to school each morning around nine o'clock, mainly on instinct as many Plainview families had no clocks. Once a family of children living on the other side of the woods arrived at school at noon. When Missis Bertha asked them why they were so late their answer was, "we took a shortcut."

(During this time, no public transportation to school was provided by the state for colored children, only schoolbuses for the white children. Daily passing us on the road in their big pretty yellow bus, they never failed to stick their heads out the windows and give us a holler or two, or more...)

Each morning before class two boys raised the school's flag, an old and ragged piece of cloth yet recognizable as The Stars and Stripes, atop the pole out in the school yard. (No girls ever got this job. If a boy didn't come to school, the flag didn't fly that day.) Then in two separate lines of boys and girls we would stand facing and, in unison, pledge allegiance to the old and ragged flag. Later, inside the classroom, Missis Bertha would read a chapter from the Bible, then each pupil would stand and recite a verse from the Bible. A religious hymn sung by us all closed out our thanks-to Uncle-Sam-and-God period before the start of classes, conducted by the assistant teacher or the seventh grade students while Missis Bertha departed to the kitchen to start cooking lunch for her children.

When Lil' Bubba and Minnie Pearl left Plainview school to go into the Navy and get married, respectively, the family Massey did a complete about face. With Harvey and Benny now in Town School and the family Mapp moved to Atlanta, the remaining Andrews and Masseys at Plainview school became close friends, never again to fight one another. Jesse, considered the toughest of the remaining Masseys, was suddenly interested in a girl, Nookie, which greatly mellowed him. There was now much less fighting, even boxing, since most of the older, teenage boys were gone, cleared out by sawmills, pulpwood, the military, marriage, and the end of the school's free lunch program. Instead of boxing matches, our recess was now spent raiding a nearby pear tree, searching out and destroying wasp nests, testing our arms by throwing rocks at trees and moving targets such as rabbits, birds and an occasional motor vehicle, and roaming the woods in search of wild fruit and nuts or the campsites of hoboes. But the older boys, especially Duke Morris, Junior Roland and Jessie, all were now more interested in girls than in doing boys' things. Sissies!

During the school year of 1946-1947, Sister's and my final year at Plainview Elementary, the end of the free lunch brought Missis Bertha, strop over her shoulder, out of the kitchen to all-day teaching in the classroom. No longer able to cook for her children, Missis Bertha seemed lost. But what she now missed in the kitchen she made up by telling us children more stories about The Old Country.

That entire summer after Sister and I finished Plainview and before we entered Burney Street, Mama, not wanting us to be behind the other eighth graders in learning, gave us lessons in American history and world geography. When we told her "Other children" didn't have to do this, she retorted with her familiar reply, "Don't worry about other children..." Mamas!

7. MANNERS & MORALS

Mama and Daddy kept us well lectured, and disciplined, on behavior, or "manners," at home and in public, an extremely important matter at the time. Within the colored community, *all* children addressed *all* adults or "grownups" as "Mister," "Missis," or "Miss," and answered "Sir" and "Ma'am" to them. If you didn't address grownups in this manner, then they reserved the right to tell your parents on you. When this happened, which was rare since children knew better than to act "mannish" or "womanish" around grownups, parents lost no time in setting their children straight, often with a switch. Grownups other than one's parents also had the authority to discipline any community child they felt needed it when their folks weren't around. Too, upon being met on the road or wherever, everyone expected a greeting of "Good morning, Good evening, Hey," or whatever. If you saw the person or persons, and were not close enough to be heard in a normal tone then you had the option of throwing a holler or a wave. If you didn't greet a person, especially a grownup, and word got back to your parents, you could be sure you would hear about it from your folks too.

Next to killing someone, the biggest local taboo, or "sin," especially for children, was cursing, or "cussing." This was, in the eyes of most grownups, even worse than fighting. Mama (whom I've never heard cuss) and Daddy (whom I've heard cuss) forbade all of us children to use a "bad word." Our house was free of such language (on occasion when real mad Daddy "slipped"), including the words "hell" and "lie" (as in fibbing or, as we expressed it, "telling a story"). We children even had to be careful around the house using the word "bull."

The baddest of "bad" words never used in our house was the expression "nigger." Mama and Daddy always made us say either "colored" or "Negro." The Brazil nut, locally called "Nigger Toe" by both colored and white, was called by us Andrews children a "Negro Toe."

Perhaps Mama's three strictest don'ts for us children overall were no using the word "nigger," no cursing, and no drinking liquor. Only grown bad men, were meant to drink, or so this was believed by many. A few women of the neighborhood drank too but they were looked upon, or down at, as being members of the "fast" crowd (like Aunt Bea and Old Missis Hill). Some older boys drank but they were out of school and working when they started. No liquor was ever anywhere around school (but much was drunk in the woods in back of church on Sundays), except at Burney Street whenever there was a party (usually Friday night). Some of the upperclass boys would go to Rudolph Moore's parked car, the only student-owned automobile on campus, and get a "nip" from his bottle of moonshine. Mama didn't touch the stuff. Daddy did. (I yet marvel at how they met and married.) In fact, Daddy quite often made and sold liquor. Aunt Bea once told about the time Daddy, as a teenager, was boiling a home brew atop their kitchen stove when the concoction blew up, spraying the whole room and leaving the entire house smelling for days afterward.

Grandmama Jessie was known for making blackberry wine and even taught us children how to make it. But I quickly learned I had little patience for wine making, letting the berry juice ferment for only about an hour before drinking it. Harvey, Benny and Sister were better wine makers than I, letting their juices ferment for nearly a whole day before drinking. Sister would always be the last to drink hers in order to "have something" when the rest of us didn't. She always seemed to enjoy whatever she had to eat or drink much more than Harvey, Benny or I enjoyed ours.

Mama, of course, wasn't too happy about Grandmama telling us children how to make blackberry wine, none of which any of us got around to letting age more than twenty-four hours. In fact, there seemed very little Mama and Grandmama Jessie ever agreed upon. And Daddy always took Grandmama's side, regardless of the disagreement between the two women, which only made him and Mama argue the more.

The first time I ever tasted liquor occurred at about age seven. One day I was standing on a chair searching for something on the mantel above the fireplace when I spotted up there a bottle of, I thought, water. Unscrewing the cap, it didn't smell like water. Smelled like Daddy's mouth on Saturday night. I tasted it. It sure didn't taste like water. A few minutes later, my burning stomach, which somehow knew this was "white lightning" streaking down, threw it, and every-thing else down there, back up. Mama must've said something to Daddy about this because I never again saw a bottle of liquor on the mantel (replaced up there by the codliver oil) or anywhere else in the house. That is, except for Christmas of 1942, when Aunt Soncie, just having been to Atlanta, came by and brought Daddy a present of a bottle of storebought or, as it was locally called, "government" liquor,

Four Roses. Aunt Soncie, a sometime member of the fast crowd, especially on holidays, insisted upon giving we four older children a taste of "Christmas cheer." Mama didn't approve but Daddy didn't object too strongly so Aunt Soncie (who was in all of our good graces for having brought out many other Christmas goodies besides Daddy's booze) gave Harvey, Benny, Sister and me a teaspoon each of government liquor. I don't recall the taste of this, my second lifetime (and last ever while living home) shot, but my stomach didn't send it back up...maybe because this was from the government...President Roosevelt's private stock.

Many children whenever out of hearing distance of grownups cussed like sinners on a Saturday night and others wanting to belong followed suit. We didn't. Too afraid Mama and Daddy might hear about it. But once when I was out in the woods all alone I mouthed aloud *every* single bad cuss or swear word I'd ever heard. Then I awaited the bolt of lightning.

Then there was the day I thought I would teach my younger brother Joe a new word I heard at school that day.

"Say 'shit.'" Joe just stared at me as if he knew it was a "bad" word.

"Come on Joe, say '*ssshhhiiittt!*'" Yet silent, the baby Joe continued to stare at me, making me feel guilty or, worse, sinful. To get his mind off of the bad word I quickly grabbed Joe, threw him down and began beating on him. Language from me he understood.

That night at the supper table with Daddy present there was no talking, just eating. The only talking that ever went on at the dining table when Daddy was there was talk he started, and ended. After a hard day of work, Daddy on this night didn't feel like talking nor hearing any. Then.

"Dit!"

I didn't look up from my plate but could feel Joe, sitting on Mama's lap at the foot of the table while being fed by her, staring at me.

"Dit!"

Daddy was too tired and hungry and Mama too busy trying to spoonfeed Joe for either to try and decipher baby talk so everybody just kept right on eating.

"*Dit!*"

Around the table was heard nothing but the sound of eating, except of course for the filthy mouth baby Joe Louis hollering down at the foot of the table.

"DDDIIITTT!!!"

XV. Madison

1. THE TOWN

The town of Madison sat about four miles north of us. When I lived here the town's population was about three thousand but before the coming of the boll weevil after World War I as many as twenty thousand people had lived there. Every Saturday folks from the country would pour into town to buy, picture show go, socialize, see and be seen, and strut. We Andrews children, every chance we got, were part of this weekly pilgrimage to Madison.

If ever a ride into town was offered by anyone driving a car or truck, no matter how slow, dilapidated, noisy or smoky the vehicle, we chose it over the mule and wagon offer every time. We'd rather been seen *pushing* a car into town than riding in aboard a wagon. The *motor* mattered. But when we started Town School I began not accepting rides (that is, not being seen coming into town) in a Model-T or a Model-A Ford, since, I considered, both too old for the young. The Model-B (the 1933 Ford) was optional.

I had my personal problems with Mister Charley Slack's 1930 Model A.

Mister Charley, Plainview's church custodian, drove his niece Nookie, who also finished elementary school with Sister and me, to Burney Street every school morning and whenever he saw just Sister and I walking along, he would stop and give us a ride in. If a non-Andrews walker was walking with us, Mister Charley didn't stop. I preferred this. I felt very "country" sitting in an outdated, old fashioned, Model-A (two steps above the mule, the Model-T being just one step above). I figured the ride was fine for Sister, a girl, and besides Nookie was her best friend.

Town held the goodies! First, to me, was the picture show. Then came the drugstore, where you could buy magazines and books. That is, only at Baldwin's Drugs and Rexall's, or the "Middle" Drugstore, as the Corner Drugstore didn't allow colored to enter, sending them instead to the window marked "colored" where their order was handed to them. Mama and Daddy told us never to go there and we didn't. The third place was the Five and Ten Cents Store, which sold toys and where Benny and I spent World War II buying (but mostly looking at and dreaming about) our one-a-month toy soldier. Then came the ice cream places, again the drugstores although my family hadn't always known of the whereabouts of ice cream being sold. As a young country girl in town, Aunt Soncie had gone into the post office asking to buy an ice cream cone. Years later, I walked into the Five and Ten Cents Store asking for the same and the owner politely pointed me to the Middle Drugstore.

The town also had its laws. Like the law. The police, or "the Man." An early recollection about the law was my hearing folks talk about the first person from Madison to ever go to the electric chair. He, a colored man, went because he killed a white policeman over a colored woman.

The policeman I remember the most was Ab Booth, a mean Man. But, supposedly, he was just as mean to the poor whites as he was to the colored. Tough only on the tough, many said. Yet there were always more colored than white beat up and put in jail by him. Even after Ab Booth retired from the police force to his farm he continued to beat up, arrest, and bring, folks into town to jail. Yet for many years there was talk about him having a well-respected colored woman for his mistress. Only a few in the county knew who she was but feared to tell.

The jailhouse, located directly in back of the courthouse, held a fascination for us country folks. It was a must-see place for us whenever we were in town. We would go down and peek in through the bars to see who was in jail. If one was lucky enough to go into town during a weekday there was always the possibility of arriving there when the janitor cleaned the jailhouse. This is when he left the front door open (though the cells inside remained locked) and anyone was allowed to follow him inside and tour the place while he cleaned. Benny was lucky enough to take this grand tour once. This was during the time Mister Martin Dorsey was in jail; according to Benny, Mister Dorsey treated him nicely but kept complaining a lot to the janitor about being in there. I was never lucky enough to set foot inside the jailhouse.

When I started going to the picture show on Saturdays with Harvey and Benny, we would often go down back of the courhouse to the jail after the movies to see who was locked up. Outside the jailhouse, unlike Harvey and Benny, I wasn't quite tall enough to stand and peer in through the bars. The only inmates I ever remember being locked up in there then were the Hester boys. Led by their mother ("Madison's Ma Barker"), the Hester boys (I don't recall how many of them there were but they were all juveniles) seemed to be in jail every Saturday that we went to the picture show. As far as I know they were in jail for stealing. Even in jail they had money, always sending Harvey and Benny to the store to buy candy to bring back and hand to them through the bars. I never knew what happened to the Hester boys...whom I never saw because of being too short to reach up to look in at them through the jailhouse bars.

The front side of town belonged to the white folks. Colored could enter all of the buildings (except for the Corner Drugstore which went out of business during the war) and could stand alongside whites but couldn't sit down beside them. Together white and colored stood but divided they sat. Sitting in the South was serious back then. In the picture show, The Madison, for example, the colored sat together in the eighty-four seats in the balcony (known to whites as "Niggers' Heaven") which had its own entrance. During sellout shows the eighty-fifth person had to wait outside in line for the next movie. The whites sat together downstairs in the much larger orchestra section. At the soda and lunch counters of the drugstores (not counting the Corner), the colored could stand at the corners nearest the door and buy ice cream cones, candies, and things you didn't have to sit down to eat (involving the use of china, glass or silverware). In there only the whites sat. Inside the grocery, Five and Ten Cents, hardware and drygood stores, the bank, post office and other such places, colored and white *stood* side by side. But *no* colored went into white restaurants since every-one in there *sat*. All the behind-the-scene, invisible kitchen help, was colored (except for the office manager who had a chair). The colored worked standing...or stooping.

A few colored, mostly older folks, would stand on the front, main, block of town talking. The two side streets running off Main were mixed, whites mostly taking over the top of each block, closer to the front of town, while the colored dominated the bottom halves, leading to the back, or "flip," side of town, the colored side. The only white person you ever saw back there was the Man.

Between the end of slavery and the coming of the boll weevil, all of the service jobs were called "nigger work" because a *real* white person didn't "stoop" to "serve" or become a "servant" to anyone, thus placing most craftman jobs in the domain of the coloreds. Besides working as domestic servants (the aristocratic South didn't trust po' white trash inside their homes and especially to care for, or train, their children) in and around the homes of Madison's aristocracy (and pre-tenders), the local colored also owned and operated the town's laundry and dry cleaner, cobbler shop, boot black stand, and barber shop, and were its brick masons and blacksmiths, all, in the eyes of those who ruled, "servant" jobs. (In the Old South, today's airline pilots, airline stewardesses, secretaries, salespersons, for example, would have been considered doing "nigger work.") Then, some say, the Lord sent the boll weevil, beheading King Cotton and sending many "real" white people looking for nigger work. Once finding it, running the niggers off, and scrubbing off the black fingerprints, these jobs became, genteelly, known as "public servant work." But it was *still* "serving work."

Meanwhile, Madison's colored shops and craftsmen eventually lost their white clientele (the domestic servant scene remained constant since someone trusted had to continue raising, and "civilizing," the local aristocratic brats).

One of the South's major crafts had always been brick masonry and since slavery this profession had been proudly passed down from colored father to colored son. Even today throughout much of the South brick masonry is still looked upon as a black profession. Slaves though these early masons were, they built the South's foundation. Old Mister Murray, a proud old colored man who raised a proud family (whose children were in school with me at Burney Street) was considered the best brick mason in the area and built the foundations, or entire buildings, for much of Madison.

On the colored end of one of the two major side streets, Mister Joe Love (whose wife, Fannie, taught at Burney Street) owned a dry cleaners. On down this street, beyond the back street, was Mapp's Undertakers (now Funeral Home) where Uncle Corris worked and which was run by his oldest sister, Olga. Mapp's was just down from the livery stable (where Mister Sid bought his blind mule each year), up from Mason's Cotton gin and up and over from the ice plant and train depot.

On the back street, running parallel with Main Street, was Thomas Cafe whose juke box, called a "piccolo" by us, brought in the youngsters, especially the high school crowd. Every Saturday the place would be "busting" out with Burney Streeters buying cold drinks, or "pops," candies, peanuts and "skins" while jamming nickels into the piccolo to dance to Louis Jordan telling all, "Ain't Nobody Here but Us Chickens," or asking, "Caldonia! What Makes Your Big Head So Hard?" or Nat King Cole warning us to, "Straighten Up and Fly Right," or to get our kicks on, "Route 66," or Wyona Harris, "Letting the Good Times Roll."

Sitting off to itself on the back street, in the next block over from Thomas Cafe, was a two-story building that housed an upstairs barbershop owned by Mister Wilson Bass, and the office of Doctor Smith, a graduate of the University of Michigan Medical School whose father had been Madison's first black doctor. Downstairs from the barbershop and the doctor's office on street level sat, or "loomed," the colored community's most renowned and, by most, feared establishment in the county: DeMoore's Dew Drop Inn, or just "DeMo's," a cafe named after its owner and known for its fried fish and fights. In the back of the cafe was a pool room.

All Christians and children stayed out of DeMo's on direct orders from God and mamas. The good just stood on the porch of Thomas Cafe and stared across and down the street at the *bad* entering and exiting DeMo's, the *ugly*. Lord, have mercy! Once, Lord, *only* once, I got up the nerve to walk past and look into DeMo's front door. The place was packed with sinful folks, most of them sitting around tables eating fried, *sinful* fish. (Every Friday, the owner bought a barrel of fish from the truck passing through Madison hauling seafood from Savannah to Atlanta. DeMoore, selling the best fried fish in the area, always sold out between Friday and Saturday nights.) Walking on past the cafe down to the open side door I looked in and, Lord, beheld men standing around a long green table of sin. Lord knows, I didn't dare tell Mama or Daddy about my daring trek past the doors of sin because their strict instructions, told to us each time we went into town, were to, first, "Stay out of the way of the white folks," and then, "Stay away from DeMo's." We could go to the picture show, buy an ice cream, funny book, toy and marbles, and stand for a while on the front and side streets, but *not* on the back street. We could of course visit Mapps Undertakers to see who died (though Mama didn't like us hanging around the jail to see who was in). We could visit the train depot to check out who was leaving and coming and visit the ice plant where we were always given a piece of ice to "chew" on. And we *always* had to get home before dark. Nobody that I ever heard of ever got into a fight of trouble in Thomas Cafe (Mama and Daddy just didn't like the name "back street," especially for us children) but on Saturday the Man would walk in every so often to let the colored folks *know* he had come to work that day. Yet I *never* saw, nor ever heard of, the Man ever entering a place on Main Street to let the white folks know he came to work that day. (Somebody once said the white folks already *knew* he was at work because they were the ones who gave him the job in the first place and could take him off of it any time he stopped doing his job, which was to keep the colored in line and not to mess with the whites.)

But, Lord, the Man earned his pay, and more, in DeMo's. Especially on Saturday night, when all the sinners were out eating fried fish

and fighting and all the Christians and children were home, respectively dreaming about and dreading Sunday in church. Amen.

Madison had two "characters" whom folks definitely didn't want their children to grow up to be like. One was a white woman, Sal Turner. Tall, slender with long white hair, snuff stained lips and no teeth, the aging Sal was seen around town always wearing the same long flowing, shapeless cotton dress. But most of all she was ignored by most whites because she spent a lot of her time around town talking to and associating with the colored. The South's *First* Deadliest Sin.

The other character was a colored man, "Heddum" (whom Mama and Daddy made us children call "Mister"). A tramp. Heddum too was always seen around town, usually sitting on the corner or the curb, wearing the same clothing. A dark-skinned, heavily graying, bearded man, Heddum was never known to bother or beg from anyone. There were those, Mama included, who said Heddum read a lot. Maybe he did but this meant absolutely nothing to most folks because his always being seen dressed in rags indicated to them they he didn't know too much.

I don't know if Sal Turner (who, incidentally, was a good friend of Grandmama Jessie) and Heddum knew one another well. Back in those days local mores didn't, outside the line of business, permit white "ladies" (what *all* white women were to coloreds) to converse with colored "boys."

Every year at the end of September or the beginning of October the Fair came to town. When Mama and Daddy were children, the circus with its animals always came to town. Later, the "real" Fair, as Mama called it, took over, with folks winning prizes for cooking, baking, canning, and livestock raising, all contests being conducted in the big exhibition building on Madison's fair grounds not too far from the A&M College. From the time I came along, the Fair had been replaced by the "carnival" with its chief emphasis on rides, games of chance, and sideshows. But everybody still called it "the Fair," which usually arrived in town on a Friday night and began setting up for a Monday night opening. Known to be sinful just by being Fair folks, each year they confirmed everyone's suspicions by working on the Sabbath setting up and, on the following Sunday, closing down. But, Lord, from Monday night through Saturday night these evil folks were fun to visit. The first five nights mostly town folks came as most country folks were home in bed after picking cotton all day. Friday night was locally known as "white night" when mostly white families attended. A few colored would show up on this night, usually those whom white folks liked and those who weren't scared of white folks.

I was about four or five years old when Mama took me to the first fair I can remember attending. She said she spent all of her money on my rides (a nickel each). What I remember most, apart from the rides, was the loudspeaker playing the song, "Flatfoot Floozie With the Floy Floy." As I got older I was allowed to go one night out of the week (in addition to Saturday) but never on Friday. Once on one of these weeknights, I got lucky. From under one of the tents in which you paid a quarter for three throws with the ball to see if you could knock all three dolls off the shelf for a present a barker beckoned and gave me a job. The behind-the-scene job of picking up and sitting back upright on the shelves the knocked over dolls. Lord, I was ecstatic! Working at the fair! Me! Many of those knowing and seeing me back there scrambling to pick up the downed dolls wanted to know from me what were my connections to land a job with the fair? I wasn't talking...as I didn't know myself. If one could call a barker suddenly looking your way, pointing, and bellowing, "Boy, you wanna job?" as having connections, then I had them. That night I also found out why the dolls weren't easy to knock over. Rather than sitting atop the shelves, like they appeared to be from where the tosser stood out front, the dolls sat in a groove running the length of each shelf making them difficult to topple. But that night I was too thrilled about working for the fair to worry over such trivia. And to top the thrill off I got *paid* for working those three hours...fifty cents! That night I knew there was a God.

The next day, Mama wasn't too happy to hear what I'd done. She told me fair folks were said to sometime kidnap young children and take them away with the fair. Sounded good to me.

Saturday the fair belonged to the country folks. They—we—would pour in from every cotton patch in the county and outside (people from Eatonton, Monroe, Greensboro, Social Circle and Monticello often came to Madison). Before going to the fair, like going everywhere else, Mama briefed us children. The first no-no was that we weren't to go into any of the side shows where there were half-dressed women (the only side shows that ever interested me). Then we were instructed not to get involved in any gambling game because they weren't meant for us to win. With only a quarter apiece (our fair allowance, in addition to our regular town allowance) we couldn't get into too many sideshows or gambling games. So I usually spent my quarter on rides, mainly the

Silver Bullet since the merry-go-round and ferris wheel were too slow for someone my age and speed.

2. TOWN SCHOOL

Hulking over behind the planer mill, across the railroad tracks, and on the dirt street for which it was named was the county colored high school, Burney Street. A two-story high, badly-in-need-of-paint, dusty brown, wooden oddity with a fire escape chute decorating one side giving it an off-balance look, this Burney Street school fronted Canaan, Madison's most populous, and popular, colored neighborhood. It was to Burney Street one early Monday morning on September 4, 1944 (cotton picking opening day) that thirteen-year-old Benny—bathed, with hair cut and combed and pimples freshly picked, took off walking up that long, four-mile dusty red dirt country road to Madison—with a pencil and tablet in one hand and a brown (greasy) papersack lunch of two fried sweet potato and biscuit sandwiches clutched in the other. Thus Benny was to become the first one of us children to attend high school. (To Benny's surprise and pleasure, he discovered at Burney Street several teachers instantly interested in his drawings which soon began appearing on classroom blackboards throughout the school...and they weren't Santa Clauses. Thus did he leave behind Missis Bertha, Herschel, and their blackboard.)

Benny at the time was the only child, colored or white, on Mason land attending high school. A problem. Word was Mister Mason didn't want any male children, especially colored, on his land wasting away precious hours sitting in a schoolhouse while there was cotton to be picked or planted in the fields. He left it up to the overseer to see to it that such treason to the cotton boll didn't occur on Mason land. But, Lord, Mister Mason didn't know Mama.

Mama was determined that as long as we children lived under her roof we were going to go to *two* places. Church and school. And, let me tell you, we went. Eventually, a compromise was reached between Mama and the overseer whereby Benny (and, later, the rest of us Andrews, or "Viola's" children) could attend high school during the rainy days or when there was no work to do in the fields. (In the South of yore, colored women came off better confronting white bossmen than did colored men. Daddy always remained silent around those whites in charge regarding our education. But *not* Mama.) Included in the

VOC (Viola and Overseer Compromise) was that in order to get the cotton out of the field as soon as possible, we Andrews children had to pick all day Saturday while the other sharecropping families got to go into town to shop, see...and strut.   Also, during the winter months Mama, instead of letting us work in Mason's fertilizer plant tossing around 100 pound bags of guano like the other sharecropper males did to make money, sent us to waste away these precious hours in school, moneyless.

Of all the many things (stories, ideas, lies, etc.) Benny brought home from Town School the most memorable came on his very first day, when he returned home and told me the shocking news that during the recess hour at Burney Street (he having right away dropped the countrified term, "Town School") the main game was not boxing, wrestling, nor baseball. Mouth open, I waited to hear what was coming next. He stood right there and told me that up at Burney Street they played a game called "basketball." Lord, have mercy!

Benny fell in love with basketball. Picking cotton, like everything else involved with school, messed mightily with Benny and basketball, but although Burney Street had no farm boys on its basketball team since cotton picking and corn pulling gave them no time for after-school practice, Benny practiced anyway and eventually made the school team.

Even on rainy days, since Burney Street had no gymnasium, all playing took place in the schoolyard on a dirt court. The court had to be tape measured, marked, and lined off with string and lime before each home game and by the time a game ended all the white markings would be all over the players, the referee, the ball, the school's official cheerleader (Bill Dorsey who upon finishing school became an undertaker), and fans or it would have disappeared in the dust or mud (games were sometimes delayed, called off or postponed by rain). Cotton and corn might have messed with Benny trying to spend time in town playing their game, but it didn't stop him from bringing the town game with him home to the country.

From a molasses, or syrup, barrel Benny took a metal rim which he shortened, shaped and nailed up a ways on the side of our house and called it a "basket." Now we younger children had seen cotton baskets, peach baskets, flower baskets, bread baskets, picnic baskets, and sewing baskets, all made of straw, wicker, reed, or wood, but we had *never* before heard of, much less seen, a *metal*, "bottomless" basket. But if that's what Benny said the Town School children thought

BENNY ANDREWS/ DEC 11, 1989

a basket looked like, then we were willing to pretend that this metal syrup barrel rim nailed to the side of our house was a basket, town-type. Now we didn't have the big round ball Benny described to us, nor could we use a ragball since he also told us that in order to play this game of basketball you had to bounce or, as he called it, "dribble" the ball. Ragballs don't bounce even if you dribble on them, so we had to use our other baseball, the tennis ball. Tennis balls bounce like crazy, even on grass, where we had to play our basketball games. (On the high school team, Benny was noted for being a good dribbler—having practiced with a tennis ball on grass hadn't hurt.)

When Benny brought basketball home from Burney Street, Harvey was no longer playing with us, having abruptly left our childhood to go play with the big girls. That left Benny to teach Sister, Shirley, Joe and me. Johnny, at two, was too short to work the boards. Playing the game every night after work, on Sunday and on winter days following school when there was less work, we Andrews kids had the rest of Plainview, especially the baseball lovers, thinking we were "tetched" in the heads.

After Harvey moved to Atlanta, he brought back a softball for us on one of his visits home. Now it was not, according to Benny, as big as a real basketball and it wouldn't bounce on dirt, much less grass, but it was much firmer than a ragball and closer to the size of a basketball than was our basket-tennis-ball. A softball thus became our basketball. Instead of dribbling the ball, we now passed. By not being the sadistic or masochistic type of player who loved hanging out beneath the basket (this was the favorite territory of Sister, with her stiletto elbows), I soon became known for my long, "way on the outskirts of town" shots—which missed mostly.

Now from the inside of the house the "plink" of the tennis ball against the outside of the house (right next to where Daddy and Mama slept) wasn't all that annoying to our parents until that early Sunday morning when Daddy was lying in bed wallowing inside of a late-Saturday-night-in-town-head when suddenly right above this same brittle head came the sound "WHONK!!!" I had just officially opened early-Sunday-morning-before-Church-basketball at the Andrews Arena with one of my outskirts-of-towners—misses—bouncing our brand new official softball-basketball up against the outside wall of Daddy's and Mama's bedroom. Well, Daddy came out on a rebound that a latter day Wilt the Stilt would've envied and told us a few things that would have banned him from the NBA for life. A few minutes later we had moved the entire franchise all the way out to the side of the barn where the grass was greener, and taller. There our two cows, after suffering the sounds of a few of my early Sunday before Church morning way-on-the-out-skirts-of-towners-up-against-the-side-of-the-barn misses, soon went right back to giving milk as before.

On September 1, 1947 (official cotton picking opening day), Sister and I entered town...er, Burney Street High School.

Town children were different. Even the smallest of them wore shoes to school during barefoot season. Some country children even *went* to town barefoot. I went to town barefoot as late as twelve years old, the year my Santa Claus balloon busted. On this, my last barefoot day in Madison, Benny and I were sent into town to the train depot to pick up a set of hand-operated cotton weighing scales Harvey had sent to Daddy from Atlanta. After picking up the scales at the depot, Benny gave them to me to carry and said he would meet me on the other side of town where the pavement ended and the dirt road began, the way back home. With cotton scales over one shoulder, I walked barefoot right through the heart of town and, like he promised, Benny met me where the pavement ended, and from there we walked home together. I found out later that Benny, then at Burney Street (and wearing shoes), hadn't wanted to be seen by any of the Town School children carrying cotton scales through town so he had had me, yet at Plainview Elementary, do so. A year later, I was at Burney Street (shod) where I quickly learned to understand Benny's feelings about everything "country." At Burney Street if you wanted to be hep, wanted to belong, you didn't act country...especially if you were from the country.

At Burney Street the next worse thing to being country was being poor, or "po'." Needless to say, there was nothing, *absolutely nothing*, on God's earth, or Satan's hell, worse than being country *and* po.' If you were, then Lord have mercy on your soul! "Country" meant picking cotton, plowing a mule, and wearing overalls, the three deadliest of sins that most of the Burney Street country kids would have gladly died and gone to hell right in front of their mamas, rather than be caught committing before those who really mattered—the town children. "Po'" meant what you wore, which meant who you (your soul) were. Besides bib overalls, which even a po' town child wouldn't stoop to wear, the poorest thing one could be caught wearing was corduroy...made from cotton.

Madison had a clothing store, Rhodes-Smith, that, because of its abundance of corduroys, became known as "The Po' Critter Store."

Mama, naturally, shopped here. Thus began my life of corduroy. When one was seen wearing corduroy pants at Burney Street he would soon be followed by some student's finger popping and hand clapping to the tune of,

"Man, where're you gonna go?"
Down to the Po' Critter Store.
Man, where've you been?"
Down to the Po' Critter Store and going again.
"Po' Critter, Po' Critter…"

What saved me from most of the Po' Critter Store jokes was the fact that Mama also shopped at the town's Army-Navy Surplus store from where she stocked Benny and I up in Army shirts. Plus, when Uncle Toodney's youngest brother, Junior Maxey, came back from the Army he gave Benny his Army combat boots. In Benny's early days at Burney Street he wore these combat boots with whatever else he had. But by the time he was a high school senior he had inherited Harvey's sent-down-from-Atlanta old zoot suit wardrobe, whose pegged trousers, yet stylish at Burney Street, he wore daily. Also, Benny became the first at Burney Street to wear to school a pair of loafers (these too sent to him by Harvey). Meanwhile, my wardrobe was brown Army shirt, black corduroy pants and (inherited from Benny) brown Army combat boots. True, the corduroys were po' folks wear, but *anything* Army automatically transcended style, or socioeconomics. Army was in, hep.

At the same time, for girls it was not hep to wear hightop shoes, cotton stockings, or long johns, despite the winter months being cold to all those not wearing these "uncool" items.

For Burney Street's Junior-Senior Prom of 1947, Mama went all the way to Atlanta to buy Benny a suit. Benny proudly hinted around school about his mama hopping an early morning train to Atlanta to shop for his prom suit. But what Benny didn't know was that Atlanta, too, had a Po' Critter Store. And, Lord knows, Mama had a nose, *and* pocket book, for po' critter stores. Benny's imported-from-Atlanta-po'-critter-store suit, besides not being of the very latest style, was too short in both the arms and legs. This meant that in order for these shortcomings not to be as noticeable, Benny spent a lot of his prom night with arms folded and, no easy feat while standing, legs crossed. The next morning a disappointed-in-Atlanta's-haberdashery Benny gave me the dated, belt-in-the-back, suit. I wore it on Sundays to church but nowhere else. Once addicted to Army shirt, black corduroys, and combat boots, the habit was tough to kick.

My best friend during my first year at Burney Street was someone I knew before starting school there. He was a cousin of June's on Aunt Marie's side, whose nickname was "Bud." The only son of Mister Clarence Hill, Bud's real name was Henderson and because of his classroom brilliance at Burney Street he was known as "Doc." Henderson was often asked "What's up, Doc?" Folks loved giving other folks names.

Doc lived about a mile up and over from us (thus being a country boy who got all of his schooling in town—a miracle) with his father, his older sister, Mary Ella (there were just two children), and Mister Clarence's mother. The only name I ever knew her to be called by was "Old Missis Hill," but we children knew her as "Doc's Grandmama." She was born a slave. There were a handful of others around (mostly women) who had been born slaves, but Missis Hill is the one I remember most. She was twenty or so years older than Grandmama Jessie and was known to talk about remembering being a slave as a young girl, about being freed, and about when the Yankees came through Morgan County. In her nineties, Missis Hill was still walking around busily working in the house, even cooking, and working around the yard. Her mind and body were both very active. Too active, many thought. She drank a bit. Not only did she drink but she ran around with a much younger, fast, set of "girls," most of them in their sixties, who were also known to drink. One of these young'uns was a distant relative of ours (in Plainview just about everybody found a way to be "kin," Grandmama and, later, Daddy, always finding us new, never-before-known kinfolks). This was Cousin Chaney (whose husband was accused of being a "gentleman" because he always wore a brown derby and was never seen in overalls), on whose breath, in church, someone once claimed to have smelled liquor. Yes, Lord, Old Missis Hill certainly ran with a fast crowd. Some said she was a "pistol."

By comparison to the grandmother, the granddaughter was a wallflower. Tall, quiet and sweet, Mary Ella was liked by Mister Sid, the blind mule owner. Once we saw Mister Sid coming up to Doc's to "court" Mary Ella. I'd always thought Mister Sid was too old to court, but there he was, wearing a pair of hightop black, shined shoes, black and white striped pants, and his white Sunday shirt and black hat, coming to court. Everybody said this was his courting outfit from the 1920s. It looked it. Once Doc and I walked into the room where

Mister Sid and Mary Ella sat on the sofa together, not saying a word to one another, just looking straight ahead at us. I wondered was this how you courted? It looked dull. Mister Sid looked funny sitting there courting, looking like he'd rather have been out possum hunting.

Mister Clarence owned his own land and farmed it, but never kept Doc out of school to work in the field (the father did most of the work himself while hiring outside help, including Mister Sid). And the oddest thing was that Doc didn't seem to mind living in the country. Also, he got along equally well with town children and country, both of whom he invited to his house regularly. We *never* invited any town kids to our sharecropper shack and weren't about to do so—though we did invite Doc who came many times.

Unlike us, Doc lived in a nice house with several rooms, all filled with pretty furniture. Mister Clarence, Mary Ella and Missis Hill were always nice to all of us children, who were forever coming around. (Mister Sid was always nice to us up there too, but he still didn't give out any nickels or pennies). Doc's house and yard, full of fowl, dogs and cats, felt like the kind of farm you read about or saw in books and magazines. Not like our sharecropper's shack. I always liked going up to Doc's.

Doc's parents were either divorced or separated, I don't remember which. His mother, whom I never saw, lived in Detroit and every so often she would send for Doc to come visit her. It was from there that Doc became a Detroit Tiger baseball fan, especially liking the pitcher, Hal Newhouser. Besides his classroom exploits, Doc loved reading about and playing sports. (He also read other books, including funny books; his collection—and scope of interests—was much greater than mine.) But when Jackie Robinson came to the white Major Leagues, Doc, like most *real* colored baseball fans, became torn between the team he first started liking and the Brooklyn Dodgers (not many Southern colored—none that I remember—rooted for the Dodgers before Jackie). I suffered the same problem, having started pulling for the Boston Red Sox because of Ted Williams (whom Doc liked also), before Jackie Robinson. As a result, I started having a National League team (the Dodgers) along with my American League team (the Red Sox). Only a fan living outside a Major League city, state or area could have allegiance to more than one team, or league.

Often when I went to Doc's there would be a gang of kids, town and country, playing, usually baseball. At Doc's we played by "town" baseball rules, the same way they played in the Major Leagues, rather than by Plainview's "run and dodge" rules. Doc always pitched (at football he always played quarterback and whenever we all went swimming he was the first one to spot the snake in the water, which would send us splashing for the banks). Sometimes when I would go to Doc's there would be just a few of us, but we played baseball and football with as few as two to a side. Basketball you could play with just one to a side.

I didn't take to basketball like Benny did, in spite of my way-on-the-outskirts-of-town shot. I cared more for football. Faithfully, I followed the college and professional games over the radio and through the newspapers and magazines. Then, when from Atlanta Harvey sent Benny and me a football (after years using as substitutes tennis balls, softballs, ragballs, two shoes tied together and tin cans filled with rocks), we took it to Burney Street. The kids who during recess couldn't get near the basketball court (dominated year round by the team's players) would kick the football. Sometimes we would play games, running, passing, catching, kicking, tackling, and blocking (along with clipping, holding and fighting) in, around, through, and over children in the crowded school yard.

Playing tackle football in the dirt yard could hurt. Benny once got tackled atop some broken glass and it put a gash in his leg that required stitches from Doctor Smith. Coming home with a limp, Benny told Mama and Daddy he hurt his leg trying to jump on the back of a moving truck and falling. Daddy, of course, flew off the handle but Benny got out of plowing for a while. Doc, our best football passer, got cut above the eye. Preston Jackson, a good runner, broke his ankle. Tackle football without pads was tough.

But the principal game at Burney Street was still basketball.

Doc and Benny, both seniors, played guards on Burney Street's 1947-1948 basketball team, which had two games rained out and one called off at the half due to rain. Doc, short and slender, was a defensive standout. In fact, in those days practically everybody on the team was a "defensive" specialist as very few players could shoot, or had "an eye" for the basket. A team making more than twenty-five points in a game was considered scoring high. For example, Burney Street lost a game that season to Monroe (on a partially grass court where Benny dribbled like crazy...but didn't score) by 12-6. Our highest point total that year came in the season opener when we poured it on Covington, 19-17, with Benny scoring the game's first two points.

Our center, George Harris, a World War II veteran (this was in the days before those over twenty-one were ruled ineligible to participate in high school varsity sports) was the tallest person in the school at the time—so tall, just over six feet, that he was called "Big Oop" and was automatically put at Center on the basketball team. Though he was good at rebounding, it was mostly from his own missed shot—he would stand under the basket missing one after the other. Oop was a much better baseball player, and this was the game he truly loved. Along with Candy Man and, later, James Thomas, also a former Burney Street basketball player, Oop was on the town's baseball team. It was his love for the game of baseball that was chiefly responsible for the long survival of Madison's team, and league, long after most towns in the area had dropped the sport.

But basketball was the Burney Street game. The school produced many good players, Monk Jones, Les Edwards, Shep Roland, Skee Jackson, Tom Jones, James Thomas, Doug Tolbert, Pappy Thomas, to name a few. But the legendary player, Burney Street's earlier day version of Oscar Robertson and Michael Jordan combined into Magic Johnson, was Jack Drake...who gets better the older I get.

Doc was the one who first told me about Athens High (whose basketball team mopped up all the smaller schools in the area). The school had a gymnasium (Doc had been inside it) where you played the outdoor game of basketball indoors. No wonder Burney Street could never beat Athens High...even at Burney Street.

A senior when I was a freshman, Doc graduated with Benny and went on to college in Savannah at Georgia (now Savannah) State. He was an upperclassman who, besides being highly thought of by his classmates and teachers, openly associated with us underclassmen, both the town and country kids. Doc was a truly remarkable soul...even if he was a Detroit Tiger fan.

What Burney Street represented most for all of us, both town and country children, *and* grownups, was education—a chance for the colored to improve, *prove,* him or herself. While I was there the school was on the list of the "unaccredited," which meant it fell below the standards on which schools in the state were rated. It also meant that those few Burney Street graduates who went on to college had a difficult time entering. But the school, like many colored schools in the area at the time, was unaccredited because of its rundown physical condition and lack of proper teaching equipment, *not* because of its teachers and teaching.

Burney Street always had a heavy supply of competent and dedicated teachers intent on education and disciplining the colored children of Madison and Morgan County. This started from the first grade with

Missis Fannie Love (who, incidentally, *loved* children). For over forty years, she taught this grade, which meant that for nearly a half-century *every* child starting school at Burney Street got introduced to education through Missis Love. Unlike Missis Bertha, my Burney Street teachers didn't tolerate unpreparedness as Mama had warned us children. If you didn't know your lessons you didn't pass in their classes and if you didn't pass, you repeated the grade...even as a senior. It was not uncommon for students to repeat grades, one girl having spent a record five years in the eighth grade...only getting out when she got married. No, Lord, my Burney Street High School teachers, led by Miss Marie Bass, Mister Randolph Binford (a World War II veteran), Miss Ruth Davis, Mister John T. O'Neal (another World War II vet), to name a few, took no prisoners. True, these teachers were tough but, most of all, they were extremely fair. You got your lesson, you got your passing grade.

It was under these teachers of the "Unaccredited" Burney Street that I learned to love knowledge not just for what monetary gains it might ensure but also purely for the sake of knowing. I remember them gratefully for teaching me this.

XVI.

THE OUTSIDE WORLD

1. THE WAR

After the recollection that Hitler started World War II in order to upstage my first day of school, my next memory of the war came from looking through *Life* magazine and seeing pictures of the bombing of London. That's when I first started thinking that war only occurred in cities.

As well as news of the war, Mama read and talked about other topics of interest, but Daddy and Mister Jim seemed interested only in war news. When Aunt Bea got her radio, Mister Jim would time his breakfast, dinner and supper so that, before eating, he could listen to the latest news over the air. When he was listening to the radio in her room nobody, including Aunt Bea's cats, went in there. After we got our radio, Daddy could listen to the war news at home. When Aunt Bea moved, Mister Jim came to our house twice a day to hear the twelve noon news and the six o'clock evening news. Yes, Lord, on Mister Jim's place there was lots of war news read and heard.

Then when the Japanese bombed Pearl Harbor everything just seemed to get busier. *Everybody* was now talking about the war. And Daddy even more so now. Harvey's, Benny's and my dream was to see our Daddy in uniform...any kind of *military* uniform. Daddy didn't share the same dream. Being in uniform was for him a nightmare. What do daddies know?

The first person of Plainview to get drafted was Edgar Allen, Mister Wes's youngest brother. Edgar was a bachelor who didn't seem to want to ever get married but once Pearl Harbor got bombed he suddenly up and married a much older woman, Missis Pinkie Broadnax, another one of our neighbor, Mister Lonzie's, cousins. But Edgar still got drafted. Not too long after going away to camp he sent back a picture of himself in uniform to Uncle Bubba and Aunt Marie which they kept on their mantel throughout the war. Edgar looked good in his Army uniform (to Benny and I everybody looked good in military uniform) and I wished he'd sent us a picture of himself as he had to Uncle Bubba and Aunt Marie. A year or so later, Aunt Marie told June and I that the picture belonged to Aunt Bea, who told her to keep it for her. I wondered why Aunt Bea didn't want Edgar's picture in his impressive Army uniform sitting on her and Uncle Toodney's mantel?

Edgar looked so good in his Army uniform to Harvey, Benny and me that we could hardly wait to see Daddy in his. Daddy could wait.

The morning Daddy went down to take his physical examination in order to be classified for the draft, Harvey, Benny and I were ecstatic. Not Daddy. A leading advocate of nonviolence outside the home, Daddy was downright scared. Harvey, Benny, and I weren't. We watched him march off to Madison that early morning in step, we were sure, to the music in our heads.

Well, to our great disappointment, Daddy didn't get inducted into World War II. He said he was turned down because of his fast heartbeat, claiming to his friends that an aspirin and a "dope" (the drink Coca-Cola was known as to the oldtimers) taken just before examination did the trick. But I think Uncle Sam figured it was better that the then thirty-one-year-old Daddy stay home and take care of his wife and seven children himself rather than letting the government take on such a huge responsibility. Whatever the reason, we children never got to see our daddy in a military uniform.

Since virtually everything in the newspapers and magazines we read, as well as most of what we heard over the radio, had something to do with the war, I grew up in a generation figuring war was the norm. We three older Andrews boys assumed the war would last long enough for all of us to join—Harvey wanted to be on a ship in the Navy while Benny and I wanted to be aviators in the Army Air Corps. We patriotically bought the war comic, Wings, and many others of this ilk. All the funny books and funny papers heroes were now involved somehow in the war effort of "smashing the Axis" (Germany, Japan, and Italy). Benny not only bought toy soldiers but from the newspaper started clipping out and collecting the daily panel cartoon "Up Front" by the G.I.-cartoonist, Bill Mauldin, for his personal Army. Every gun, bullet belt, helmet, and canteen, for example, that appeared in the cartoon, Benny kept a list of for his military arsenal, which he counted daily. Every military uniform we saw worn on the streets of Madison we mentally recorded (and long after the war remembered) the soldier's rank. (During his 1944 4-H Club week-long trip to Savannah, Benny saw so many uniformed military men that he nearly lost his marbles trying to remember all of the many ranks he felt chosen to see.)

And, yes, the war movies. After Harvey got interested in girls, and left Benny and me to fight the war alone, Benny and I looked at World War II as being one gigantic, continuous movie. We saw every war movie we could. Starting with Don "Red" Barry (an earlier day Western "Red Ryder") in Remember Pearl Harbor, we had many war heroes.

This included the biggest one of them all, General Douglas MacArthur, who was even a big favorite of Missis Bertha Douglas . Yet with movies Benny and I were caught up more into the story than the star in films like *Guadalcanal Diary, Destination Tokyo, Bataan, Wake Island, A Wing and a Prayer, The Commandoes Strike at Dawn, God Is My Co-Pilot, Objective Burma, Escape in the Desert* and many more.

Contrary to today's belief, John Wayne did not win World War II. Errol Flynn did. John Wayne only won the war after it ended. I remember only three Wayne war movies, *Flying Tigers, The Fighting Seabees* (who did almost as much work as fighting) and *Back to Bataan*, and another one *They Were Expendable,* showing right after the war. In 1949, long after Errol Flynn (with moral support from Benny and me) had won the war while it was still being fought, John Wayne appeared in *Sands of Iwo Jima* to begin winning the long post-war. During America's fighting overseas, John Wayne was still busy winning the West in films like *In Old California, In Old Oklahoma, Flame of the Barbary Coast, Dakota* and *Tall in the Saddle,* thus leaving it up to that All-American boy next door with the Australian accent, Errol, to win World War II. Another star, Van Johnson, was always in uniform but apart from his role in *Thirty Seconds over Tokyo,* he spent most of the war on leave kissing girls.

Oh yes, Helmut Dantine (the Austrian-born actor) lost the war for Germany while Richard Loo (born of Chinese ancestry in Hawaii) failed Japan.

Many colored males from Morgan County were drafted into the Army, yet some were kept out of the military by their white bossmen— Mister Mason and Mister Nolan, for examples—because they were considered essential to the home front. Unless working for one of these rich white men, it seemed, one's work wasn't essential enough to keep one out of the war as was the case of those (especially living in town) colored men who worked for themselves or for lesser known whites. Thus these not-owned-by-a-rich-white-man coloreds proved far more patriotic, judging by the number of them going off to fight, than were the Mason and Nolan Niggers.

Despite all the colored of Morgan County (and other counties around the country) who went into the Army and off to the war never did I ever see a colored face in all those war movies. I remember once wondering why?

Besides showing our patriotism by buying war funny books, seeing war movies and buying toy soldiers, Benny and I made a big donation to the war effort one day by contributing old car tires (from Uncle

Bubba's and Mister Wes's autos) and scrap metal, hauling several loads of this stuff into town on our backs. At the end of this long day we both got paid for our patriotic efforts a whole dollar, together. Praise the Lord and pass the ammunition!

When the war ended in the summer of 1945 everybody the world over, according to the newspapers, magazines and radio, seemed happy the fighting had ended. That didn't take into account almost fifteen-year-old Benny and eleven-year-old me who'd spent the past nearly four years hoping that whoever was in charge of the war would keep it going long enough for us two to get into it and right up on that big war movie screen. A world without a war was a world we didn't know.

Soon, the soldiers were coming back home. Some came with many stories to tell, some with just a few stories and others never said anything about the war...they just drank. One of these was Edgar Allen...another was Uncle Few.

Benny and I were eager to hear *any* story about *anything* military, during fighting or peacetime, so we hung around the veterans every chance we got. All to the dismay of Daddy who tried to keep Benny and I away from these former soldiers, whom he claimed were too full of "outlaw" talk. They cussed. They said nothing we had not heard on the school yard; they just said it more often. But what the veterans had that the children on the school yard didn't have...and Daddy knew...were the pictures. Pictures of naked white girls the veterans had brought back with them from overseas.

Mama was happy the war was over because all of the killing had stopped. Daddy was happy because now he didn't have to go over and get killed. When he found out Benny and I (Harvey was now in Atlanta) weren't too pleased over what we considered the abrupt ending of the war, he tried to console us by telling us not to worry because for us "There would be another war." What, we asked ourselves, did daddies know?

2. THE PRINTED WORD

Our original link to the outside world was the mailbox where the mailman brought us the newspaper, The *Atlanta Constitution*, and, later, *Life* and *Look* magazines. While living on Mister Jim's place, Daddy had started subscribing just for the daily, which meant no Sunday funnies. During these years when the mailman delivered the newspaper we always had to go over to Mister Wes's place on Monday to see the Sunday funnies. For Sunday funnies on Sunday, Daddy would send first Harvey, then Benny, and then me into town early (before church) every Sunday morning (through rain, shine, sleet or slime...or all combined) to buy the *Atlanta Journal*. This way we got to know their funnies (The Phantom, Red Ryder, Tim Tyler's Luck, Bringing up Father, The Katzenjammer Kids, Little Annie Rooney, Prince Valiant, Flash Gordon, Mandrake, The Lone Ranger, Blondie, et al) as well as ours, the *Constitution*'s (Dick Tracy, Little Orphan Annie, Mary Worth, Smilin' Jack, Gasoline Alley, Superman, Tarzan, Moon Mullin, The Gumps, Terry and the Pirates [Benny's and my favorite] , Steve Canyon [our next favorite] to name some). Missis Mattie, Aunt Soncie and Aunt Bea (when J.B. wasn't around) always put aside the funnies for me to read, or look at.

By the time we were living on Mason's, "going to the mailbox" had become an important part of us children's lives. When we weren't working in the field or in school, two or three or more of us would go to the mailbox early to await the arrival of the mailman's car. With the newspaper and its daily funnies, along with the weekly *Life* and biweekly *Look*, being the "first" one to get to the mailbox became extremely important. While working all morning in the field, we children would be eagerly awaiting the twelve noon "dinner bell" that would ring from up at the Big House.

(Oh yes, the term "afternoon" didn't exist for us. The day consisted of three parts, morning, evening, and night. Also, our three meals were breakfast, dinner and supper. Lunch was something you carried to work, or school, in a—usually greasy—paper sack, or empty lard bucket, because you were too far from home to go eat dinner at twelve o'clock noon.)

There were less than a handful of watch owners on Mason's, but during the summer months everyone could tell when twelve noon, or dinner time, was near. When you could stand up straight and stick out a leg that touched the head of your shadow, it was twelve o'clock. At the first ding of the bell, we children would drop whatever we were holding—cotton sack, hoe or whatever—and race at full speed straight for the mailbox, about a quarter of a mile away. Though always trailing in the field, I was quite often the first one to reach the mailbox. Daddy many times expressed the wish that we, especially me, worked as fast in the field as we did in running to the mailbox. When coming back to the field, and work, after eating and being torn away from our reading, we children always let Daddy lead the way.

Competition got so fierce among us on these mad dashes to the mailbox that tempers would often flare, leading to pushing and punches, but mostly hollering, accusations and, of course, tears. This inevitably led to Mama assigning each one of us a specific day to go the mailbox, thereby ending those dinnertime mad, fun dashes.

My immediate family was addicted to the printed word. Daddy was the village closet reader, as in Plainview *real* men didn't read...or didn't know how to. But Mama openly read and read a lot. Our house was always filled with reading matter that we got "somehow." Besides subscribing to the *Constitution*, *Life*, and *Look*, on occasion we managed to buy *Collier's* and *The Saturday Evening Post*, magazines Mama liked. Daddy, in addition to reading anything dealing with the war (plus the funnies and our funny books), read detective, western and adventure magazines and books...along with *Film Fun*, a magazine filled with half-naked women that he thought he kept hidden from us children.

I read voraciously. Looking back it was predominantly junk but it was all I had. When I first learned to read I was so thrilled at being able to identify and pronounce (the Andrews version of) many of the printed words that I was less concerned with their meanings. When I would read Daddy's police detective or western magazines, I didn't know the meaning of the word "continued," so I would read straight through the magazine as if it was one complete story. Benny eventually enlightened me about the meaning of "continued on page..."

Often I proved an embarrassment to Mama when she would take me as a young boy on visits to neighbors. Many cracks between the wall boards of Plainview houses were filled with newspapers to keep out the winter cold. Easily bored, if I couldn't go outside to play I would sit listening to the grownups talk for a while before starting to look for something to do, or read. That's when I would attack the cracks in the wall to pull out the narrowly folded newspapers and spread them open to look for funnies, movies, radio, or sports...all, of course, to the horror of the host and Mama. Many houses were wallpapered with newspaper (sometimes even the funnies!), which would have me standing on chairs to read. Into every house I was taken I went looking for something to read, but with few exceptions the reading material in all of these houses was on the wall...or in the cracks. Mama eventually stopped taking me with her.

Mister Emerson Wales, a kindly, soft-spoken man, worked in and around the homes of several white families in Madison. From these homes he would collect magazines and books intended for the trash and give to Daddy about once a month a croker sack full of this saved-from-the-garbage-dump printed matter. I still remember Daddy bringing home those croker sacks full of goodies. I *know* Mister Emerson Wales is now in heaven.

I was even happy to see Mama go into town to the doctor, for whenever she did she returned with an armload of waiting-room reading material. She would, of course, ask the doctor for these magazines, but it would not have surprised me if the doctor thought our Mama was getting pregnant with one of us just to make sure the rest of us had something at home to read.

But undoubtedly Benny's and my greatest achievement in sniffing out the printed word occurred the day when the two of us found ourselves, for some unremembered reason, walking past the fairgrounds en route to downtown Madison (not our regular way of entering town), when a gust of wind suddenly blew our way the pages of a newspaper. Printed words! During that time it wasn't a common practice to litter, nor did people have much to litter with, so we were curious as to where the paper came from and went investigating. The trail led us to the big exhibition building, where we peered in through the window. (It was the only structure over there on the bare, litter-free grounds where the fair hadn't come for that year.) God Almighty! The building, larger inside than the Upper and Lower Churches combined, was stacked wall to wall and nearly floor to ceiling with newspapers, magazines and books! I thought I was peeking into heaven.

Opening the window and climbing into this paradise of print, Benny and I went immediately to work. Of all this suddenly discovered booty, we could only take away what we were able to carry in our hands, under our arms and in our pockets (the exhibition building didn't supply shoppping bags). But the very next day (this happened to be lay-by time) we went back prepared. Armed with two croker sacks, *apiece.* Our chief interests here were the *Atlanta Journal* funnies and the many magazines we'd never seen, nor even knew existed, like the many movie star magazines. We worked until near dark before heading home, walking the four miles toting on our backs the two croker sacks apiece, each well over half filled. We figured at this rate, working a full day every day, we'd have the exhibition building emptied of all we wanted in about a month.

So agog were we over our startling discovery that at the time we were totally unaware of anything or anybody else around. Mama even asked us where were we getting all of these magazines and papers from? We told her, and believed so ourselves, that they had all been discarded and stored as trash over at the fairgrounds. Well, the next day with the family's blessing, Benny and I, croker sacks armed, marched off back to the fairgrounds. Only to find the exhibition building boarded up! Good God Almighty, Paradise was locked! The world came to an end, for the first time, for me that day.

Later, we found out that the local (white) Boy Scouts of Madison had gone all over the area collecting this paper matter and storing it in the exhibition building until it could be hauled away for the war effort. Meanwhile, Benny and I were busy hauling away (a piddling of) this printed matter for the "Andrews effort." Someone, apparently, spotted us (probably thinking we were the enemy agents, Helmut Dantine and Richard Loo) hauling away this war ammo and reported it. Whatever, the gate to heaven was permanently boarded up.

In addition to our newspaper and magazine subscriptions, each Saturday Daddy would faithfully buy the *Chicago Defender* and the *Pittsburgh Courier* from a colored Madison man, the only person in the area selling these two weekly colored newspapers, which were sent (in some instances "smuggled") South. (We were to learn that in many areas of the South—Mississippi in particular—selling or possession of either could get one beaten up, or worse, by the KKK. In Madison, I doubt many, if any, whites knew these papers existed.)

Through these newspapers we were able to follow much that was happening in the colored world of America, particularly the South. Atlanta's *Constitution* and *Journal* each carried only a small amount of colored news, which was located in the crime sections in the back of both papers. In the weekly *Defender* and the *Courier* we were able to follow the area's colored struggle to earn the right to vote, which was causing a whole heap of beatings and lynchings of coloreds by whites, particularly in the deep South (South Carolina, Georgia, Alabama, and, especially, Mississippi). Information of this sort was rarely, if ever, found in the *Constitution* or *Journal*, not even back in the colored news.

When the colored magazine *Ebony* came out, Daddy started buying it from this same colored man too. Daddy was the man's best customer. I can still remember the magazine's pictures from an early issue on the politician and reverend, Adam Clayton Powell, Junior, and his wife, Hazel Scott, one of the most beautiful females I'd ever seen. She was right up there in the same class with Pauline and Miss Johnson.

When Harvey visited from Atlanta, he would often bring us copies of the *Atlanta Daily World,* a daily colored newspaper covering events in the lives and times of Atlanta's coloreds that also didn't make it back to the *Constitution's* and *Journal's* crime sections.

By the age of eleven I had cut back drastically on my funny paper and funny book readings because for me, the stories were becoming too predictable. Now I was into reading movie and radio magazines…and sneaking and reading Daddy's "not for us children" magazines and books. Daddy kept this personal reading (and looking) material under his and Mama's bed in a locked wooden box he had made himself. But I knew where he (thought he) hid the key.

From the movie and radio magazines and Daddy's adult library, I moved to the sports pages and magazines to, Lord, the novel! Tom Swift! Followed closely by Nancy Drew and the Bobbsey Twins. There came many more of these types of books whose main characters' names have long left my memory but a good number of whom, I do remember, were being enrolled in Northeastern prep schools prepping for Yale. Then came my up-until-that-point favorite novel, *The Little Shepherd of Kingdom Come.* The story involved a young orphan boy growing up in Kentucky just before and during the Civil War. I remember that the author wrote about the individuals, the families, and the state splitting over which side to support when the war started. This was perhaps the first serious book I ever read. And it is my misfortune for having forgotten the name of the author.

Plainview school had no library. The county gave the school a few library books, mostly nursery rhymes, such as *The Three Little Pigs, Little Red Riding Hood,* and *Little Black Sambo.* Missis Bertha, when not telling The Old Country stories, sometimes read these books to us pupils and we could read them ourselves while in school, but she would never let any of us take the books home. Burney Street had a small room (not much larger than a closet) designated as a library, but I don't remember much about the books in there. Students used this space mostly for a study (and giggling and spitball-throwing) room. (I do remember the book from which I copied an Elizabeth Barrett Browning poem which I sneaked to my secret love, Yvonne, as though it were my own words: "How do I love thee? Let me count the ways…")

The town of Madison had, for a while at least, a small one-room library for the colored above Mapp's Undertakers. But, at least when I learned about it, the librarian was the county's colored school superintendent, who kept the room locked while she was out attending to school business, which was most of the time. When returning books one often had to deposit them with the undertaker downstairs. From this town library I borrowed and read *Treasure Island*, but when I returned the book I found the library had closed for good. All I could do was leave the book downstairs with the undertaker...and hope he did not bury *Treasure Island*.

I believe my early experience with libraries—or lack of libraries—is why I rarely visit one today unless I have no choice. Of course, this is a bad attitude on my part, as I do firmly believe in public libraries and in support of them. (Many years later, when I lived in New York City for nearly twenty-seven years, I visited the main public library, perhaps America's best, only once. I discovered on that visit that one couldn't browse, which is understandable there for many reasons. Since I could not select the book I wanted, or did not want, myself, or just browse, I never bothered returning. While in this astrodome of books I felt just as restricted, and helpless, as I did sitting downstairs in the undertaker's waiting for the county superintendent to return from her many other duties and open the one-room library upstairs.) Early on I developed the habit of wanting my own books.

At the magazine racks of Madison's two drugstores, young boys often sat reading the funny books. They were all white except for an occasional town colored or two. Included in Mama's and Daddy's strict "stay out of the whitefolks' way while in town" instructions was not to go into any white-owned store unless going to buy something. So, unlike the white kids and a brave town colored or two, we didn't use the drugstore magazine-rack area as a reading room (though, Lord, we longed to). We felt we could only stand for a few minutes flipping some magazine pages before we had to decide what we could afford, buy it, and leave. Sometimes, against Mama's and Daddy's "when in town" laws, with no intention (or money) to buy I would walk into the drugstore and stand flipping through pages wistfully before walking out. I've always loved browsing through bookstores (the only stores I've ever enjoyed entering; others were entered purely out of need...Do the new video movie stores attract browsers?), and, if possible, libraries, even in foreign countries where I didn't understand the language but just enjoyed being among books.

In 1944, I believe, *Life* ran a picture series in one of its editions of colored actors acting out parts from a book called *Black Boy*, written by Richard Wright of Chicago, a colored man. This was the first time I'd ever known of a colored person writing a book. Later on I found out Richard Wright was born in the South—Mississippi.

184

Not long following this there was talk about another book (which might also have appeared in *Life*) called *Kingsblood Royal*. This was a story about a prominent white male citizen of a northern American city who in tracing his family tree discovers he has colored blood, a fact he makes public, and all hell breaks loose in his upper-class neighborhood. This book was written by a Sinclair Lewis, whom I automatically assumed to be colored. I didn't find out differently until more than a dozen years later.

From Tom Swift, Nancy Drew, and others, I went to the pocketbook, or paperback. Reading in this medium I got totally involved in the detective and murder mysteries of Erle Stanley Gardner, Earl Derr Biggers, Agatha Christie, Ellery Queen, Raymond Chandler, Dashiell Hammett, and James M. Cain (my favorite). Then there were the westerns of Max Brand, Luke Short, Zane Grey, William McCloud Raines and Clarence Mulford, to name a few. All heavy duty stuff! Literarily, I felt I had arrived!

3. THE PICTURE SHOW

When Daddy was a boy he went to the picture show often. He once told us children about how many of the older folks seeing a movie for the first time would react to the screen (and this was during the days of the silent film), especially when there was plenty of action. With guns shooting and horses running straight at the camera, many of these folks thought the bullets and beasts were coming off the screen right at them and would go running and screaming out of the theater.

As children, Daddy and Aunt Bea went to the picture show most of the time together, but when he married Mama, Daddy quit going so he could concentrate on being a *real* man. (Picture-show going, like drawing pictures and reading, was for children, girls, and "sissies.") Aunt Bea continued going to the picture show on into adulthood...yet I never heard anyone say she wasn't a *real* woman. She took us children with her some of the time, but other than the Tarzan movies, which she liked, I didn't like the pictures she was always taking us to see, in which the men and women were always kissing and a whole lot of crying was always going on. Rarely, if ever, was there a decent gun or fist fight. So at about age seven I started going with Harvey and Benny to see *real* movies, cowboy pictures where nobody kissed and nobody cried. (Although in Gene Autry and, later, Roy Rogers pictures there was *always* a girl, though she seldom if ever cried and sometimes was even the cause of a good fistfight.)

At the time movies cost a nickel for those under ten and nothing for those under five. Soon it was a dime for everybody, and not too long after the bombing of Pearl Harbor the price leaped to eleven cents. This was a fact of life that we discovered at the ticket booth and Harvey, Benny, and I had to drop out of the line to go borrow from somebody, somewhere, a penny apiece if we wanted to get into that Saturday's picture show. We eventually got the three pennies from a schoolmate, "Bro" Williams, and saw Wild Bill Hickock that day. (For years following, Bro constantly accused me of not having paid him back his penny, which I thought I had, though I don't remember doing so. Besides lending me that penny which he, apparently, never got back, Bro' gave me my first, and last, chew of tobacco. He handed the candy-looking bar of tobacco to seven-year-old me one Saturday on the way home from town, and I bit off a chaw…chewed…and *swallowed*…and don't remember the rest of the day, or night, as everything spun around and around and around and…I puked, and…). After that the picture show price began to soar, first to fifteen cents and then, by war's end, all the way up to a quarter! From then on the cost just got outrageous…By the time I left Madison in 1949 admission to the picture show was an unheard-of thirty-five cents!

Toward the end of each month the Madison movie theater would mail out a calendar listing all the films showing in the next month. On Monday and Tuesday, the same movie was shown; on Wednesday, a regular film plus a chapter from a serial ran; on Thursday and Friday, the movie was the same; and on Saturday a cowboy movie and another picture could be seen. At first, this other Saturday picture was a chapter from a serial (different from Wednesday's), but it was later dropped for a "B"—usually adventure—movie. There was no picture show on Sunday. Monday, Tuesday, Thursday, and Friday the serious, grownups' movies played. They were all at night, with the first show starting at seven and the second and last beginning at or near nine and ending at or near eleven. Wednesday's show, most often a lesser-known main movie, had the same seven and eleven starting and ending times. In the years after the war, a Wednesday matinee began being shown…after school.

On Saturday, country day in town, the picture show started at noon (or perhaps an hour earlier) and ended at or about eleven that night, thereby supplying approximately twelve hours of solid adventure, mostly gunsmoke and horseshit. Once my cousin T.J. went and sat through the entire twelve hours, and when he returned home late that night and told where he'd been, a nearly-worried-to-death Grandmama Jessie wanted to know why he had stayed in the picture show so long. He replied, "They didn't turn out until late." On all of these days, or nights, along with the regular film(s) would be featured a weekly newsreel (except on Saturday), a short (quite often one by Leon Errol, Robert Benchley, the Three Stooges, Our Gang, or Pete Smith), or one or more animated cartoons, and always a week's worth of previews of coming attractions.

In my beginning picture-show years, Mama and Daddy let me select from the Madison Theater movie calendar one Saturday show to go into town to see each month. "Through the week" pictures were off-limits to me, unless I went with Aunt Bea to see one of her "kissers and cryers" movies, which I early outgrew. Until I was ten, my once-a-month-to-the-movies was to see the likes of Buck Jones, Deadwood Dick, the Three Mesquiteers (who I thought were the original Three *Musketeers*), Hopalong Cassidy (not overly popular in my circle because of his gray hair), Tim Holt, Johnny Mack Brown (most everyone's favorite), Tex Ritter, Wild Bill Elliott (another big favorite), Rocky Lane, Hoot Gibson, Bob Steele, Don "Red" Barry, and, of course, those two singers, Gene Autry and Roy Rogers. (True, Tex Ritter would sing, yet he did more fighting than did Roy and Gene...and was never as involved with girls as were the latter two.)

It was Mama who first told me. She told me on a Monday morning down near the spring at the washplace while I was bringing up buckets of water for the pot and tub she was using to do the weekly wash. Buck Jones was dead. Killed in a nightclub fire in Boston that previous Saturday night. How was that possible, I stood stunned thinking, Buck Jones *dead?* In the serial "White Eagle" I had seen him with my own eyes get out of much worse predicaments than some nightclub fire. Besides, what was Buck Jones, or White Eagle, doing in a nightclub? A saloon, yes, but a nightclub? I was finding what Mama had told me hard to believe about the Buck Jones I knew. But when she told me he had saved some twenty people from the fire and had gone back for more...and didn't return, I felt a little better. But, Lord, a *nightclub?*

After reaching the age of ten I was permitted to pick out and go to see two movies a month. This included the through-the-week, "grown-ups'" pictures at night, at which Harvey and Benny had more than a two-year head start on me. Thus, on Wednesday, November 1, 1944,

Daddy let me leave the cotton field a few minutes before quitting time to go running the four miles, alone, into Madison to see Preston Foster, Victor McLaglen (the man who once lost a boxing match to Jack Johnson), Anthony Quinn, and Lois Andrews in "Roger Touhy, Last of the Gangsters" (later retitled just "Roger Touhy, Gangster"). After the first show ended at nine, I had to come face to face with reality...returning the four miles home, walking, alone, in the dark. In the confines of Morgan County at the time there was no prevailing sense of fear of anyone harming you, not even a white person if you "stayed in your place." The fear ten-year-old I had that night had nothing whatsoever to do with another human being, nor an animal. But *haints!* Not that I believed in haints, but there were several stretches of the long, dark road home, especially below the several hills, where true followers of the spirits claimed haints hung out, and on my first night out alone that far from home I wasn't taking any chances. So just as soon as I got down to the last street light at the end of the pavement leading out of town, I started to run and ran all the way home. En route I saw nothing but darkness and heard nothing but my running footsteps and pounding heart. I never mentioned this end of the night to anyone, just told about the picture show part.

Once I started going to see through-the-week movies, it wasn't long before I was transformed into a complete film junky. Eventually, Mama and Daddy let me select three movies to see per month, and before reaching the age of twelve I was allowed a movie a week. All of what little money I managed to earn, or had given to me, was now spent going to the picture show or buying movie magazines. Funny books were out. Of the movie mags there were *Modern Screen, Silver Screen, Screen Guide, Photoplay, Movie Mirror, Movie Album* (or *Screen Album*) and others, but my two favorites were *Screen Stories* and *Movie Stories*. These two monthlies carried the entire story of several films in each issue. Many of these movies I never saw, but after reading their stories in these two mags, I could talk about them as though I had.

"Did you see the movie?"

"No, but I read the story," became a common reply of mine, although many other children thought I was odd to be "reading" movies.

In the beginning days of my going to see "serious" movies, Benny and I more often than not went together because we liked many of the same films. Seeing the previews of coming attractions enabled us to decide which pictures we would see. If the previews showed a gun, we would go see the movie. (Basing the decision to see a picture on whether or not it had guns in it sometimes brought about close calls—

we almost missed *To Have and Have Not* since in the previews a gun wasn't shown until the last scene. Whew!)

Benny was a big fan of Alan Ladd and I liked Humphrey Bogart, both of whose pictures were usually filled with lots of gunpowder. My favorite movie during this time was *Northwest Mounted Police,* with Gary Cooper and an all-star Cecil B. DeMille Paramount Pictures cast. (When I was going to Saturday afternoon pictures only, I had rated *Law of the Range,* starring Johnny Mack Brown, as the greatest movie ever made. Many, many, years later I saw this film on television...and was no longer so sure about my earlier rating. I'm hoping I never see *Northwest Mounted Police* again.)

After about a year of our trips to the movies at night ranging anywhere from one to four times a month, Benny suddenly lost interest in going to the picture show—at least, going to the picture show with me. He started going there with girls! First Harvey and now Benny—turncoats! The "movies" (as he now called them) that he and those girls were going to see were those o' pictures where everybody either sang, danced, kissed, or cried. As bad as Aunt Bea!

Now I was back to going to the picture show by myself...though at the brave old age of eleven I walked, *not* ran, home from the movie in the dark.

There was a good friend of mine in Plainview who for awhile followed the movies nearly as closely as I did. This was Arthur Ward, or "Sonny." Unlike most Plainview young boys, he and I followed more than just the movies' cowboys and Tarzan. We kept up with the films of the big named stars as well as buying and swapping movie magazines (along with funny books). Willie Lee Jackson, who went to Plainview Elementary for a while, also followed the movies closely, but he was older than Sonny and I and soon moved out of the community. Sonny, also older than I by about two years, followed the movies into his early teens. Then, overnight it seemed, he stopped and started following girls. It was then bye-bye picture show, Sonny.

Another person I remember from my cowboy and Tarzan movie days was a young boy my age who lived in Mason's peach orchards down near Putnam County. He was the youngest child and only boy in a house full of girls. The nicest and prettiest of his sisters left home one year to go live in Atlanta. Less than a year later she was back. Bringing home a husband. A good-looking, dark-skinned man, her husband had mean-looking eyes. I never saw him smile. Only sneer. He didn't seem to like his wife's family, friends, or anyone else for that matter. In the pretty young wife's eyes you could always see her making excuses for her husband's behavior...which never changed anything, as he often hollered at or even hit her. But they yet seemed to love one another.

The husband especially didn't like white folks. This made it hard on the wife's father (a good man, everyone said, to tolerate a houseful of women), who was held responsible for the ways of his son-in-law, who didn't seem to like the father either.

I figured the man must've lived in the country before he lived in Atlanta because he knew how to drive a tractor. He drove the tractor, hauling peaches (in crates stacked atop a flat-bedded wagon) from the orchards to the awaiting trucks to be hauled into town to the big Peach Shed. But after the man came to live with his wife in the peach orchards, the young boy (now the husband's brother-in-law) suddenly stopped talking to me about cowboy movies. One day the young boy wanted to fight me...and did. I won the fight (I think) but lost a friend. I never could prove it, but I still cannot help but believe that the brother-in-law had something to do with the young boy and I never again being friends.

Following our fistfight the young boy never again spoke to me (nor I to him) and every time I saw him after that he was always in the company of the mean-eyed-looking man from Atlanta.

During World War Two the country, thoughtlessly, did not provide a children's Army Air Corps. If it had, I could have been a child fighter pilot. Now, at the age of eleven, I realized there was not even a war left for me to look forward to growing up to fight in. That's when I turned my eyes toward Hollywood, deciding on becoming a child movie star.

I began to follow closely the careers of child stars of the 1940s like Darryl Hickman, Skip Homeier, Scotty Beckett, Roddy McDowall, Butch Jenkins, Bobby Driscoll, Dean Stockwell, Bobby Blake, and even the girls, Margaret O'Brien, Elizabeth Taylor and Peggy Ann Garner (on whom I had a secret crush). I didn't wish to be one of them; I wanted to be a child star *like* them. But to become a child movie star I knew I had to *be* in Hollywood and *not* Madison. That's when I decided what I would do.

After having seen the films *The Uninvited, Salty O'Rourke,* and *The Unseen,* I'd fallen madly in love with Gail Russell (this was much more than the crush I had on Peggy...this was serious). So I wrote a letter to her, in care of Paramount Studios, explaining my situation—

age, love of the movies, her number one fan—but not mentioning my love for her. I ended by asking her to please send for me to come and live with her and her family in Hollywood, where I could become a child movie star. Then I waited.

I never told anyone about what I'd done, but while waiting for Gail's answer (which I expected to come in the form of a uniformed chauffeur appearing one early morning in front of our three-room Mason sharecropper shack to whisk me back to Hollywood...and Gail...by limousine), I mentioned to Mama one day about wanting to become a movie star. That, Lord, is when she told me. "Colored people can't be movie stars." This hit me right smack dab where I lived! I'd *never* before thought being a movie star had *anything* whatsoever to do with one's color, or race! Then Mama went on to explain about how a colored person could appear in the movies under "certain" conditions, yet never become a *real* movie star. But I wasn't listening. I didn't want to be a movie star under any "certain" conditions! I wanted to be a movie star like all the other movie stars, under "movie star" conditions! *Nothing* less! That limo from Hollywood never did show up... nor did Gail ever answer my letter.

Mama's shocking revelation about who could be and who couldn't be a movie star and who the *real* movie stars were had set me to thinking. Back in 1943, the town of Madison had gotten a new movie theater, the Grande—a colored picture show. Located across from DeMo's, the Grande had a big downstairs where sat the colored. There was a balcony, with about four or six chairs, for whites. It was always sold out up there. Sitting downstairs for the first time I saw how big the movie screen was! From the Madison theater balcony, especially at the rear of the balcony, the screen looked much smaller (not much larger than today's twenty-one inch television screen), but down here one looked *up* at the movie while seeing all of the big screen's warts (grains). I right away preferred the far-back view, where the picture looked much sharper.

Unlike the Madison, the Grande had very few recent movies. But for the first time I saw all-colored films. Besides those few made by the big (white) studios (the old standbys, *Hallelujah*, *Green Pastures*, *Cabin in the Sky*, and *Stormy Weather*), the Grande showed all-colored-cast movies made by colored studios. I didn't see all of these, but presented at the Grande over a period of time were the colored-made movies *Sunday Sinners*, *Tall, Tan, and Terrific*, *Murder on Lennox Avenue*, *Paradise in Harlem*, *Go Down Death*, *The Black King*, *The Devil's Daughter*, *Lying Lips*, *Murder with Music*, and *The Spirit of Youth*, which I remember very well as it had Joe Louis in it. But the film I remember most of all was the *Bronze Buckeroo*, with colored cowboys, led by Herbert Jeffrey. There were also colored crooks. But no colored Indians.

With these films appearing in Madison and by receiving the periodicals *Chicago Defender, Pittsburgh Courier, Atlanta Daily World* and *Ebony*, I discovered there were many more colored movie stars than just Lena Horne, Bill "Bojangles" Robinson, Paul Robeson, Hattie McDaniel, Louise Beaver, Butterfly McQueen, Edward "Rochester" Anderson, Mantan Moreland, and Steppin' Fetchit. The Grande introduced to Madison such never-before-heard-of names as Nina Mae McKinney, Fredi Washington, Francine Everett, Lorenzo Tucker, Noble Johnson, Albertine Pickens, Charles Lucas, Evelyn Preer, and many more.

I have no idea who owned the Grande, but after a few months in business it went from operating six days a week to operating only four days (Monday, Wednesday, Friday, and Saturday). Shortly thereafter it dropped Monday...then Friday...and by early 1945 it went out of business altogether. Besides the all-colored films, which were few, the Grande showed many (of the few made) movies with a colored, or more, in them. But as far as the rest of the Grande films went, they were badly dated, being mostly from the1930s and including many B movies. The Madison picture show, in contrast, always ran Hollywood's latest films and many local colored moviegoers attended both theaters, often on the same night, or Saturday afternoon.

I hated to think it, but Mama had been right. Looking back, the *only* coloreds I could ever recall seeing in the Madison picture show, where the real movie stars shone, were there under "certain" conditions, either as servants or singers, and too often they were depicted as scared or lazy. World War Two had ended without my help, and now I couldn't be a child movie star. Lord, life had suddenly become complicated, *unreal*, to eleven-year-old me.

My attitude toward the movies, especially the stars, began to change. I'd never before associated movie stars with something so insignificant as "color." I'd assumed they were "above" such pettiness (this sort of pettiness, I'd always thought, only interested white Southerners). Truthfully, when I was eleven I believed movie stars were above *everything*...even something so lowly and unimportant as sex (the stars not even bothering to own the "parts" needed to participate), a concern so low down on life's scale of meaning that only the poor folks of Plainview, and Morgan County, indulged in (and talked about) it. Or so I believed.

In most of America it was, "Where were you when Pearl Harbor was bombed?" In the South it was, "Where were you when *Gone with the Wind* (GWTW) came to town?" When I first heard of GWTW (I don't recall the exact year) I was strictly a Saturday-picture-show-goer and wasn't at all interested in movies where people died without first being shot. But I do remember some grownups talking about GWTW being "an old slavery time picture" that they weren't interested in seeing. No one I knew at the time went to see it. Not even Aunt Bea. The feeling was that this was a "white folks" picture and if you weren't a slave (or at least dressed like one) you wouldn't feel too welcome at the Madison theater. Besides, Clark Gable was no Buck Jones.

I didn't see GWTW until March of 1948, when it played at the Madison on Thursday and Friday nights with a special matinee shown on that Friday afternoon. The town's schoolchildren (white and colored) were excused from classes…but only to see the movie. What I remember most was sitting through the entire picture wondering just why in the world Scarlett was so much more interested in the weakling Ashley than in the more adventurous Rhett? Didn't she know Rhett was Clark Gable? Her attraction to Ashley, or Leslie Howard, made no sense whatsoever to thirteen-year-old me. When Rhett finally wised up and walked out on Scarlett at the end I was overjoyed, especially at his parting words (or word) to her.

Oh yes, I liked all the GWTW action scenes… I was hoping the Civil war in the movie would last longer.

By the time I was twelve years old my interests had their feelers out in search of something else…and I found it. Lord, Joe Louis was back and Billy Conn got him…in a fight that Joe was to win by a knockout in eight rounds. Goodbye to the movies and its celluloid world… Hello to the *real* world. Sports!

4. SPORTS

The earliest national sport I followed was boxing, because of Joe Louis. Joe went into the Army during World War Two, and a picture of him in his military uniform holding a rifle appeared in the *Atlanta Constitution* on the same day as the news of the death of Clark Gable's wife, Carole Lombard, who was killed in an airplane crash. There followed many pictures in magazines and newspapers showing Joe in

Army uniform, but the most memorable one for me was him in full battle dress posed for action with a bayoneted rifle pointed at the unseen enemy while he was quoted (supposedly) saying, "We'll win because we're on God's side." If Joe said it then there was no doubt in my mind about who was going to win the war. With Joe Louis and Errol Flynn on our side, how could we lose?

Joe's first defense of his title following his Army discharge came, expectedly, against Billy Conn, whom he knocked out, unexpectedly, easily in the eighth round. This fight we listened to at Mister Lonzie's because our radio battery had died just a week or so earlier. Mister Lonzie, no radioman or fight announcer, let Daddy turn the knobs and call the fight through the static back over his shoulder.

On the Saturday before the Louis-Conn second fight, the *Chicago Defender* carried the story about Jack Johnson, who loved driving fast, having been killed in a car accident earlier that week in North Carolina. That's when Mister Will told us all about Jack Johnson and I discovered that Joe was just the second colored Heavyweight Champion ever. Until then I'd always thought Jack Dempsey and Max Baer were colored.

Also, through the *Defender*, *Courier*, and *Ebony* I was to learn to my astonishment that other coloreds around the country were claiming Joe—especially in a section of New York City called "Harlem." It seemed to us country folks that city folks felt they and not we owned Joe. We could understand the city of Detroit claiming Joe, since he moved there from Alabama—the country. But New York?

When Joe defended his title in December of the following year he did so against a colored fighter, "Jersey" Joe Walcott. Our radio battery having died in mid-November sent Daddy alone to town and Aunt Bea's to hear the fight. I didn't bother going because I didn't figure it to be much of a contest while, sadly, Benny was now more interested in girls than in Joe. As it turned out, Jersey Joe knocked down the "real" Joe twice in the fight before Louis managed to win a fifteen-round decision. But according to Daddy, who *heard* it all, Jersey Joe won the fight. (Daddy was just mad at Louis for not having knocked Walcott out early like he was "supposed" to.) I got mad at Jersey Joe for trying to whip our Joe, whom I felt was the colored man Walcott's Joe as well. I just didn't understand why Jersey Joe would want to do such a thing...try to beat Joe Louis. An impossible thing for another colored man to want to do. I thought.

At the time coloreds were very aware of the nation's few colored public figures. During the 1940s the handful of coloreds in the national sports world was led by Louis in boxing and, later, Jackie Robinson of the Brooklyn Dodgers baseball team. Other colored sports figures were boxers Sugar "Ray" Robinson, Henry Armstrong, Beau Jack, Ezzard Charles, and, of course, Jersey Joe Walcott, the man who tried to ruin it all. (Archie Moore was boxing at the time but I don't remember hearing of him until the early 1950s.) Jackie, who came to the Dodgers in 1947, was followed on the team the next year by Roy Campanella, a catcher, and Dan Bankhead, a pitcher. Don Newcombe, a pitcher, joined the team in 1949. In the other Major League, the American, Larry Doby, an outfielder for the Cleveland Indians, became the first colored to play over there, joining the club in 1947, shortly after Jackie started with the Dodgers. The following year, Leroy "Satchel" Paige, a pitcher, became a Cleveland Indian. Luscious "Luke" Easter came to the Indians in 1949. In 1947, the American League's St. Louis Browns had for a brief period two coloreds, Henry Thompson and Willard Brown. Henry, or "Hank," joined the New York Giants in 1949, along with Monte Irvin. These ten were the only colored players in the white Major Leagues during the 1940s.

The big-name colored football players on white college teams (as they were called by us then) were Claude "Buddy" Young, Ike Owens, and Paul Patterson at the University of Illinois; George Taliferrao of Indiana; Emlen Tunnell of Iowa; Len Ford, Bob Mann, and Gene Derricotte of Michigan, and Levi Jackson, who became the first colored football captain at Yale. In 1946, Kenny Washington became the first colored to play in the National Football League since Negroes had been barred following the 1933 season. Washington signed with the Los Angeles (formerly Cleveland) Rams their first year on the West Coast. He was followed on the team by Woody Strode, who later became an actor and, like Washington and Jackie Robinson, played college football at UCLA. Buddy Young dropped out of Illinois to play professional ball in the new, now defunct, All-American Football Conference (AAFC, which started to play in 1946) with the New York Yankees. In 1949 the league's San Francisco Forty-Niners signed Joe Perry. But the team known for their coloreds were the Cleveland Browns, also of the AAFC, with Marion Motley, Bill Willis, and Horace Gillom. Shortly after the league was formed their head coach, Paul Brown, was supposedly told by members of the Miami Seahawks that his team would never do much winning as on it he had "too many niggers." The Browns won the AAFC title that year (plus the next three years of the league's existence) while the Seahawks, after one losing year in Miami, moved to Baltimore, where they continued losing.

We'd all heard of the track star Jessie Owens, whose hand Hitler refused to shake following the runner's victories in the 1936 Olympics in Berlin. But during the 1940s the track star I remember most was Harrison Dillard from Baldwin-Wallace College of Ohio. Though never a track and field fan, I knew of Dillard simply because he was colored. As with opera and Marian Anderson.

The only national colored basketball players I can remember from the '40s were the Harlem Globetrotters—though I didn't understand why they had the name "Harlem," as they seemed to play everywhere but there. Or was it like it was with Joe—that Harlem claimed everything colored?

A colored in those days was expected by other coloreds to root for the teams with coloreds. If you didn't you were considered worse than a traitor...you were considered a colored wanting to be "white." The colored community baseball teams were the Brooklyn Dodgers, Cleveland Indians, New York Giants, and St. Louis Browns, the "good" teams. The "evil" teams were the St. Louis Cardinals (who in their actions expressed their dislike for Jackie Robinson) and the New York Yankees (who, besides having no coloreds, always beat the Dodgers). The Cleveland Browns was the pro football team of the coloreds. In college football the Big Nine (earlier, and later, the Big Ten) was the "colored" conference. We learned early whom to pull for and whom to pull against.

In the summer of 1948, the real Joe knocked out the traitor Jersey Joe in the eleventh round (Daddy said he should've done this the first time and not "scared" folks like that) and retired the next spring after nearly twelve years of holding the title and defending it successfully twenty-five times. Thus boxing, for me and many others, was never again the same.

Besides listening to boxing matches with the real Joe, we, Benny and I particularly, listened on radio to weekly boxing every Friday night ("The Gillette Cavalcade of Sports"). Here we followed Sugar Ray. Outside of Louis and Robinson fights, Benny's and my favorite matches of the '40s were the three between Rocky Graziano and Tony Zale in '46, '47, and '48. Benny pulled for Rocky and I for Tony.

With the exception of Joe and Sugar Ray fights, Benny and I always pulled for opposite sides in sports. For example, Benny liked the college football teams of Notre Dame, Georgia, and Illinois, while I liked Army, Georgia Tech, and Michigan. In baseball, Benny's team was the Brooklyn Dodgers and his league was the National League. I liked the American League and the Boston Red Sox (even after Doby came to Cleveland I remained faithful to Ted Williams and the Sox).

Even during the 1947 World Series I traitorously pulled for the American League Yankees to beat the National League Dodgers...though only Benny and I knew this. But by the time the two teams met in the 1949 World Series I was a full-fledged Yankee hater (a team my brother Joe was now following)—a Yankee hater not because of what they did to the Dodgers in the Series, winning this one four games to one, but because of their having beaten the Red Sox out on the last day of the regular season for the 1949 American League pennant. This was hands down the third biggest disappointment of my young sports-following career. The second biggest disappointment had occurred on November 6, 1948, when Georgia Tech, unbeaten and untied through six games that season, met and lost to a twice-defeated and once-tied Tennessee team, 13-6. Up until that doomsday Saturday afternoon I'd always thought "upsets" happened to other folks' teams.

My biggest sports (and life's) disappointment up to that time occurred when Max Schmelling beat Joe Louis in 1936...a fight I didn't remember but felt I should've.

In addition to the World Series and American-National League All-Star games on radio, for baseball we got the Atlanta Crackers (a Double-A Minor League team) games plus the Major League Game of the Day, recreated. Besides Georgia and Georgia Tech, the airwaves on fall Saturday afternoons and nights were filled with football games from around the South and country, especially Notre Dame and Army. The professional football team we heard play every Sunday afternoon during the season was the Chicago Cardinals because of Charley Trippi, a former Georgia All-American who played for the Bulldogs in 1942, 1945, and 1946 before turning pro with the Cards in 1947. We also heard the games of the Washington Redskins with "slinging" Sammy Baugh.

In addition to hearing boxing, baseball, and football over the radio, every Friday night I listened religiously to the fifteen-minute sports show of Bill Stern, who told glory-filled, heartbreaking stories of athletes and their mothers. And I believed him too.

XVII. REALITIES

1. RACE AND POLITICS

I don't recall the exact moment, or day, I found out I was colored. But I do remember the day Sister, Margaret, and I were over in the field across from Mister McIntire's house "Roxie Ruth Watching." On this particular day, I was more interested in the tractor plowing in the field, which was being driven by Mister Glenn Paul, Mister McIntire's over-seer—a white man. Seeing me standing at the end of the row watching him drive the tractor, Mister Glenn Paul gave me a ride up and down the row on one of his rounds, with him holding me on the machine between himself and the steering wheel. Seeing me riding, Sister auto-matically wanted a ride too and got it. While Mister Glenn Paul was riding Sister down the row on the tractor, Margaret and I watched. That's when she said to me, "He won't give me a ride 'cause I don't look white like you and Sister." I didn't know what she meant...especially after Mister Glenn Paul dropped Sister off the tractor, picked up Margaret, and rode her up and down the row too.

Later, as waterboy in the cotton fields and peach orchards, I learned quickly that you *always* carried the bucket to the white folks first be-cause no white person would drink "behind" a colored person.

White folks were different from colored folks. Their only problem or worry in the world, I always thought, was us coloreds. Yet I could never understand why they worried about us, who couldn't do any-thing but "stay in our place" and "out of their way."

Personally, I knew little about white folks, but I often watched them. For example, when in town I would stand outside watching and envying the white teenagers entering and leaving Baldwin's and the Middle Drugstores. They all seemed to have been having such a good time and they looked so happy. Lord, I thought, white folks have all the fun!

It was impossible to separate race from politics. To most coloreds politics in Georgia of the 1940s meant "Talmadge"—Eugene, or "Gene," and then his son, Herman, or "Humman." They both preached hatred of coloreds while campaigning for governor of Georgia. The colored didn't get the vote until after World War Two, and even then the vast majority of them didn't talk about voting since politics was considered to be *owned* by the white folks. Yet several teachers at Burney Street were always talking to us schoolchildren about voting, telling us to encourage our parents to do so too. But in Plainview children *didn't* tell their parents what to do, and voting was just not a part of the community's tradition. Voting to these folks always meant trouble. Talmadge, Theodore Bilbo of Mississippi, the Ku Klux Klan...all spelled "white folks trouble," the *worst* possible trouble for a colored person to be in. It could mean a beating...or death...and *nobody* could, or would, help you. Even God. Like that time in Monroe.

The town of Monroe is a few miles northwest of Madison and it was there that in the summer of 1946 four coloreds were lynched by a mob of whites. (Whites always seemed to come to beat or kill a colored in numbers...never alone.) The mob had started out to lynch one colored man who, supposedly, had pulled a knife or gotten into a fight or an argument with a white man (all no-nos of the day). But they ended up hanging four people (the man, his wife, and a married couple who were friends of theirs who happened to be visiting that night). The NAACP rushed into the area and brought back several people to Atlanta who had witnessed the lynchings and were being tracked down by the mob. Many of these were children. Nothing was ever done, and very little said, in the white world about this lynching. But the coloreds in the region have never forgotten it. The Monroe lynchings made it clear to me at the time that *any* white person could kill *any* colored person *anytime* he saw fit without *anything* ever being done about it. A colored life was a shred. God, I thought, must've loved white folks better than he did colored folks.

(But Mama always said that while we went around thinking and talking about white folks all the time they rarely, if ever, thought about us...unless they needed something to blame us for. In fact, she said, they wished we weren't even here. I wondered why, as I'd always thought we were nice to the white folks.)

Madison's first two public schools, a white and a colored, both began classes in the same year, 1895. Both began with ten grades and eventually added an eleventh. The white school, located on Main Street near the town's heart, was named for the town. But the colored school, way on past the town's heart over across the railroad tracks, was named after the street it was on, Burney. (While enrolled there I occasionally wondered, why hadn't the school been named Madison? Other colored schools in the area, such as Monticello, Greensboro, Covington, Conyers, Elbertson, Union Point, Monroe, Winder, and even Athens, all were named for their towns.) In the early 1950s when Madison got a new colored high school, it, too, was named after a street, Pearl Street.

In sports, as mentioned before, Burney Street had only boys' and girls' basketball, without a gymnasium. But the white high school, in addition to boys' and girls' basketball, had not only a gym, but a football team. (About the only thing Burney Street had that Madison High didn't have was the town's first school yearbook.) To the best of my recollection, Madison High ceased playing football at some point during World War Two and didn't bring back the sport until 1947.

Other than Mister Jim, one of the first to attend the school, I never knew anyone personally when I lived in Morgan County who went to Madison School. In those days it was extremely rare for a white child and a colored child to so much as converse with one another, and when such did happen it usually occurred among those not connected with any school—po' folks. (Coloreds were constantly aware of whites, as most of us had to be, but few whites were ever aware of us...unless, of course, one of us got out of "our place"; then they became *over* aware. So in order to keep up with Madison High sports I read the town's two newspapers, the *Madisonian* (the town's only newspaper today) and the *Morgan County News*. The game I recalled reading about most in the year of 1947 was Madison High football team's loss to Monticello, 76-0.

At most of Burney Street's basketball games a few white males would cross over the railroad tracks to watch. I even attended my first football game by going to see Madison High play—the Greensboro game of 1949.

Madison had lost only once, coming into their final game of the season against an underdog Greensboro team on that Thanksgiving Day. I went to the game with a town kid about my age named Morgan. As effervescent as he was good looking, and bow-legged, Morgan had dropped out of school a term or so earlier to go to work at one of the stores in town. But what I remembered, and envied, most about Morgan was all the time that he, along with several of the town's white boys, spent at Baldwin's Drugstore magazine rack, sitting and reading funny books without ever buying any. It was said that Morgan "knew his way around town" (equivalent to being "street smart" today), particularly knowing what went on in the white sector.

Morgan was the one who coaxed me into going to that Madison-Greensboro football game and led me to the stadium. (At this time the town's white high school department had left the elementary school behind in the building on Main Street for the old Madison A&M College site out beyond the fairgrounds and near the football stadium.) We bought our tickets and entered the stadium at a separate gate from the white customers. The gatekeeper said to us, "Don't get in anybody's way."

Rather than sitting, Morgan and I, the only two coloreds in the half-filled stadium that Thanksgiving Day, had to stand watching the game on an embankment away from the stands...out of everybody's way.

I didn't mind standing, nor did I mind where I was standing, since all I wanted was to see my first football game. But standing on the bank that windy Thanksgiving Day, what I remember most about my first football game was not that Greensboro upset Madison, 19-2. I remember the gatekeeper's words, "Don't get in anybody's way," ringing in my head and I wondered, were we coloreds *always* getting in white folks' way? Did white folks *ever* get in colored folks' way?

That's what I remember most about my first football game.

My parents didn't vote and never seriously discussed voting with us. They were the children of the colored disfranchisement. Daddy didn't vote because he was afraid to, which is the reaction that disfranchisement created among the vast majority of Southern colored during those fifty years of not being able to vote. And this fear (thanks mainly to the KKK) eventually led to indifference toward politics...as in Plainview in the 1940s. Mama, I believe, being ever conscious of her children's well-being, didn't want to bring the wrath of the white man down on her family. (Although it was said during the 1940s that Madison's leading whites didn't permit the KKK to operate within or near the town, still, few coloreds dared vote.) Like many Southern colored parents of the day, Mama wanted to raise her children safely, after which, hopefully, they would leave the South for the North (the Promised Land?).

Mister Will Roland followed politics, but I don't know if he ever voted. Many Morgan County coloreds talked about politics, but few talked about voting. In later years, the young Plainview deacon, George Williams, Junior, and his wife, Olivia, residents of Madison, were to become very active in politics, especially local politics.

Besides schoolteachers, the only other colored person I can recall voting during this time was Aunt Soncie, who in the national election of 1948 cast her ballot for the Republican candidate, Thomas Dewey, because, she said, "The Democrats have never done anything for the colored folks." Well, Lord, maybe not, but many folks wondered about Aunt Soncie's sanity in having voted against the party of the late President Franklin Delano Roosevelt (the first president since Abraham Lincoln whom coloreds felt good naming their children after). Some felt Aunt Soncie voted the way she did because she married a divorced man...some felt it was because she was known to take a drink...others knew it was because she had no children.

(During the 1960 presidential election campaign, while living in New York City, I went to the place of registration in my Manhattan neighborhood. The person in line ahead of me was asked by the registrar where was he born and when he replied, "Brooklyn," he was waved on through without having to write or read something to prove his literacy. When I was asked moments later by the same registrar where I was born and answered, "Georgia," she handed me a pen and told me to write my name on the writing pad on the table in front of her. "Why didn't he write his name?" I wanted to know, motioning in the direction of the person who had gone before me in line. The registrar let out a sigh, shook her head, and rolled her eyes toward the ceiling before telling me, "*He* was born in New York and *you* were born in Georgia!" To satisfy her suspicion of *my* kind, I signed a capital "X" and never went back.)

2. GIRLS AND THINGS

I had a whole lot of girlfriends...99.9% of whom never even knew it. An "older woman man"—or boy—I was, beginning with Pauline, then going on to Miss Johnson, and proceeding with many, many more. (Even after Gail Russell didn't answer my letter...or send her chauffeur...my Hollywood loves continued with Leslie Caron, Dorothy Dandridge, Jean Simmons, Dorothy Malone and Gina Lollobrigida...though none of these I ever wrote to sent their chauffeurs for me.) I was especially hooked on pretty schoolteachers...women who knew all the answers in all the books. Also, as I got older, I found myself enjoying seeing these teachers teach sitting down rather than standing. This was a better way to see more. When I was little I never understood why I wanted to look where I *knew* I shouldn't (under a dress) but, besides it making me feel different from any other feeling I ever felt, I couldn't help myself. So, ignorantly, I looked on.

The older I got the more aware I became that girls were "different" from us, normal, boys, but I couldn't exactly understand or explain why. In my class at the time and about two or so years older than I at age ten was Robert "Duke" Morris. A good-looking boy, Duke, while sitting in the back of the classroom where most of the boys sat, would

often take out his thing beneath the desk and tie it in a knot around his left wrist. Nobody else in school could do that. Also, Duke, rather than playing with the rest of us boys, would spend most of his time at school around the girls. Because he didn't play with us boys and seemed to love being with girls, we figured Duke was a sissy.

Then one recess hour he told the rest of us boys about why, and exactly *how*, girls were different from us...explaining the *what* about them he liked better than being with us. Listening to Duke explain in hardcore detail about the birds and bees that day, I was stunned...especially when he explained the girl's "thing" to us. I came away wondering what was inside it that kept the big boys *always* talking about "getting it"?

The young girls closer to my age whom I first liked were Nookie, and later, at Burney Street, Yvonne Pitts. But both of these girls were more interested in the school's uppergrade, "older" boys. So I set my sights on the senior class girls...who liked college boys. Seems I was "the boy who *misread* girls." When they said "don't" I didn't, and didn't; I always tried to be "nice," which never appeared to work. The big boys always talked about "treating them rough and they'd love you," but I was not interested in mistreating anyone, which was proba- bly why I was never the Casanova at Burney Street that I wanted to be. (In looking back, I wasn't always nice. There was a girl at Plainview who liked me and one day when I wasn't at age ten was Robert "Duke" Morris. A good-looking boy, Duke, while sitting in the back of the classroom where most of the boys sat, would often take out his thing beneath the desk and tie it in a knot around his left wrist. Nobody else in school could do that. Also, Duke, rather than playing with the rest of us boys, would spend most of his time at school around the girls. Because he didn't play with us boys and seemed to love being with girls, we figured Duke was a sissy.

Then one recess hour he told the rest of us boys about why, and exactly *how*, girls were different from us...explaining the *what* about them he liked better than being with us. Listening to Duke explain in hardcore detail about the birds and bees that day, I was stunned...especially when he explained the girl's "thing" to us. I came away wondering what was inside it that kept the big boys *always* talking about "getting it"?

The young girls closer to my age whom I first liked were Nookie, and later, at Burney Street, Yvonne Pitts. But both of these girls were more interested in the school's uppergrade, "older" boys. So I set my sights on the senior class girls...who liked college boys. Seems I was "the boy who *misread* girls." When they said "don't" I didn't, and didn't; I always tried to be "nice," which never appeared to work. The big boys always talked about "treating them rough and they'd love you," but I was not interested in mistreating anyone, which was probably why I was never the Casanova at Burney Street that I wanted to be. (In looking back, I wasn't always nice. There was a girl at Plainview who liked me and one day when I wasn't at school she told all of the other children that I was her "boyfriend." The moment I arrived at school the next day I was told by the other boys that they knew who my "girlfriend" was. More than mad at this girl for publicly embarrassing me I, without hitting or "cussing" her out, told her off in such a manner that she cried. She rarely ever spoke to me again. I never forgave myself for what I said to her. I hope she forgave me.)

The summer June and I turned thirteen and the girls weren't falling at our feet like we felt they should have been, we got together and had a man-to-man talk about the woman situation. In the middle of a long, graphic discussion on the subject of girls, and *things*, he and I, the virgin two, agreed unanimously that we were *never* going to demean our manhood by putting *our* things into the the things of girls. Yuk!

That was the last heart-to-heart talk June and I ever had... Soon after that, most of our time was spent falling at female feet.

Boys usually started out on the "girl hunt" around the age of fifteen. Meanwhile, girls (whose bodies and minds matured earlier than boys) didn't start courting, or "receiving company," until they were sixteen. My first (not counting the Pauline years) courting date came about two months shy of my fifteenth birthday—the night I went courting Grace.

Grace, the youngest of three girls, was the daughter of Mister Zeke Williams and his wife. Mister Zeke was a big, muscular man with a kind soul. The family Williams moved to Barnett Farm in late 1948, just up the way from us, and they immediately hit it off with the community. This was due to Mister Zeke's size and his three pretty daughters, Dorothy Kate, Irene, or "Reenie," and Grace, considered by most the prettiest of the three. The fact that the manly-sized Mister Zeke didn't have a son was inexplicable to the community, and it meant his three daughters, in addition to housework, had to plow, lift, chop wood, etc., all work meant for sons. Despite his three daughters and no son...given his size...no one ever reminded Mister Zeke of his shortcoming. Also, even though his daughters were doing "sons'" work, they were still the most sought-after females in the community.

There were no telephones on Barnett Farm or in Plainview, except for the family McIntire's. So, when going courting, the boy just went to see the girl, often without first asking, or warning, her. Courting usually occurred on Sunday afternoons following church, or at night. On Sunday many girls' houses would have several males coming to court them (especially at the house of Williams with its three girls of courting age), with the overflow spilling out onto the porch and into the yard. This was when, particularly on beautiful days, there occurred among this male overflow much outdoor activity like marble shooting, foot racing, horseshoes and horsing around wrestling, and, every once in a while, a fistfight. Besides being rough on Sunday clothes, going courting could be dangerous.

The first time I went courting Grace came on a weekday night following Easter Sunday, 1949, during cotton planting time. Two of my peers, Robert or "Bhug" White and Roosevelt Mitchell, went with me that night to see the three Williams sisters. Arriving, Bhug and I went inside the house while Roosevelt, suddenly smacked by a case of shyness, stayed outside and played with the dog. Mister Zeke and his wife greeted us but the father didn't appear too happy to see boys coming to court his daughters on a weekday night in the middle of the cotton planting season when they had to be up at sunrise the next morning. But nothing stops courting. I sat beside Grace, but not touching, while Bhug sat near Reenie, and all Bhug and I talked about the whole night, and to each other, was Roosevelt sitting outdoors playing with the dog. Bhug and I even went out to get him to come inside and court Dorothy Kate, but hearing us, he ran and hid. Laughing, Bhug and I went back inside and talked about Roosevelt running and hiding. I don't remember what the girls talked about...or if they talked at all.

When from the other room Mister Zeke, at ten o'clock sharp, hollered "Bedtime!" we ended our courting and left, Roosevelt patting the dog goodnight and coming with us. Thus ended my first night of courting. If it hadn't been for Roosevelt it would have been dull.

Meanwhile, moving into the house out of which the family Roland had just moved was another Williams family (no relation to Mister Zeke's), headed by Mister Albert. A short, thick man with a heavy mustache, Mister Albert woke the neighborhood every morning with his loud, deep, and soulful spiritual songs. At Plainview church he sat, and sang loudly, from the Amen Corner. Mister Albert and his wife had several children, predominantly girls. One, Clara Bell, about my age, was a lot of woman to be a little girl. And Clara Bell liked me. But I liked Grace. And Grace liked somebody else...who probably liked somebody else, who...Clara Bell was of few, or no, words...but lots of motion. Her body, coming at one from all directions, scared me. I think. Whenever I was around her she made me feel like she was about to *make* me do something I wanted to do. Scary! The probable reason why Clara Bell didn't make me do that something I wanted to do (besides not grabbing me) was that I liked girls who talked. Clara Bell only giggled.

While Clara Bell giggled and jiggled, I kept going back, mostly alone, to see Grace. Then, Lord, came the Sunday night of the full moon when Grace hauled off and kissed me, leaving on my mouth a heavy smudge of lipstick which I licked off all the way home while feeling I had "scored."

I never went to see Grace again. Not that I didn't want to go, but Grace, a year older than I, was being courted by older boys, and men, who had cars and jobs. Serious courters. Thus, unable to compete or cope with these older males, I lost my first official girlfriend, Grace.

Then, before Clara Bell got the chance to shake some real fear on my soul, someone stepped in between her giggle and jiggle and me and she got herself pregnant. Now it was back to Burney Street for me—back to Yvonne, whom I never saw outside of school. In school, I continued to admire her from afar while she continued to strut her stuff around the older boys, and teachers.

In 1948, Sister struck sixteen! Courting age! And, Lord, Sister lost no time! The Sunday of her sixteenth birthday, Daddy ran home from standing outside church and told Mama, "Sister is walking home from church with a *boy! You'd* better talk to her." Mama said, "As long as she's with the boys where you can see them there's nothing to talk to her about. She's sixteen now."

"Sixteen! *Our* lil' Sister?" was all Daddy could say.

But Sister's courting turned out to be more of a pain to us three younger children—Shirley, Joe and myself—than to Daddy. At least one of us had to chaperone, or "watch" Sister and her boyfriend *all* the time, following them back and forth to town, to the picture show, to school parties, and to wherever else they tried to sneak off to. When boys came to see her we took turns entering the "courting" room at ten-minute intervals to put wood on, stoke the fire, check the kerosene in the lamp, or just look out the window (a haint check?). *All* on orders from Mama. The boys coming to see Sister *hated* us and we *hated* Sister for turning sixteen. But what I hated most of all was Sister being the cause of all these town kids coming out to see first-hand our country shack. Yet I never heard a single one of them remarking one way or the other about our country conditions. Maybe they were too busy hating me for always suddenly walking into the courting room just to clear my throat.

They came walking up from the bus station. There were two of them. One step in the lead was the short, heavy, dark-skinned one with the ivory-toothed smile. He was doing all the talking. The trailing one was tall, skinny, light-skinned, and quiet. It was a Saturday and they both headed for the back street where, while standing outside Thomas Cafe, the fat one with the wet smile told a young boy back there that he had "nice hips." Word quickly spread that two "sissies" were in town, and folks began congregating on the back street to see and hear the sissies. The short fat one talking, laughing, arguing, smiling, flirting, cursing, and giggling while fielding questions from the audience and the tall skinny one standing silently to the side looking sad, the two sissies stood surrounded by a crowd outside Thomas Cafe for the rest of the afternoon.

Madison already had two sissies, most of us children figuring they were called such because of their love for doing girl things, specifically cooking. But as that Saturday grew on, and the more the chubby one talked, it began appearing that these two sissies were *different* from our sissies. These two rode the bus from town to town throughout the area, and the way the chubby one talked *and* looked at you that day made you feel they hadn't come to Madison with cooking on their minds. But before I could hang around and hear what these two sissies were interested in if not cooking, it got too near sundown and came time for me to head home.

Something Plainview Baptist Revival night Christians never talked about came in the year of 1946. With Daddy and Mister Charley Jackson outside talking crops, the mourners' bench was back to normalcy this Revival, packed with juvenile sinners. One night, about midweek of Revival, when the preacher was approaching the climax of his sermon and had every saved soul in the congregation willing to die right that moment in his or her own seat and fly off to heaven without a question, all were brought abruptly back to earth by the explosive sound detonated in the men's Amen Corner. A Satan sound? One of God's Children over there had broken wind (Junior Roland, today a deacon in Plainview's Amen Corner, later that night and right on the church grounds, called it a "fart"). The preacher kept preaching as if nothing had sounded, but for the remainder of the sermon much of the congregation kept its eyes off the men's Amen Corner in order to maintain its holy composure. But not us young boys, who when able to keep from laughing kept looking over at the men's Amen Corner trying to figure out which Child of God sitting there had let one go? Most of the dozen or so men occupying the three Amen benches were old, and some would nod off even during the height of the sermon, but this sonic boom sound of Satan had awakened everyone over there, and now they all sat upright staring at the preacher, stonewalling it. Though we had our suspicions, we young boys never found out for sure who in the Amen Corner that Revival night pulled the trigger to break the spell of the Holy Spirit.

It was time for our cow to "come in." To have a calf. But before the "dry" cow could have a calf, and once again give milk, she had to spend the night up at the Moore Boys' farm. With Harvey gone, I went with Benny to walk the cow the half-mile up to the Moore Boys' place.

When we reached the farm house the porch was filled with menfolk talking while watching us coming up the drive with the cow. As we were passing the porch on the way back to the barnyard (our cow now leading the way, as, unlike me, she'd been on this trip before), one of the men on the porch hollered out to me,

"Boy, you're 'bout old enough to fuck that cow yo'self!"

The rest of the men on the porch exploded in laughter, along with Benny. I didn't laugh, just kept walking while wondering what did our bringing our cow up here have to do with my being old enough to do that "bad word"?

XVIII.

THE LAST RADIO BABY

"Turn back to that song we heard last night."
Missis Annie Durden, while listening
to a radio program she didn't dig.

Of our links to the outside world, radio, next to the printed word, affected me most. Like the printed word, radio left it entirely up to the listener's imagination to put in the picture. With no restrictions (unlike film and the funnies, which provided the pictures), my imagination with the "heard" word had unlimited freedom to romp, roar, and soar.

In my family, Aunt Bea, Daddy, Uncle Bubba (after moving up on Moore Boy land), and later, Mister Jim, in that order, bought radios. All of these radios were battery operated until 1946, when Uncle Toodney and Aunt Bea moved to town into a house with electric lights, and she bought the family's first "'lectric" radio.

When the batteries at one house weren't working, everyone went to one of the other family houses to hear the radio (though no one went to Mister Jim's house to hear except me). So in the summer of 1941 when Aunt Bea's and Daddy's radio batteries were dead, we all (except Mama and the little children) went the mile or so up to Uncle Bubba's to hear the first Joe Louis and Billy Conn Heavyweight fight. Up there Uncle Bubba controlled the dials and announced the fight through the static back over his shoulder while Daddy sat with the rest of us listening until Joe finally got to Billy in the thirteenth round.

In our early years of owning a radio we, of course, always had to listen to whatever Daddy wanted to hear (except at those times when he wasn't home and Mama let us turn on the radio). Besides the news (war, weather, and cotton prices interested him most), Daddy loved listening to police, detective, and murder mystery programs. His two favorites of this ilk were "Mister District Attorney" and "The Mystery Theater." He also liked the joke show "Can You Top This?" and the (mostly) Saturday night barn dances: the "National Barn Dance" from Chicago (with Lulubelle and Scotty and the Hoosier Hot Shots), the "WSB Barn Dance" from Atlanta (with Herman Horsehair Buzz Fuzz), the "Renfroe Valley Barn Dance" (with the Duke of Paducah), the "Louisiana Hayride," and the "Grand Ole Opry."

Daddy listened to these singing, playing, and dancing shows because, unlike most coloreds, he liked hillbilly (today called "country") music. But no doubt his favorite song and music programs were those few available featuring colored singers and musicians. Not one bit religious, Daddy nevertheless loved spirituals. Without fail (unless the radio battery was dead) every Sunday morning he woke up the house with the spiritual sounds of the Golden Gate Quartet, the Sprokos, or some similar group or singer. When Daddy had on music he loved, he figured everyone else loved it too (or should have) and he would turn the radio volume on loud.

Every afternoon, Monday through Friday, during the war, "Strictly in the Groove" was broadcast from Atlanta, with all colored music. Not spirituals, but the "Devil's" music. Blues. Here I first heard blues sung on the radio, with Louis Jordan (backed by his Tympany Five) singing "I'm Gonna Move to the Outskirts of Town" and "Ration Blues." Two other memorable performers from this show were Cab Calloway and Fats Waller. Then there were the songs (of which the fifteen-minute program played three to four per day) "G. I. Jive," "Reet, Petite, and Gone," "That Chick's Too Young to Fry," "Caldonia," "Salt Pork (or Polk), West Virginia," "Is You Is, or Is You Ain't My Baby," "Ain't Nobody Here But Us Chickens," "Somebody Done Changed the Lock on My Door," "Boogie Woogie," "Saturday Night Fish Fry," "Hey Ba-Ba Re-Bop," "Let the Good Times Roll," "Open the Door, Richard," and many, many more. Then, right after the war, especially on Friday and Saturday nights, Daddy would get "Randy's Record Shop" on the radio from WLAC in Nashville, which carried rhythm and blues, gospel, and hey-lordy-mama-gut-bucket blues. The disc jockey for all of this colored music coming out of Nashville was a white man, Bill "Hoss" Allen. About a year or two following this came other all-colored singing programs with their white disc jockeys, like Jack the Bell Boy out of Decatur and Zenas Sears from Atlanta.

One time Daddy had the radio on and said to us, "That's Marian Anderson singing." We knew Marian Anderson from pictures, and in the colored world she was right up there alongside Joe Louis. Almost. But her singing didn't impress us, not sounding "colored" at all. "She's singing that 'high class' opera," Daddy continued. Nor did it sound like Grand Ole "Opry" singing either. None of us, including Daddy, understood the words she was singing, but because it was Marian Anderson we all sat quietly and respectfully listening until she finished her song before Daddy turned to something less high class.

(Many years later, while walking down a street in New York City, I passed a colored man who was crying and screaming out the fact that

Marian Anderson had just gotten married...to a white man.)

Mama had her favorite radio programs too. One was the variety/ quiz Wednesday night "Kay Kyser Kollege of Musical Knowledge." She also liked Jack Benny. Besides Benny, on Sunday night we listened to the "Fitch Bandwagon" with Alice Faye and Phil Harris (singing his "That's What I Like about the South"), the "Edgar Bergen and Charlie McCarthy (and Mortimer Snerd, my favorite) Show," and the "Fred Allen Show." I didn't think Fred Allen was funny because I didn't understand what he was talking about, but I did enjoy his trips each week down "Allen's Alley," especially when he interviewed the southern Senator Claghorn. Sometimes Mama would listen to the fifteen-minute daytime soap opera "Stella Dallas."

(As a young woman, Mama read the magazine *True Stories*, along with movie magazines. She was the one who first told me about the beautiful Jean Harlow having died at age twenty-six—on the day after my third birthday...and fifteen days before Joe Louis won the World Heavyweight Boxing Championship, the latter a juxtaposition Mama hadn't realized. The sad news about Harlow sent me into mourning seven years after her funeral. Mama sometimes talked about other movie stars too, among them John Barrymore, Rudolph Valentino, Delores Del Rio, Douglas Fairbanks, Senior, Mary Pickford, Clark Gable, and Carole Lombard. But the older Mama got, the less she talked about the movie stars, claiming she had no time for so much "make believe." With the passage of years she seemed more and more concerned about us children and our schooling and what she called the "real" world. But in one rare, unguarded moment I remember her telling me that as a young girl she had gone to the fair in town and saw on a stage outside a tent several young women dancing so beautifully that for a moment—or longer?—she had wanted to be one of them. Never again did I hear her mention this incident. She only talked about—and this only infrequently—her childhood dream of becoming a good wife to a loving husband, living on a big farm of their own that would grow everything but cotton, and raising a houseful of children... Only the last part of her dream came true, but in life, I suppose one out of three ain't bad. Years later, Mama mentioned to me that she had wanted to write a novel about living on a farm in Russia. When I asked, Why Russia? she said she'd always romanticized about writing about Russia. That's when I told her that if she was going to write about someplace it should be somewhere she knew, like Georgia, U.S.A., and not Georgia, U.S.S.R. She understood and, choosing reality over romance, began writing, as much for the family as for publication, about the South she knew...and knows—her autobiography.)

Besides the Joe Louis fights, perhaps Daddy's, and the community's, favorite radio show was "Amos 'n Andy," initially a fifteen-minute nightly (Monday-Friday) program that later went to a half-hour just on Friday nights. Mama wasn't an Amos 'n Andy fan. She said the show made fun of colored folks. When Daddy disagreed, Mama said that the day they put on radio a "serious" show about coloreds, depicting a colored doctor or lawyer like they did for whites, then she would listen to Amos 'n Andy. Mama never got around to listening to Amos 'n Andy.

Every Saturday night Benny and I listened to "Your Hit Parade" with its weekly top ten popular songs. It was on this show that I first heard one of my yet all-time favorite songs, "Accentuate the Positive."

Once Mama told me the voices on the radio were coming from real people, I immediately became curious as to who were they? What did they look like? In the Sunday newspaper, and occasionally in the dailies, particularly on Fridays and Saturdays, pictures of radio stars would appear. But, to me at least, more often than not the star's face didn't match, or live up to, the voice. Yet in the long run the face came not to matter to me, as most important was the voice which I had come to love or, occasionally, hate. In fact, framed in my imagination was my own picture of the face behind the voice, and thus I disassociated most radio voices from the published pictures of their owners.

For more pictures of and information about the stars I would from time to time buy a copy of the monthly *Radio Mirror* magazine, where everyone was usually pictured standing behind a microphone. But to me what radio stars looked like was nothing near as important as what movie stars looked like.

While working in the fields I, beneath my breath, also did radio shows, including announcing the news, boxing matches, and football and baseball games. (I never was a basketball announcer.) Then, when I started reading pocketbooks, I would often sneak one to the field (especially when plowing) and steal reads from it among all the other activities I had going on among the cotton stalks. Having the comic strips, motion pictures, radio shows, and sports readings to keep me busy in the cotton field, it's a wonder I picked as much cotton as I did. In fact, I've never understood how I managed on that October day in 1948 to break the one-hundred-pound barrier. I don't recall doing anything different, like picking faster. Maybe my mind was carrying a lighter schedule than usual that day. (Incidentally, I celebrated my one and only one-hundred-pound picking day by going to the picture show that night to see Victor Mature in *Fury at Furnace Creek*. The next day

I picked sixty-odd pounds, closer to my average, thus returning to normalcy.) The day I picked my (and Plainview's) all-time low of *nine* pounds of cotton, my mind's schedule had been running on overload. Daddy, whose blood presssure shot up, didn't let me go to the picture show that night, or that week.

The radio and the funny papers (which generated daily suspense and anticipation and thus led me to prefer them to funny books) fed my early imagination more than anything else. After reading one day's funnies I would continue each strip's story by imagining how I thought it should go on the following day (talking it out to myself). Of course the script's story *never* followed the script in my mind, but such poor foresight on the part of the cartoonist in no way prevented me from telling *their* story *my* way.

Radio was also full of funny paper and funny book characters. The first one I remember was "The Lone Ranger," coming on Monday through Friday right before the six o'clock evening news. But my favorite radio characters were "Hop Harrigan" (a World War Two fighter pilot...what else?), "Dick Tracy," and "Terry and the Pirates." I followed these three daily fifteen-minute shows religiously. There were several other shows I heard, like "Captain Midnight," "The Green Hornet," "The Shadow," "Jack Armstrong," "Superman," "Buck Rogers," and "Flash Gordon," to name a few. (I never got into Buck or Flash. In science fiction it always seemed to me that technology was more important than the story. There was—is—nothing humorous...or humane...about technology, unless it doesn't always work, and if that had been the case, then Buck and Flash would have ended up crashing in somebody's—our?—cotton field.)

Having to continue my favorite comic strips along with the radio stories on a daily basis kept my imagination on overactive most of the time with the heavy responsibility of keeping these stories moving to a conclusion. (The cartoonists and radio producers only had *their* particular story to be concerned about; like God, I had them *all* to worry about.) While working (?) in the field with (and always way behind) others, I would talk, or mutter, beneath my breath so that those (everybody) working ahead of me, especially Daddy, couldn't hear. But when in my storytelling-to-self I had to demonstrate—performing fistfights and so on—I would drop my cotton sack, hoe, plow handle, mop, or whatever, and with fists, arms, and legs flailing, act out the part (I did all my own stunts). Daddy, in particular, hated these parts of my stories. They would start him to hollering back down the row at me to "stop cutting the fool and go to work!!!" Daddy never realized the heavy schedule I daily carried in my head.

Naturally, I preferred being alone when continuing my version of these funny paper and radio stories, and quite often I managed to be. I would go down into the woods in back of our house and walk for miles through the trees, underbrush, even water, talking aloud to myself, my imagination running on limitless. Hunters didn't like me in the woods because they claimed I scared off the animals. I never thought the animals were scared of me since in my stories I only shot crooks.

Even walking down the road I would have a story going. Sometimes in the middle of the road I'd break into a wild fistfight or shoot an enemy plane from the sky or sink one of their subs or ships in the nearby ditch, with all the sounds of warfare provided. But sometimes I wasn't on the road alone. Whenever someone heard these funny paper, radio, or motion picture continuations coming at them down the road in the form of me talking aloud, scooting here and there at full speed, falling down, jumping up, and leaping over ditches, all while chasing, or being chased by, the enemy, they usually figured I just had "the devil in me." Once discovering I had an audience (no one but myself and all those playing a role within my mind was ever invited to attend these strictly personal performances), I would immediately jump out of my head back onto the dirt road, whistling and acting like nowhere in sight was there an enemy...or the devil.

One day not too long after the war ended and while we were in the field picking cotton, Daddy told us children that someday soon radios would have pictures on them, just like in the movies. Even I couldn't imagine how a picture show could possibly fit in anyone's house, especially ours, and thought nothing more of Daddy's talk of the future.

About a month after finishing Burney Street High in May of 1948, Benny went to Atlanta to get a job. While in Atlanta he learned he had won a 4-H Club scholarship to Fort Valley State College, which he entered that fall. What I remember most about Benny's first year at FVSC occurred during his first week of school—freshman hazing. Benny didn't appreciate this harassment by the school's upperclassmen and wrote a letter home saying he'd had enough and was coming back. Benny didn't know our Mama. He was reintroduced when Mama wrote back to him telling him, "Not to this house are you coming back." In her letter, Mama made it clear to Benny that he being the first one from the immediate family...and the first of Mason's sharecroppers...to go to college, he owed it to us *all* to stay, no matter *what* he had to go through to do so. Benny stayed. When he came home for Thanksgiving that year he talked about hazing, but only in a joking manner (Benny rarely ever complained about anything...he was always too busy *doing*). But mostly he talked about "Eudora." Even though I wanted to discuss Fort Valley's football team record of that year, which was seven victories out of eight games, losing only to Morris Brown of Atlanta, 21-6. But *all* I heard was "Eudora...Eudora..."

On that rainy Sunday of November 27th following Thanksgiving Day of 1948, Sister and I got soaked walking to town to see Benny (who was just as wet) off at the Greyhound bus station. While we waited for the bus to take Benny back to college, from where I sat in the station's "colored" waiting room, I could see through the window of the clerk on duty over into the "white" waiting room. And, Lord, over there on that rainy, chilly Sunday afternoon, the white folks were all sitting staring at the same "something." Moving closer to the window I then saw what they all were staring at. It was a little picture show box right there in the bus station! From where I stood I could see a part of the "little bitty" screen they all sat mesmerized by. On it was a football game played way over in Athens the day before between Georgia and Georgia Tech (Tech lost, 21-13). While I stood watching this little bitty picture show, Daddy's cotton-field prophecy about the picture show on the radio came rushing back home to me. Standing there looking at those looking, I figured that with a screen that tiny the "real" picture show...or radio...was in no danger of *ever* being replaced by this new, little, "picture" box.

Thus prognosticated the last radio baby.

AFTERWORD

On the early, overcast, and chilly Sunday morning of December 4, 1949, toting Grandmama Jessie's cardboard suitcase and wearing my Sunday, summer best, I left Madison for Atlanta. Joe walked to town with me to the Greyhound bus station. This would be my first time traveling more than five miles from home. All of my life I'd wanted to travel but was just now getting the chance. Many of my peers had been to such faraway, exotic spots as Appalachee, Buckhead, Godfrey, Rutledge, and Swords. A few had even ventured outside the county. My *only* claim to being a world traveler was once having gone "near" Rutledge. I missed seeing the downtown skyline (both stores) by a mile or two, something I *never* told anyone, letting them go to their graves believing I'd *been* to Rutledge. Now, here I was going on the Greydog for more than *sixty* miles to the big city of Atlanta! Take that, Rutledge!

My main reason for leaving home was that sharecropping was being phased out of the area (and my family). The new cotton picking machine was coming to Morgan County, which meant there soon wouldn't be any need for human cotton pickers (something I'd always felt).

I was fifteen years old when I left home to go to Atlanta to live at the Butler Street YMCA, where Harvey lived, and to work and attend night high school at Booker T. Washington. Years later, Mama told me that because I was so young when I left home, she had always felt she'd never done as much for me as she'd done for the other children, who all left at older ages. The truth was, I told her, she'd done all she could for me because *nobody* can do anything for, or with, a fifteen-year-old. If I hadn't learned the Viola Andrews Method by the time I was fifteen, I'd never learn it.

(When I was fifteen I wasn't quite a "know-it-all" teenager. But by the time I was seventeen I was. As a teenager it's a must to know *everything*—except what's in your textbooks—because all of your peers do. Otherwise, you're a square, or nerd, or "different"...the *worst*. But by the age of thirty I knew *nothing*. And now, at fifty-six, I know even less and am unlearning by the day.)

Originally, I'd wanted to include my Atlanta years in this book but later changed my mind, for the reason that, starting with Atlanta, in spite of my mere fifteen years, I entered the world of the adult. *The*

Last Radio Baby is about childhood, growing up. Living at Atlanta's Butler Street YMCA (right off "Sweet" Auburn Avenue and down from the original "sin" street, Decatur Street, Atlanta's answer to Memphis's Beale Street), working days, and attending school at night turned me into an adult long before my twenty-first birthday. I think.

A forthcoming book, to be titled *Once upon a Time in Atlanta*, will cover my Atlanta period, 1949-1952.

I hope you have enjoyed reading *The Last Radio Baby*. I certainly had fun writing it...and have many good memories of having lived it.

RAYMOND ANDREWS